Authentic Movement

of related interest

Foundations of Expressive Arts Therapy
Theoretical and Clinical Perspectives
Edited by Stephen K. Levine and Ellen G. Levine
ISBN 1 85302 463 5

Movement and Drama in Therapy, Second Edition
Audrey G. Wethered
ISBN 1 85302 199 7

The Metaphoric Body
Guide to Expressive Therapy through Images and Archetypes
Leah Bartal and Nira Ne'eman
ISBN 1 85302 152 0

Introduction to Dramatherapy
Theatre and Healing
Ariadne's Ball of Thread
Sue Jennings
ISBN 1 85302 115 6

Authentic Movement

A Collection of Essays by Mary Starks Whitehouse,
Janet Adler and Joan Chodorow

Edited by Patrizia Pallaro

Jessica Kingsley Publishers
London and Philadelphia

First published in the United Kingdom in 1999 by
Jessica Kingsley Publishers Ltd
116 Pentonville Road
London N1 9JB, England
and
325 Chestnut Street
Philadelphia, PA 19106, U S A

www.jkp.com

Copyright © 1999 Jessica Kingsley Publishers except where indicated.

Second impression 2000

Library of Congress Cataloging in Publication Data
A CIP catalog record for this book is available from the Library of Congress

British Library Cataloguing in Publication Data
Authentic movement : essays by Mary Starks Whitehouse, Janet Adler
and Joan Chodorow
1.Dance/Movement therapy – Psychological aspects 2.Jungian psychology
I.Whitehouse, Mary Starks II.Adler, Janet III.Chodorow, Joan, 1937–
IV.Pallaro, Patrizia
615.8'5155'019

ISBN 1 85302 653 0

Printed and Bound in Great Britain by
Athenaeum Press, Gateshead, Tyne and Wear

Contents

Dedicated to the memory of my mother, Bertilla Zuanon,
to Mary Starks Whitehouse and to my teachers, Wendy Wyman,
Janet Adler and Joan Chodorow, who have taught me much
about the experience of authenticity,
and to my husband, D.A. Sonneborn, who wholeheartedly
supports me and challenges me to such experience.

Acknowledgements

Janet Adler and Joan Chodorow for their enthusiasm and collaboration; Feather Whitehouse King – daughter of Mary Starks Whitehouse and copyright holder of her mother's work – for believing in this project; Gilda Franz, Frieda Sherman, Neala Haze, Tina Stromsted and Nancy Zenoff for their timeless interviews; Carolyn Caddes, D.A. Sonneborn and Cara Moore for soulful photographs; Angela Fischlein-Rupp and Marie Louise Oberem for early conversations with Joan and Janet about the need to make these papers available to the European community; The Authentic Movement Institute for its support of this project; A Moving Journal for its unwavering dedication to this work; D.A. Sonneborn for his patience with and belief in me; Barbara Banchero for always being there with her remarkable presence; All my fellow movers in the training and practicing circles for standing right beside me.

The following have been here reprinted with the kind permission of each author, editor and respective publisher.

Frantz, G. (1972) 'An approach to the center: An interview with Mary Whitehouse'. *Psychological Perspectives* 3, 1, 37–46. © 1972 by *Psychological Perspectives*. Reprinted with permission of Gilda Frantz, *Psychological Perspectives* and C.G. Jung Institute of Los Angeles. (Mrs Frantz was a friend of Mary Starks Whitehouse. She is a Jungian analyst practicing in Santa Monica, California.)

Sherman, Frieda (1978) 'A conversation with Mary Whitehouse'. *American Journal of Dance Therapy* 2, 2, 3–4. © 1978 by American Dance Therapy Association. Reprinted with permission of the American Dance Therapy Association and *American Journal of Dance Therapy*, Plenum Publishing Corporation.

Whitehouse, Mary Starks (ca. 1956) *Creative Expression in Physical Movement is Language Without Words.* © ca. 1956 by Mary Starks Whitehouse (F. Whitehouse King). Printed with permission by F. Whitehouse King.

Whitehouse, Mary Starks (1995) 'The Tao of the body'. In D.H. Johnson (ed) *Bone, Breath and Gesture,* pp.241–251. Berkeley, CA: North Atlantic Books. © 1958 by Mary Starks Whitehouse (F. Whitehouse King). Reprinted with permission of F. Whitehouse King, D.H. Johnson and North Atlantic Books.

Whitehouse, Mary Starks (1987) 'Physical movement and personality'. *Contact Quarterly,* 16–19. © 1963 by Mary Starks Whitehouse (F. Whitehouse King). Printed with permission by F. Whitehouse King and *Contact Quarterly.*

Whitehouse, Mary Starks (1977) 'Reflections on a metamorphosis'. In R. Head, R.E. Rothenberg and D.Wesley (eds) A Well of Living Waters: Festschrift for Hilde Kirsch, pp.272–277. Los Angeles: C.G. Jung Institute, 1977. © 1977 by C.G. Jung Institute of Los Angeles

Whitehouse, Mary Starks (1977) 'The transference and dance therapy'. *American Journal of Dance Therapy 1,* 1, pp.3–7. © 1977 by American Dance Therapy Association. Reprinted with permission of F. Whitehouse King, the American Dance Therapy Association and American Journal of Dance Therapy, Plenum Publishing Corporation.

Whitehouse, Mary Starks (1977) 'C.G. Jung and dance therapy: Two major principles'. In P.L. Bernstein (ed) *Eight Theoretical Approaches in Dance/Movement Therapy,* pp.51–70. Dubuque, IA: Kendall/Hunt, 1979. © 1977 by Mary Starks Whitehouse (F. Whitehouse King). Reprinted with permission of F. Whitehouse King and Kendall/Hunt Publishing Company.

Haze, Neala and Stromsted, Tina (1994) 'An interview with Janet Adler'. *American Journal of Dance Therapy 16*, 2, 81–90, Fall/Winter. © 1994 by American Dance Therapy Association . Reprinted with permission of N. Haze and T. Stromsted, the American Dance Therapy Association and *American Journal of Dance Therapy,* Plenum Publishing Corporation.

Adler, Janet (1972) 'Integrity of body and psyche: Some notes on work in process'. *Proceedings of the Seventh Annual Conference of the American Dance Therapy Association,* October 1972. Columbia, MD: ADTA. © 1972 American Dance Therapy Association. Reprinted with permission of J. Adler and the American Dance Therapy Association.

Adler, Janet (1987) 'Who is the witness? A description of authentic movement'. *Contact Quarterly,* pp.20–29, Winter. © 1985, 1987, 1996 by Janet Adler. Reprinted with permission of J. Adler and *Contact Quarterly.*

Adler, Janet (1992) 'Body and soul.' *American Journal of Dance Therapy 14,* 2, 73–94, Fall/Winter. © 1992 by American Dance Therapy Association. Reprinted with permission of J. Adler, the American Dance Therapy Association and *American Journal of Dance Therapy,* Plenum Publishing Corporation.

Adler, Janet (1994) 'The collective body'. *Proceedings of the First International Dance/Movement Therapy Conference 'Language of Movement'.* Nervenklinik Spandau, Berlin, Germany, 1994 and *American Journal of Dance Therapy 18,* 2, 81–94. Fall/Winter. ©1996 by American Dance Therapy Association. Reprinted with permission of J. Adler, Marie Louise Oberem, Director, First International Dance/Movement Therapy Conference 'Language of Movement,' the American Dance Therapy Association and American Journal of Dance Therapy, Plenum Publishing Corporation.

Zenoff, Nancy R. (1986) 'An interview with Joan Chodorow'. *American Journal of Dance Therapy, 9,* 6–22. © by American Dance Therapy Association. Reprinted with permission of Nancy R. Zenoff, the American Dance Therapy Association and American Journal of Dance Therapy, Plenum Publishing Corporation.

Chodorow, Joan (1974) 'Philosophy and methods of individual work'. In K. Mason (ed), *Dance Therapy: Focus on Dance VII,* 24–26. © 1974 American Alliance for Health, Physical Education, Recreation, and Dance. Reprinted with permission of J. Chodorow and American Alliance for Health, Physical Education, Recreation, and Dance.

Chodorow, Joan (1978) 'Dance therapy and the transcendent function'. *American Journal of Dance Therapy,* 16–23, Spring/Summer. © 1978 by American Dance Therapy Association. Reprinted with permission of J. Chodorow, the American Dance Therapy Association and American Journal of Dance Therapy, Plenum Publishing Corporation.

Chodorow, Joan (1982/1995) 'Dance/movement and body experience in analysis'. In M. Stein (ed) *Jungian Analysis,* pp.391–404. La Salle, IL: Open Court, 2nd ed., 1995. © 1982/1995 by Open Court Publishing Company. Reprinted with permission of J. Chodorow and Open Court Publishing Company.

Chodorow, Joan (1984) 'To move and be moved'. *Quadrant 17,* 2, 39–48, Fall. © 1984 by *Quadrant.* Reprinted with permission of J. Chodorow, *Quadrant,* and the New York C.G. Jung Foundation.

Chodorow, Joan (1986) 'The body as symbol: dance/movement in analysis' In N. Schwartz-Salant and M. Stein (eds) *The Body in Analysis.* The Chiron Clinical Series, pp.87–108, 1986. © 1986 by Chiron Publications. Reprinted with permission of J. Chodorow and Chiron Publications.

Chodorow, Joan (1991/1996) 'Active imagination'. Adapted from the original published in *Dance Therapy and Depth Psychology: The Moving Imagination,* published by Routledge, 1991. Printed with permission of J. Chodorow and Routledge.

For the use of lines from Christopher Fry's poem 'A Sleep of Prisoners' published in Christopher Fry's (1977) *Plays,* © 1951 Chrisopher Fry, the editor gratefully acknowledges the permission granted by Oxford University Press, Inc.

For the use of lines from Daniel Quinn's novel *Ishmael* published by Bantam Books, 1992, the editor gratefully acknowledges the permission granted by Bantam Books.

Photo credits:

Mary Starks Whitehouse © ca. 1970 Carolyn Caddes. Courtesy of Janet Adler.
Janet Adler © 1997 D.A. Sonneborn.
Joan Chodorow © 1982 Cara Moore. Courtesy of Joan Chodorow.

Introduction

Patrizia Pallaro

Movement is life. I did not really, consciously know this until I engaged in the study of Dance/Movement Therapy and Authentic Movement at UCLA in the mid-1980s. Studying authentic movement with Wendy Wyman opened up a new life for me. I remember the funky smell of the studio where we used to meet and I remember the darkness of the space, even though a few years later when I revisited that room rainbows of light shone through its grand windows. I remember fear in my body as it moved from corner to corner and joy and a swelling in my pelvis as I let go of my fears. I remember sitting on the steps of the Dance Building, avidly reading Mary Starks Whitehouse's papers, looking for answers to my questions. I remember meeting Janet Adler, one of our guest lecturers, who presented her paper on witnessing. I remember feeling I had finally come home. Once in the San Francisco Bay area, I remember my supervision hours with Joan Chodorow and a sense of wonder and bewilderment sweeping over me at times. I remember the endless hours spent moving in cold Berkeley studios, in Valley Ford's sun-filled schoolhouse and dancing in my own living room.

To my own students and supervisees I often recommended Mary Starks Whitehouse's, Janet Adler's and Joan Chodorow's articles. And I remember thinking one day – I could not find a paper by Mary Starks Whitehouse – that it would be really great if all the papers written on authentic movement could be found in one place, all together in one book. And I remember thinking 'Maybe I must do just that!' The seed for this project had sprouted. Over the years during which it has grown, I have encountered the support of many to whom I feel profoundly indebted.

The time has come to present movement students and seekers with this priceless collection of essays. This first volume presents the historical documents on authentic movement, from Mary Starks Whitehouse's talks about the wisdom of the body, to Janet Adler's contributions on the developing relationship between moving and witnessing, to Joan Chodorow's continuing development of movement as active imagination. Each author shows a marked evolution in their thinking about authentic movement as she has deepened her practice.

Each author complements the other in describing different aspects of this work. All have tremendous faith in the body and in moving the unconscious. Mary Starks Whitehouse opens the door for creative movement expression, the reunion of body and mind, the importance of a guide who shows the way to the mover. In her 'movement-in-depth' approach she discovers that movement which is authentic. Janet Adler moves from a therapeutic standpoint to a teaching stance, while carving a space for the mover's consciousness as well as the witness' consciousness to emerge in the circle. She brings her work from a descent into the personal unconscious to the embrace of the collective embodiment to the transformation of a mystical practice rooted in the transcendent body. And while witnessing thousands of movers, she also witnessed the birth of Authentic Movement as a discipline. Joan Chodorow brings together the wisdom of the body and the wisdom of Carl G. Jung as she makes her scholarly contribution to the two traditions of dance therapy and analytical psychology.

So many riches, so many pearls, so many ways of embodying the self and moving to life.

Mary Starks Whitehouse

Mary Stark Whitehouse's Papers

The following papers by our teacher, Mary Starks Whitehouse, appear here, published within one book for the first time. This event is enormously important for those of us who were Mary's students, for the people with whom we work, and for present and future generations in which the body's wisdom made conscious becomes mandatory for the development of the Self. Mary's contribution to fields as diverse as analytical psychology, dance-movement therapy, dance, somatic epistemology and meditative practice is immeasurable, timely and essential.

Mary's essays span a period of perhaps twenty-five years. She began to write them when she was in her forties and her last paper was written shortly before her death at the age of 68. Her writing shows a development over time as she gained a more differentiated understanding of the relationship between expressive movement originating from an unconscious source and Jungian thought. Her early papers were presented as lecture-demonstrations to members of the Analytical Psychology Club in Los Angeles and at UCLA.

'Creative Expression in Physical Movement is Language Without Words', begins with the spontaneous, wholly embodied experience of the child. In contrast, she describes the myriad inhibitions of the adult. It is published here for the first time. In 'The Tao of the Body' (1958) her approach to movement comes alive as she describes her work with many individuals. She gives examples of how awareness of the body leads to self-knowledge and addresses the essential distinction between moving and being moved. 'Physical Movement and Personality' (1963) identifies the specific inner impulse that is the source of expressive movement. Mary described how different students learn to open the channel between impulse and action. 'Reflections on a Metamorphosis' (1969) is an autobiographical essay that explores the great change that occurred in her work when she realized she did not teach dance, but rather that she taught people. 'The Transference and Dance Therapy' (1977) was presented first at an ADTA conference. Here Mary discusses with honesty and courage her understanding of transference and countertransference when working with movement. In 'C.G. Jung and Dance Therapy' (1979) we are gifted by the exploration of her role within the therapeutic process and how she understands the subtle and complex relationship between some of Jung's most important ideas and the experiences of authentic movement and active imagination.

Mary wanted very much to complete her book about her work, which she called *The Moving Self.* She was heartened by the outpouring of interest and support from her colleagues, students and friends, including a grant from the Marian Chace Memorial Fund. Her great desire was to bring to fruition the depth of her discoveries. Her pioneering work is evident now, not only from her writing, but in the efforts of those who continue consciously to explore the experience of the body in many parts of the world. We turn now to her splendid papers which speak for themselves.

Janet Adler and Joan Chodorow
January 1998

CHAPTER I

An Approach to the Center
An Interview with Mary Whitehouse[1]

Gilda Frantz

Mary Whitehouse, a pioneer in movement therapy, spent a couple of afternoons talking with me about her art and her ideas. What follows is an extract of those conversations. She is a graduate of Wellesley College and holds a professional Diploma from the Wigman Central Institute in Dresden, Germany (an institute of dance), and is a charter member of the American Dance Therapy Association. Her rich background of professional dance training, teaching and performing, which includes the Jooss Ballet School, Bennington Summer School, the Martha Graham School and others, qualifies her to speak with authority about Dance.

She has taught at colleges on both the East and West coasts, was on the Dance Faculty at the University of California at Los Angeles and has studied at the C.G. Jung Institute in Zürich, although she is not a graduate of that institute. Her membership in the Analytical Psychology Club of Los Angeles grew out of her personal depth analysis. Her studies in analytical psychology, as well as her personal analysis, have influenced her development of a psychosomatic approach to personality.

Mrs Whitehouse conducted both a private movement therapy practice and a movement therapy teacher training program in her Los Angeles studio until recently.

I was a student of hers during her early exploratory days. I came to her home once each week, seeking a better understanding of my own body through movement. It was a one-to-one experience during which she would

---

1   Interview previously published in *Psychological Perspectives*, Vol. 3, no. 1, Spring 1972.

play rhythms or beat a drum (subsequently, she used many types of musical approaches with people) and I would sit or lie on the floor and move as directed from within or follow her directions toward physical movement. During these sessions I had a dazzlingly explicit revelation of how little I knew my own body and how it moved. This knowledge was like a door opening that exposes buried treasure, for I could now see the possibilities of being able really to move.

I stayed with Mary Whitehouse only a short time, but the experience of becoming conscious of my entire physical self has stayed with me to this day. During our talks we discussed many things, but it was discussion of her work with movement therapy, which is called 'movement-in-depth,' that occupied most of our time.

I: 'Do you feel that your work is directly related to Jungian psychology or is it a compilation of different disciplines?'

MW: 'Now that's a very ticklish question. Without my own analysis, and the subsequent broadening of my own horizon as a result of bumping into analytical psychology, I would never have done it. I can also see that the roots of this work, and everything that I was becoming and had been, was all there long before analysis. The way I did improvisation, when nobody else did, and my insistence that people follow their impulses even when it was the strictest kind of dance form, my value system, implicitly belonged to the attitude that I was able to consciously find when I got into analysis. So the answer is yes, but it was so very much mine that it didn't begin there. Analytical psychology gave me a way to understand and think about the instinctive procedures that I had always used without knowing what they were'.

I: 'Is movement therapy helpful in resolving sexual problems?'

MW: 'I wouldn't put it that way. I would say that the movement therapy brings up the sexual attitude in the person very early and then the question becomes how can one relate to the discovery of one's own sexuality, just as one learned to relate to the discovery of one's emotions. Where the presence of sexual feelings become apparent, it creates a problem sooner for men in mixed group than for women. A woman tends to diffuse this feeling and mix it with other feelings. On the other hand, when she experiences her own sexuality in her own body as she moves, it can be a hair-raising admission to her that there is no man there making her feel like a sexual being and that it hasn't a cause which needs to wait until tonight or next week when she meets her lover. The knowledge that she is a sexual human being, and the process of her getting used to that idea, is the beginning of a different relation to herself. In that sense, it resolves putting all of her sexuality on a man or men.

A great deal of the shame and embarrassment which people carry around with them through life is also resolved with this realization. I constantly hear such things as: "I don't like my breasts because they are too large" or "my fanny is too wide." These parts of the body are related to the basic problems of male and female. Much of this goes back to one's parents and their attitude to the child's body, which is, of course, a simplification. Many factors are involved when there is a rejection of the body but in an adult sexual man or woman there can be a relaxation of anxiety with regard to actual physical sexual feelings. Again, the body becomes real instead of imaginary'.

I: 'Is an individual's total inner development possible through "movement-in-depth" or is movement therapy more useful as an adjunct to psychotherapy?'

MW: 'This is a question that kept coming up in me in the early years of my work. I kept saying "of course it can't do it all by itself," which was, in a way, false modesty and fear. How do you translate the understanding and principles of analytical psychology into physical movement? This was a mistake on my part, for it meant that in those early years I was trying too hard to read, interpret and organize what I saw so that it could be said in the language of analytical psychology and so I could understand it in this other language. Oh, what sins of interpretation were committed in those early days. Like somebody analyzing dreams who knows nothing about them.

Because of my work with movement, there were people who got cracked open and became interested in what you have called "an approach to the center". They could not have cared less about any other way of waking up. They awakened and it was enough that they had this to struggle with. There were other people who, as soon as they cracked open, were really aware of themselves. I would then say "Go to Dr So-and-So," not only because I had no business handling them but because I really felt the verbal-dream part of it belonged to what they were dealing with.

I felt that although they could do a lot with movement, it was a matter of depth. Physical movement is an analogy to the psychic movement that leads to the center. This process can carry the personality, if the person they are working with understands that'.

I: 'What relation do you feel movement in depth has to C.G. Jung's theory of active imagination?[2]

MW: 'I think that body movement is active imagination in sensory or sensation terms, just as a painting is active imagination in visual images. When it is done on that level, it is pure active imagination and has nothing to do with which areas of the body are involved or one's stiffness or whatever. It has to do with the flow of the unconscious material coming out in phys-ical form. Dear Papa Jung did not know this, and the reason he didn't was because he assumed (as anybody brought up in that generation would assume) that you had to have the struc-ture of the outside form of the dance, which one had to learn and to be able to repeat, and then you could ask questions. Perhaps Jung didn't know that it flowed like a painting does and that anybody that knew movement could see the images

2   'By "active imagination" we understand a definite attitude toward the contents of the unconscious whereby we seek to isolate them and thus observe their autonomous development. We may also say that "we make them come to life," but this is incorrect in as far as we merely observe what is happening ... It is not unlike watching a film or listening to music, where in each case one sits back and "takes in" something which one has not made but which happens, with a concentration which is a definite kind of activity. Only the difference is that in active imagination the "film" is being unrolled inside.' (Adler 1948, p.43).

appearing as they came. They didn't have to be repeated or repeatable.[3] One docs not need to move in circles in order to create a mandala pattern with physical movement. In movement it is not that specific'.

I: 'Does the person doing the movement, which can be called an active imagination, recognize it as such or is this something which only the observer realizes?'

MW: 'Part of the answer depends on whether the person is in Jungian analysis or not. After all, the term "active imagination" is associated with analytical psychology.

However, many present-day techniques use fantasy. Therefore, there is a moment at the end of a sequence of movement when I wait to find out what relation to the inner images this person has. Often, it takes the form of a specific imaginary situation.

For instance, I remember one woman who crouched in the corner of my studio looking across the space to the other side. After a bit she begins to creep and crawl across, sometimes sitting still and playing with what is obviously water and sometimes making a pathway with her arms. Afterward she told me that she was crossing a reedy swampy place through a lot of shallow water and growing green reeds. The interesting part was that no matter what else she did (rolling in it, splashing it on her body, lying down in it), she never let her head go down into the water or be touched by it. As a matter of fact, when she was near enough to the other side she got up on her feet and walked away. This is the first episode in a fantasy development that occupied three subsequent periods.

Almost immediately afterward she became aware of the stoppage of the flow of images and of a great dryness in her daily life. Another person might feel as though they were in a whirlpool or a cave or beneath the sea. When the image is

---

3   'Those who are able to express the unconscious by means of bodily movements are rather rare. The disadvantage that movements cannot easily be fixed in the mind must be met by making careful drawings of the movements afterwards, so that they shall not be lost to the memory' (Jung 1916, p.84).

truly connected in certain people, then the movement is
authentic. There is no padding of movement just for the sake
of moving. There is an ability to stand the inner tension until
the next image moves them. They don't simply dance around.
At the end of the session there is a choice. If they know what
they have experienced in this movement just completed and
are obviously ready to talk about it, I wait quietly and they
talk and that is what I relate to. Perhaps something scared
them, or surprised them, or they wanted to go on with a particular image, but something happened to stop it. You relate
to what they are doing, not to the active imagination.

If they are not aware of it and look either blank or puzzled, I
find that it is possible to ask very gentle, pointed questions
such as: "Did you have an image at any time?", "Did you feel
you were anywhere but in the studio?", "What was your relation to me?" and I can tell by the answers to the questions
whether to go on with it or not. The questions either spark
something or else the person looks more puzzled and stares at
the floor endlessly.

Whether the person talks about active imagination and is surprised at the depth of the experience, or perceives purely
physically what was going on, I am forced to use my instincts
as to how to help them go on with the physical aspect of it,
not the psychological.'

I: 'I remember from my experience in body movement with you
         that I lay on the floor and was still forever long. It was not my
         idea of movement as I did very little moving. How did you
         arrive at the place where you had students lie down and "sink
         into the earth", as I remember calling it? I thought about this
         a long time afterward, remembering how supportive the floor
         felt and how free I felt when I finally did get up and begin to
         dance and move and feel.'

MW: 'In the beginning I was looking for something. I had always
         done improvisation and I had had the best training in the
         world for the kind of dance that I taught. I had studied at the
         Wigman School and learned that part and parcel of what they
         did there was both improvisation and respect for the material

of each individual dancer. We American students were always fighting about this. On the one hand we wanted to have ballet and, on the other, we thought we ought to improvise. When I was young it was a tremendous conflict. After I studied there I came back and did the "other half" with Martha Graham because she was really the American equivalent. You must realize that when I knew and studied with these women, it was direct personal contact. I know intimately the similarities and the differences between them and what their work really amounted to.

What I began to understand during the beginning of my work in movement in depth was that in order to release a movement that is instinctive (i.e. not the "idea" of the person doing that movement nor my idea of what I want them to do), I found that I had to go back toward not moving. In that way I found out where movement actually started. It was when I learned to see what was authentic about movement, and what was not, and when people were cheating, and when I interfered, and when they were starting to move from within themselves, and when they were compelled to move because they had an image in their heads of what they wanted to do; it was then that I learned to say "Go ahead and do your image, never mind if you are thinking of it" and when to say "Oh, wait longer. Wait until you feel it from within." So much of what I do is intuitive, it is sometimes too discouraging'.

I: 'Could you explain what you mean by an "authentic movement"? And what is cheating?'

MW: 'An authentic movement is in and of the Self at the moment it is done. Nothing is in it that is not inevitable, simple. When it is authentic, I can almost tell you what is coming next. When I see somebody move authentically, it is so real that it is undiluted by any pretense or any appearance or images. Often, it can be the movement of just one hand turning over, or it can be the whole body. To get to this authenticity a sacrifice is involved. At first it is a discovery of all of the tricks, needs and demands that separate you from what would be genuine in yourself. Then, after you have discovered what this trick is and what it prevents, it must be sacrificed, as must each subsequent one as it is discovered. The reality of impulse and movement come from such a different place in oneself that when it is experienced, the person comes to know when it is there and when it isn't, and then she can stop cheating. What I call "cheating" would be the personal arrangement of movement on many levels. Unfortunately, just when you get over one and think you are being "real" you get hit with another form of it!'

I: 'Because body movement is independent of voice and words, would an inarticulate person benefit more from movement than an articulate person?'

MW: 'No. This brings up something that is a little too much like a formula, but perhaps it will help to clarify what I feel. People that come to me can be seen on a scale of extreme opposites, at one end people who complete a movement and won't talk about it at all because it is too precious and words would spoil it. At the other extreme are the people that know all about it and can put into words immediately just what they did or felt. Those who are inarticulate need to be able to say something about it because it is not conscious until they do. To those who are enthusiastic and verbal I say "Look, you're talking it all away, go home and don't say anything about it." I must take a chance on having these people lose the impact of the movement because they may not talk about it, as opposed to the inarticulate person who profits more by the attempt to describe in words what it felt like'.

I: 'Would you call yourself a teacher or would you say that what you do is therapy?'

MW: 'I have a resistance to calling it therapy because of the public image of dance therapy'.

I: 'What is that?'

MW: 'The overtones of the words "dance therapy" in this country mean mental disturbance, emotional limitations, hospital setting, doing something to people. What I am interested in is a process that furthers personal growth. That is true whether the person is developing toward their artistic statement or toward the interest and self-knowledge that we mean by therapy or analysis.

An old friend once told me that I was going to have to decide whether I wanted to go in the direction of people, in which case he would use the term therapy, or whether I was going to help the artist. He felt that I could have a place which would be important to choreography and that I could work exclusively with dancers. It didn't go that way for me.

I have had UCLA students that brought their dances to me, and, thank heaven, I had the dance background. It enabled me to start right where they were. They could bring me a final dance and I could begin to work on that dance without touching anything about their personal lives or psychological problems. If, however, their reason for coming, whether conscious or unconscious, went deeper than their performance, we soon got into the raw material which involved their personal growth'.

I: 'Is it possible that a young teacher, in trying to apply your methods, might run into difficulties?'

MW: 'Young people and teachers have recognized from the power of the atmosphere when working with movement therapeutically, and the unusual things that happen, that people may break down or break through, or whatever one wants to call it, and they have asked: "What do I do?", "How do I know what to do?" And this is terribly tricky. My assets, I have come to feel, are that I am much older than most of the people who are trying to work with movement. My analytical experience was painful enough, and important enough, so that whatever else by way of ego-trips I may have indulged in, I had a healthy respect and overpowering feeling for the reality of the unconscious appearing in others as well as in myself. Consequently, when things happened in the course of a session, I did not make the mistake of assuming that I personally had done it. In movement there is a stimulus that is absent when an individual is sitting in a chair in an office. If they burst into tears, they are still in a chair, but in a studio you have a person running around the room, yelling and then bursting into tears. Only your own capacity to carry it for them, and your own lack of fear, undergirds how long you can let that go on. It gives you the freedom to sense when it is helpful and when you are letting them beat their heads against a wall, so it is really terribly important to respect your own tolerance. If I had queasy moments or was scared, I was on the spot where I had to feel my reluctance to see or hear what was going on as my limitation. Or, at the same time, I could feel it as a danger to both of us and could act on it.

I had a boy once who was very borderline. He would come in and dance and dance and dance. His movement was often weird and yet he was a born dancer. He was absolutely unwilling to take any lessons or learn any structure. He would bring the music with him and we would put it on and only his being willing to stop and talk about it before we went on cushioned the fact that he'd gone into some very difficult and tremendously violent things. Once in a while, I had to use my instinct whether to go and touch him and stop it that way or whether to go and be near enough so he would see me.

There is this, however, and I think it is true: the depth of the leader corresponds to the depth that she or he can bring out in a person. In other words, a younger person without the experience is not going to trigger the same depth that I have from years of both personal and analytical experience'.

I: '"Movement therapy" gives a feeling of exhilaration and well-being, but some say that its benefits are transitory'.

MW: 'I feel that the people who say that it is transitory are referring to the superficiality of many approaches that are taken for movement awareness. When it is catharsis and release, it cannot be anything but transitory – you have to come back and do it again. What you get is relief of tension and no consciousness. If the process in which you and your student discover things is made conscious, it is no more transitory than other kinds of self-knowledge. The carry-over depends on whether the value is placed upon raising something to consciousness or whether it is placed on getting "out" something.

I find quite the opposite in my kind of work. The place where I would have questions about it being transitory may come as a result of an intensive experience, such as a weekend or a workshop, but over the long haul of digging at it week after week, well, I think that is anything but transitory. I find it builds a self-recognition that has its roots in the physical body, and this doesn't go away'.

I: 'Mary, in the past fifteen or twenty years you have taught privately, taught women's classes, teachers, mixed or couples classes, had weekends at Esalen, lectured here and abroad. In all this work and activity there must have been a progression in your development. What would you say the next step was for you after all of this?'

MW: 'I was now beginning to have the feeling of knowing about weekends and wondering what was next for me. All of this is only a year or two ago. I had begun canceling weekends a year before I came to this feeling, partly because, and in a way I am ashamed to say it, but that's the way it was, my work went on in chapters of self-learning. When I had been compelled to try something new, either in exterior form or in my relation to it, and I began to be completely familiar with it, I found myself always feeling as though I had absorbed that and would now have to move on and do the next thing! I was always scared during these periods but I always felt compelled to try. For me, this compelling feeling has two sides. One is self-interest and self-learning. Without it, you don't change, you just give, and give, the same thing. The other is because you want to give somebody something and want to convey a continuity, give a sequence of experience to other people. Without wanting to provide continuity, one has no order in one's work and an organic development fails to appear. One jumps off into a variety of things simply because one is interested.

Of course, over the period of years, I found myself on one side of the fence or the other. It's not possible to balance all the time, but one tries. You could say that my motivation was selfish but, at the same time, it was the only way I could have learned'.

References

Adler, G. (1948) *Studies in Analytical Psychology*. London: Routledge & Kegan Paul.
Jung, C.G. (1916) 'The transcendent function'. In *The Collected Works of C.G. Jung* (1969) (vol. 8). Princeton: Princeton University Press.

CHAPTER 2

Conversation with Mary Whitehouse[1]

Frieda Sherman

MW: 'What I want to say most strongly is the fact that you can only do your own work if you are going to be authentic. You can only do it the way it suits your psyche. No matter what you've learned, all the learning has to drop away – you know, how they say that in order to write or dance you do it and then you learn the technique and then forget it, this is very much the same thing.

If you are going to have it, mediate and work with movement from inside yourself in an integrated way, then, as you get to the actual moment, you are able to go on with that person because you've been there. The process of getting into your own depths is the process that makes you able to accompany someone else into their depths. And they are not going there unless you've been there'.

I: 'Clarify the point about having been there. The old saw about psychiatrists was that "They all had to be crazy in order to want to work with crazy people." That's not what you are talking about, is it? No, OK. It's not that you have to have experienced everything that the other person has experienced'.

---

1 Interview about pre-conference seminar held at the 1978 American Dance Therapy Association Conference in Seattle, Washington and previously published in *American Journal of Dance Therapy*, Vol. 2, no. 2, Fall/Winter 1978.

MW: 'Oh no, not at all. The reality of the inner life is where I work
        and it comes out in movement. I make a connection between
        the reality of the psychic life and my experience, and the real-
        ity of my own psychic life is the prerequisite to my allowing
        the other person to have theirs. If I don't know my own and I
        have never been there, I am doing it all by techniques and by
        having been trained and by lip service in my head and that
        has nothing to do with my own experience of myself, which
        is the only way I can know that they have a right to their
        experiences of themselves. And my not being scared of that is
        a prerequisite of their not being scared because I have to have
        had the experience of "Yes, you're scared, but…" in order for
        them to be willing to go deeper because they have never been
        there. So, it has nothing to do with being crazy. It has to do
        with an unknown area of oneself which Jung calls the uncon-
        scious'.

I: 'And that unknown part of oneself doesn't have to be the
        same, it is only the unknown part'.

MW: 'That's right. And it can come up quite differently because
        what you had to work from is your experience of your awe
        and surprise and emotional reaction to the unknown part of
        yourself, so, when that is introduced, those emotions on the
        part of the person working are somehow familiar, but what is
        unknown is important'.

I: 'How does this work with the unconscious relate to the body,
        to the movement? This came up with the witness, with the
        observer, when you and Sharon [Chaiklin] were talking about
        watching the body move'.

MW: 'My hunch is that Sharon, as an example, not a person,
        observes differently than I do. What I am looking at is the
        physical movement as revelation, as a show of the inner thing.
        Therefore, I am not saying "The shoulders are up, the mouth is
        this way…". I take that in but it is minor. What I am looking
        at is the psychic attitude displayed by the physical movement.
        That is a different way of observing from what we are training
        all these kids to do. It's a different way of trusting yourself

and it's based on being willing to be wrong, being willing to make mistakes and misread, knowing perfectly well that was a possibility – what you saw. Most of all, it's based on your inner experience and your respect for your own life, not individually as a "special" something but as the mainstream of the human experience.

Is movement therapy what you see the body do, as in Effort/Shape, or is it also what the person feels in relation or response to that movement? I don't care what the body does! Heresy! I don't care! Effort/Shape is marvelous. It's one more thing to know about, like Feldenkrais and everything else – they all have a tremendous amount to offer. But, for me, what are we doing the thing for? Not to fix the body or to fix the soul but to introduce people to the fact that movement is a way to get in touch with yourself – the invisible part. The thing that I am struck by in having people come to a practice is that the people who want to be in touch with themselves are thrilled at this way of working and that's why I see introverts – they are more comfortable with me – they go much more quickly to what it is to them while the extroverts get "out there" and want to know how I did it and why I did it'.

I: '[What] about [what you said] at the conference: "Don't expect that the thing you do today will be the thing you do tomorrow."'

MW: 'That brings up the whole thing of getting to the place where you don't protect yourself by planning, that you fall on your face as much as you need to. I'm not saying stop making don't-s or stop planning or anything like that. I am just saying work toward the moment when you will have so much trust in your own inner relation to what you see and be willing to be wrong that what you do comes then in the moment and only then. Therefore, it can't be the same as it was yesterday. I've done it both ways. I've found something that delighted me on Tuesday and I've done it on Wednesday. By and large, it does not work. Sometimes it works but every day is different. I have a marvelous example in an article in my book where I gave the same thing to two women in a period in my life in my studio when I was doing many more forms and exercises and "do this now freely", which is different. The form could be the same but the "freeing up" that the women did with it was diametrically opposed. That's not true here, the way I work now, because people come not to move. They'd be shocked to hear me say that. They do move and it comes through the movement attitude, but I don't think that what we are doing is movement – physical movement – it's the inner movement of the psyche we're working on and trying to free.

Non-movement is movement too. The movement means the growth. There is a paradox – the growth or change, the unstatic quality of the whole person which goes back and back from the outer physical movement to the most invisible being.'

CHAPTER 3

Creative Expression in Physical Movement is Language without Words[1]

Mary Starks Whitehouse

We no longer know it but there was a time when movement was our language. It was long ago and we can't remember, but we were born into an alien world in which the first movement was breathing – that sharp inflation of the lungs that brings the first cry. From then on, we struggled and grew into movement, learning on our own, without being taught, how to stretch out and double up, how to hold up our heads, roll over, sit up, creep, crawl and, one triumphant day, to stand, walk. Our learning was nothing we did on purpose. At first, our movement was random, erratic, but as our eyes focused and our awareness increased, we became able to reach out, grasp and look around us. We were busier moving than anything else in the world, and long before we had words we communicated how we felt through our bodies. Our smiling was total and explosive. When we said 'Yes,' everything in us said 'Yes.' When we said 'No,' everything in us said 'No.' We were undivided.

Where did it all go? What happened? How are we now? Well, for one thing, the teaching which was out of our own selves gave way to being taught. We learned to buy and sell with our behavior, hoping for love, learning disapproval. We learned to curb our instant reactions and we unconsciously imitated the movement around us. We picked up the set of our parents' bodies, absorbing, without knowing it, their attitudes and connections with the body. We succumbed to the requirements of our teachers, their insistence on a certain kind of behavior, requiring, without knowing it, restrictions and limitations. Worst of all, we learned very slowly,

---

1   Unpublished paper, date uncertain, *c.* 1956.

but almost completely by the time we were in our teens, to move for a reason, to isolate our motions. When we were young and looked up into the sky at an airplane, the whole body looked up. (Do it). When we bent over to look at a bug, the whole body bent over – but, gradually, only the eyes, with a restricted movement of the neck, looked. When we reached for something, only the arm reached. When we walked, only the legs walked. The bodily stir, the total action of the whole organism, broke up into separate gestures. The lovely flow of energy, the connectedness, was gone. Our smiling became of the mouth only. Our crying, when we allow it, is held in and kept down. Our anger turns into tension. We may be very efficient and very active but we are physically inexpressive and, therefore, uncreative – our gestures are stereotypes of feeling, limited and unoriginal. We kiss by putting our cheeks together and are angry by being polite. Who can imagine an adult turning his back when he dislikes someone, skipping for fun, or clapping for happiness? By this I mean, who can imagine an adult allowing his own spontaneous creative expression in physical movement?

Once, two adults went for a walk with a child. The child ran on ahead for no reason but the fun of running, while the grown-ups walked themselves along under their talk. After a while they caught up to the little girl. She was sitting on the curb, feet in the street. She looked up at them and called out: 'See me sitting.' What adult feels in the body: see me anything?

But there is more. We were, as little children, put at desks for hours at a time, increasingly, and told to keep still and learn, just as children are today. This is based on the assumption that learning is for the mind, a mind separate from the body, that we grow up, as we acquire ideas and knowledge, by means of words and concepts. The expression of feeling is relegated to a sketchy experience in the arts and the experience of movement is assigned to required gym or athletics. Our major skill, the primary value of our culture, is communication through words. We are a verbal culture. We understand through words. We depend on words for contact with each other. We think in words. We can even talk without listening to ourselves and listen to others without hearing.

Because hearing people, and especially children, is also seeing and feeling what they are saying, and for that one needs a different kind of awareness, a sensitivity to gesture and movement. It is the movement of a child that speaks for him and of him. I have heard grown-ups greet a child by asking 'How are you?' Usually, he has no idea what to answer. One look at the way he stands and how he holds on to his mother, at his eyes which are down-cast or lifted to meet yours, and the grown-up need not have asked the question.

An adult answers the same question with: 'Fine, thank you.' (Do it.) But a contradiction comes through. What is really being said is often quite different. The body may be saying 'I'm tired' or 'I'm frightened of your questions.' (Do it.) Sometimes we catch on – the handshake in which the hand is a dead fish, the regular tapping of a foot (beating what?), raised shoulders (raised against what?), a drooping chest (apologizing?). We register and we get a feeling from that person which we can't put into words; it influences us without our realizing where it comes from. It comes directly from the movement and gestures – the body does not lie. We are like our movements, for the movement is ourselves living: vital and experiencing or tense and restricted, spontaneous and flowing or controlled and inhibited.

Professor Hocking of Harvard once remarked that we are born with the body God gave us, but by the time we are forty we have the body we have created for ourselves. And this body that we have created is less expressive, less alive than it could be, because it is not experienced by most of us. It is 'the body' or 'my body,' conceived as an object, in the way a table or a chair is an object. I use it but I am only dimly aware that it is myself. If it is stiff and unyielding, I am somehow stiff and unyielding; if it is tight and prim, I am tight and prim; if it is sloppy and heavy, there is that in me which is sloppy and heavy. It is an important truth that whether I know these things of myself or not, they are, nevertheless, communicated, especially to children. In many a classroom it is the gestures of the teacher which speak to the child, rather than what she is saying. When the teacher's physical timing is hurried and her gestures are sharp and sudden, no words of encouragement will enable the child to respond and she may well be puzzled, when she offers encouragement, to find that he is balking and sullen. Her body is saying 'I am impatient with you' and he is reacting to that message.

Any change has to come through consciousness, awareness, first of one's actual condition and, second, of the possible meaning of that condition. Physical activities are helpful – gym classes, sports – at least they help us to move. They increase the circulation and improve co-ordination. But they don't connect us with ourselves because they still have a motive external to the experience of ourselves. They still put us in the position of moving our bodies for a purpose, instead of becoming aware of ourselves. You can play golf or tennis until you are expert, but I do not believe your habitual, organized physical attitudes or personal gestures will change one bit.

Let's try an experiment. At this moment you are sitting listening to me in a particular physical way. Let's find out what it is. Please close your eyes. You may feel slightly embarrassed or self-conscious, but since everybody has his eyes closed, the embarrassment is not located on the outside, it is not because someone else is looking but because you are. The looking is an act of attention. Don't move or change your position. Just be where you are. Now, begin with your feet. Where are they? Are they touching the floor, and if so, what part of the foot is pressing on the floor? Are they touching each other? Are they alike or quite separate and different? Wiggle your toes inside your shoes. Can you feel them? Now, travel up to your knees and do the same thing. Are they crossed over each other? Is the back of either one or both touching the chair seat? If not, at what point do the backs of the legs rest on the chair? Travel along underneath and behind yourself. How much of you is touching the chair? What are you sitting on? Go on to your back. Is it rounded or straight? Are you leaning back? Where? Are you sitting more on one side than the other? What are your arms doing? Where is each one? Finally, how does your head feel? Can you feel it or do you just know it is there? Now try to be aware of yourself all at once, of all these things at once, so you can recognize 'I am sitting this way'. Now open your eyes.

It would be surprising if you connected this first time with the total feeling of how you were sitting, but perhaps something about it struck you as familiar — or unfamiliar. If it seemed familiar, I would ask you: 'Do you suppose you sit this way often when you are listening to someone?' If there was something unfamiliar, something strange about it, could it be that you never knew before that your way of sitting was like that? At any rate, your sitting, at the moment you became aware of it, was a statement. You were saying something. How you were sitting was not just an accident but an actual feeling condition. What you were saying would be hard to get into words but would be just as real as words. If the simple act of sitting conveys a feeling, think how much our way of moving and gesturing communicates. Who was it who said 'What you are speaks so loudly, I cannot hear what you say.'?

Becoming aware of movement as a kind of non-verbal language, finding out what and how you are speaking has many surprises in it and is not accomplished all at once. Have you ever had the experience of hearing a tape of your own voice? Was it not a shock? That's the way I sound! Seeing a film of yourself moving would be analogous. Perhaps you have. But neither the tape nor the film would be anything but the initial surprise of finding out.

Changes, including changes in the voice, take place only in a process of development, the development of your awareness, your capacity to observe, your willingness to feel. It is this process that is the creativity.

It always strikes me as a commentary on the lack of this awareness in our time that men and women have to sign up to come to my studio for a weekend workshop in the experience of movement when the truth is that we are alive because we move and we move because we are alive. In the deepest sense, movement is the flow of energy that belongs to all livingness. We move twenty-four hours a day and, because we do, because it is natural for us to move, we can discover a great deal about ourselves. We can explore sensations and feelings that we did not know we had. We can extend the range and freedom of our physical gestures. We can learn to trust and express our own spontaneous reactions. We can allow our movement to be creative.

How deep the experience goes, of relating to ourselves, moving, is illustrated by the fact that very frequently in my private work people moving about in the space for the first time find themselves emotionally stirred in a way that surprises them. It is a feeling of wanting to cry or suddenly feeling sad, and both men and women experience it. I believe it is a spontaneous nostalgia for an earlier time when walking about, skipping, stretching the arms up to the sky or bending over were all natural impulses freely allowed. Something has come alive and no matter how one disapproves or says 'Isn't that silly,' one has been touched, one is moved from within, not only physically. The body has become real, it is ourselves feeling.

There is a major, and general, symptomatic condition in the body which I would like to describe to you because I think you will recognize it instantly. People in our time are mostly highly verbal; they mostly run their lives with their heads. There is a great emphasis on reason, thinking and understanding, knowing in an intellectual way, explaining, controlling. The heart and the guts are often left out. This is physically visible in almost everyone who comes to me. It takes the form of a head which is always held on to, which moves very little, creating neck tension, which creates shoulder tension. The head is not a part of the body, moving easily with the rest of one's self, but somehow different and separate.

I remember one young woman who had a very wide range of movement, flexible and varied. She was dancing to music. It looked marvelous but there was something wrong; it was not free, no matter how much she moved. I looked and looked and, finally, I caught it. She was like a marionette – the arms and legs lifted, fell; the torso bent over and back. She crouched down, sprang up, but there she was, sitting up in her head, manipulating everything else, with the result that the head and neck hardly moved. (Do it).

It's as if the body belongs to the head, instead of the head belonging to the body. Did you know that the average head on an adult weighs sixteen pounds? Imagine the work you are doing with your neck to hold all that up the whole time.

Let's try one more experiment. Place both feet on the floor, straight ahead. Now set the hips back against the chair seat so that you are on your sitting bones, not on your spine. Now sit up gently and lean against the chair back, putting your hands at your sides. Drop your head forward on your chest – only your head. Now close your eyes and imagine a small sandbag on the top of your head. It is pulling at your neck, it is so heavy. Let go of your shoulders, they want to follow your head. Can you feel your back rounding? Let the weight pull you forward and down, just follow it, letting the arms slide forward and hang down too. Feel how the back of the neck and the back stretches? Now, very slowly, begin at the lowest point where your back is touching the chair and start climbing the ladder of your spine from below, one vertebra, one inch at a time. Press your back up like building a tower. When you get to your ribs, lift them and let your shoulders drop into place and your head will come up and balance. Was it not a long journey? And the head belonged to the back. This can be done standing too, folding downward until you are hanging from your hips. It is the movement that stretches, not any effort you make.

Two of the simplest words in the language are the trickiest. We all have occasion to use 'Yes' and 'No' many times each day. Say 'Yes' with your head, say it inside and mean it while you nod. Make it bigger, emphatic. Now say 'No', shake your head – remember when you were a child and you said, 'I won't!'? Really say it – not politely – 'No, no, no!'

That's another condition. We often say 'Yes' when we want to say 'No' or 'No' when we are afraid to say 'Yes,' with the result that we stiffen and are not convincing. Our bodies do not go along with our game, they pay us back in tension because we are not sincere – that is, our real feeling is not expressed.

It is possible to find a total way of saying 'Yes' that is using the whole body and a total way of saying 'No' which would mean that we really know what we were saying and felt it. I often work on this experience in weekend workshops. As people become freer in finding ways to move these words, we add the sound of ourselves saying them out loud. One night a man got going across the floor, shouting and stamping 'No,' and there came a change in his body which indicated that he was really saying 'Yes,' although his voice teasingly continued to say 'No.' The contradiction was so clear that everyone watching broke into laughter at the recognition.

But not everyone can take movement workshops. What can be done for ourselves, by ourselves? How can we become more aware of our own movement? How can we begin to allow our own naturalness? I would like to suggest several seemingly small things you can try. At least once a day, turn your attention to the actuality of your body attitude at that moment. It can be anytime, anywhere. You may be driving a car, doing the dishes, making a bed or reading a book. Simply focus your attention on what that action feels like and, in much the same way as we worked on your way of sitting, explore yourself doing something. Do not criticize, nor assume that you ought to be doing it differently, just notice how you are doing it. At the moment of really noticing, if you can then allow even the smallest change, the body itself will give you the impression that it knows what it wants. For instance, if you are standing at the sink and you discover that you are bearing down heavily on one leg, so that your back feels thrown into a curve which is slightly uncomfortable, you will become aware of an impulse to center the weight over both legs. If you find this difficult to believe, close your eyes and deliberately stand heavily on that one leg until the impulse comes. (Do it.)

In the same way, when you discover that you are tightly gripping the steering wheel while driving, don't close your eyes but see the involuntary change that will loosen the hands as a result of your noticing. Practice this little moment of finding out more and more frequently and you will begin to see what habits of straining and slumping you have unwittingly acquired.

Treat this experience as genuine adventure, bring to it curiosity, allow yourself to become conscious of yourself. In addition, when you are working on something which makes use of very restricted movement, as in typing or writing, become aware of any aches or tensions – they usually center in the shoulders – and give yourself the gift of stopping what you are doing, standing up, reaching over your head as far as you can, then shrug the shoulders, nod the head, even clap the hands, and sit down again. (Do it.) In the morning, when you wake up, instead of forcing yourself out of bed with your eyes tightly shut, take a moment to feel yourself waking up, roll over, stretch, yawn, pull yourself up to a sitting position, letting your legs hang over the edge of the bed, and, when you are ready, stand up. Most of us stagger like zombies until we have had our first cup of coffee. There is no real awakening.

You can go beyond these little things by embarking on further adventure. Play music while you are doing something in the house and, whatever it is, do it in time to the music. Gradually shift from the task you are performing to moving around in the space in whatever way the music makes possible. I would use strongly rhythmic music such as folk tunes or percussion at first. A strong rhythm makes it much easier. When you get past the point of feeling silly because you are allowing yourself to 'dance,' try lying down flat on the floor and using slower and less rhythmic music to help you to rollover, curl up, stretch out.

I think you will find that this is all far more natural than you expected and that your sense of yourself will increase sharply. Perhaps you will even go so far as to become aware of the kind of handshake you have, of the way in which you do not look directly at another person, of how you stiffen when someone touches your arm, and you can begin to allow greater spontaneity in yourself and in other people.

This spontaneity would be of the utmost value for you as teachers. If you are not afraid of your own movement, you will not be afraid of the tremendous need of children to move wholly and organically. You might even be willing to interrupt your demand for their attention, to let them stand up, to clap and stamp and reach, to walk and trot around the room, before you ask them to begin again with their tasks. As you begin to allow this freedom, you will also become sensitive to their movement toward you and away from you. When they move toward you, your own body will become welcoming, even including a hug or a hand on the head. (Do it.) When they move away from you, you will be able to avoid following or pressing after them, unless you can do it with warmth and reassurance in your body. (Do it.)

We are beginning to place enormous emphasis on creativity, but there is a tendency to think that being creative is limited to 'producing' something. I would suggest to you that the basic creativity of the human being consists in his working toward his own fullest development, the realizing of his own potentials, the allowing himself to grow. What we create first is ourselves and it is out of ourselves that the producing comes.

CHAPTER 4

The Tao of the Body[1]

Mary Starks Whitehouse

Movement is the great law of life. Everything moves. The heavens move, the earth turns, the great tides mount the beaches of the world. The clouds march slowly across the sky, driven by a wind that stirs the trees into a dance of branches. Water, rising in mountain springs, runs down the slopes to join the current of the river. Fire, begun in the brush, leaps roaring over the ground, and the earth, so slow, so always there, grumbles and groans and shifts in the sleep of centuries.

So too all living creatures. Birds and fish and insects, animals, snakes and snails have their being in movement, exist by virtue of it, show forth their nature through it. In the words of the old song: 'Fish gotta swim, birds gotta fly.'

And man? Whoever he is, wherever he is, he too lives in movement. His body is a world of movement in itself. Breathing and circulation, digestion and reproduction are all unconscious movement processes, the wonderful motor pattern of his life. Within this pattern he lies down, he sits, he stands and, standing, walks and runs. He sleeps, eats, copulates, fights, weeps, laughs and talks. Most of all, in our twentieth-century civilization, he talks. Words have become his primary means of communication and realization – words that he says, words that he listens to, words in books, words that he thinks with. And slowly, slowly, without his knowing it almost, the words and the talking, which are only one kind of movement linked to one kind of

---

1 Paper presented at the Analytical Psychology Club of Los Angeles, 1958. Previously published in D.H. Johnson (ed) *Bone, Breath and Gesture*. Berkeley, CA: North Atlantic Books, 1995.

understanding, take the place of another quite different awareness of himself and others.

Two things about physical movement are striking. One is that movement is non-verbal and yet it communicates – that is, says something. Our impressions of people are gathered fully as much from physical attitudes and gestures as from words and clothes. Nervousness often shows itself in little extra movements of hands, feet and face; tension, in raised shoulders as well as voice; depression in downward drooping lines of the whole body; fear in limited and carefully controlled movement; and so on indefinitely. They are all communicated to us by others and by us to others, whether we know it and can describe it in words or not. Often, other people are more aware of our condition than we are able to be ourselves. Which brings me to the second thing. The body does not, I would almost say cannot, lie. The human being, as he actually exists at any moment, cannot be hidden, by words, by clothes, least of all by wishes. No matter what he is doing or saying, he has his own way of doing or saying it and it is the way that reveals what he is like. The physical condition is, in some way, also the psychological one. We do not know in what way the psyche is the body and the body is the psyche but we do know that one does not exist without the other. And I would go so far as to suggest that just as the body changes in the course of working with the psyche, so the psyche changes in the course of working with the body. We would do well to remember that the two are not separate entities but mysteriously a totality.

It is difficult to know where to begin. What I want to do is to describe, and, later on, to let you see, some of the ways in which movement can become direct, subjective experience and to suggest certain kinds of self-knowledge which are available through it. I am confronted by the necessity of talking about something which is essentially inaccessible to words, but I will try. I have an approach, not a method, much less a theory. In fact, I often feel that the serious and deep things which take place in this way of working with the body happen much more out of what I do not know than out of what I do. Perhaps the fact that they happen is what is important. I well remember my initiation into this truth. I had only reluctantly begun individual appointments. A woman stood alone in the center of the studio. It was her third or fourth appointment. We had been working very simply with stretching, bending, standing and walking. Her movement in general existed in a cloud over her head – the face and eyes nearly always turned up to the ceiling, the arms and hands repeatedly extended overhead, the weight lifted up on the toes, everything going up, nothing down, everything going out, nothing held. I suggested she clench her fists and bring them up from her sides in front of her. The first time, the hands closed but there was very little tension in the muscles of the arm, they still floated. The second time, she waited longer and pulled harder. Very slowly the arms bent at the elbows, closing upward in front of her body. As the fists approached her face, her expression became one of intense sorrow and strain and, at the point of almost touching her own mouth and cheeks, the whole body turned and pitched downward onto the floor in a violent fall and she burst into long sobs. A barrier had been pierced, a dam broken, her body had pitched her into feeling.

The core of the movement experience is the sensation of moving and being moved. There are many implications in putting it like this. Ideally, both are present in the same instant, and it may be literally an instant. It is a moment of total awareness, the coming together of what I am doing and what is happening to me. It cannot be anticipated, explained, specifically worked for, nor repeated exactly.

In order that it may happen, one must have a bodily awareness of movement. It is astonishing how many people are almost completely unaware of themselves physically. Our personal ways of sitting, standing, moving, eating, smoking, talking are so habitual as to seem natural and hardly worth noticing. The wonderful joy in movement, which children have, has been lost. Movement has become a means to an end, usually a rational and purposeful end, and takes place automatically in response to hundreds and hundreds of mental images of going someplace and doing something. To be sure, first parents, and then friends have always commented freely on our faulty posture and lack of grace – 'Pull in your stomach,' 'Stand up straight,' 'Don't slouch' – and, sometimes, when we catch an unexpected glimpse of ourselves in a mirror, there is the vague beginning of a realization of something not satisfactory, not alive, but it is gone again even as it comes. After all, this is what we look like and no amount of trying will change it. This latter, incidentally, is accurate since 'trying' seldom changes anything basic – only becoming something different changes what was. It never occurs to us that we have unwittingly lost the body by not experiencing its truth and that, to the extent that it does not and cannot move easily, freely and totally, it is dead; for movement is the life of the body. This life includes the life of the mind but it is not limited to it.

There is a technical term for feeling one's body move – it is called the kinesthetic sense – and it is just as valuable as the five which inform us of the physical world about us. The kinesthetic sense is the sensation which accompanies or informs us of bodily movement. Athletes have it, and dancers, also actors, though they often forget to work with it – all the people whom we describe as having natural timing and co-ordination in motion. It is likely that some people are born with a greater degree of it than others, just as there are greater and lesser visual and auditory gifts, but we all have it. I have an idea that it is connected with the extraordinary capacity of the blind man to move in a world which he cannot see but can feel moving, and that it accounts for the equally extraordinary adaptation some people are able to make in response to serious or permanent crippling. The recent case of a high school girl, paralyzed from the neck down, who has learned to write with a pencil held between her teeth, is an example.

But if the kinesthetic sense is never developed, or seldom used, it becomes unconscious and one is in the situation I have already described, a situation that I can only call living in the head, which fact the body faithfully reflects, since it must move, by acquiring a whole series of distortions, short circuits, strains and mannerisms accumulated from years and years of being assimilated to mental images of choice, necessity, value and appropriateness. At this point, movement is 'in spite of' instead of 'with the help of' the mental life.

There is a further interesting reflection in connection with this. In our time there is a widespread repression of all physical emotion – that is, all bodily expression of joy, grief, anger, affection, fear – and an equally widespread fascination with the body's appearance and function. Advertisements of cures for nerves, constipation, colds, headaches, that run-down feeling; recommendations for slimming, trimming, building, developing; diets, gadgets, vitamins, how to sleep, how to wake up, how not to perspire, how to avoid bad breath – the list is endless and body-centered, all polarized by sex plastered interminably on bill boards, in magazines, movies, newspapers, in the form of the female body as exposed and as unlikely in proportion as possible. We are embarrassed and irritated when confronted by any form of physical intensity in our personal lives. Joy in the voice and face is all right, grief in the voice and face is understandable, anger in the voice and face will pass, but an exuberant enveloping arm thrown around our shoulders, the sight of a body rocking back and forth with grief, the sudden eruption of a stamped foot or a book slammed violently down on a table, all upset us. Could it be that the body is the unconscious and that in repressing and, more important, disregarding the spontaneous life of the sympathetic nervous system we are enthroning the rational, the orderly, the manageable, and cutting ourselves off from all experience of the unconscious and, therefore, of the instincts, which then take their revenge in the form of an exaggerated, compulsive fascination with the body and all its works? The less the body is experienced, the more it becomes an appearance; the less reality it has, the more it must be undressed or dressed up; the less it is one's own known body, the further away it moves from anything to do with one's self.

Working with movement is an initiation into the world of the body as it actually is, what it can do easily, with difficulty, or not at all. But it is also, or can be, a serious discovery of what we are like – for we are like our movement. People discover what parts of their bodies are not available, do not move, are not felt. The woman of whom I have already spoken sent me a description, much later, of her first experience. I quote it:

> Together we went out to the studio. [My teacher] said she wanted to see me walk to see how I was built and how I moved. I walked and as I see myself now, it was as if my body did not belong to me – the very fact of being alone with someone watching me brought a little light to the surface. Putting my feet together was a new experience and I never shall forget the feeling of wholeness my hands expressed when I put them together, thrusting them out into the space. Perhaps I did not know it, but my hands contained all that my body did not.

She worked in private appointments weekly, until she felt ready to try a class. Shortly after she began, she gave this account of another discovery:

> I see an image emerging out of the earth. It is a masculine image with arms outstretched to the blue space all about him. His legs dangle in the earth. He must come out of the earth and walk in the blue space that only his upper body knows. He needs legs in relation to his upper body so he can dance in space and love it.

It is interesting that it is a structural element in movement, a principle of definition and order. Walking is a means of moving about in space. It is entirely suitable that the masculine principle be set free to use space as structure. She goes on:

> I realized the only way I could live now is in this space. I began to dance to the music of primitive peoples. I discovered that my legs were not like

the upper part of my body – what a terrible feeling – I am only half a person but to know I'm only half a person was not a small thing to me. I had visions of my legs moving like my arms do – so I sat down on the floor and decided I was going to work with my legs. It may take a while I thought but the vision of moving in space as a whole thing seemed worth working for. My gosh, my legs felt like two pieces of sticks sticking out of my body. I had found a way for my hands to talk and tell me things, perhaps I could get my legs to do the same. I began to move the legs letting them do whatever they wanted to do, being sure it was only the legs doing it. It was amazing to see how little they could do – they were so helpless that I was desperately sorry for them. They needed to be cared for like a child. To do this I needed my hands. Now, another thought came to me. I had to find my hands first so I could take hold of my legs and help them out of the earth. Something inside of me jumped for joy when I discovered I have something to work with instead of something working with me.

And from another woman:

I feel most of the time a head and shoulders supported by legs that begin just south of my rib cage. Feeling of nothing in the middle has persisted through five different physical culture courses of one kind or another…

She went on to speak of her husband as a natural born dancer, I quote again:

…rhythm, flow, light, beautiful, sensitive. Me, all these [things] inside but not connected up with the body. Infuriating to us both as I do feel it as keenly as he does…he knows it and I do but it just can't get out. I know why. It is because I haven't a body. It is that something in the middle that's lacking… Bad balance and awkwardness I used to blame on feet. Now [I] realize it's imbalance inside, and [I] am convinced recently it is something missing in the middle.

The kinesthetic sense can be awakened and developed in using any and all kinds of movement, but I believe it becomes conscious only when the inner – that is, the subjective – connection is found, the sensation of what it feels like to the individual, whether it is swinging, stretching, bending, turning, twisting or whatever. People can learn movement in a variety of ways. They are not necessarily enabled to feel it when they do so. It is the concrete, specific awareness of one's own act of moving which is so satisfying. The physical culture courses of which our friend spoke, work with the body as object, not as subject, and while a general release takes place, there is no corresponding experience of the personal identity, its quality and its movement. This seems to mean that something more is needed than simply body mechanics, that the feelings hidden in the body, the source of all its movement, must be involved. People in general are not very interested in abdominal muscles, the diaphragm, the shoulder girdle and the pelvis, but they care deeply about the world in which they must find a way to live and about themselves who must do the living.

You will remember that much earlier I spoke of the ideal moment as the coming together of myself moving and myself being moved. There seem to be two extremes of people. I could describe them psychologically as those who are overwhelmed by the unconscious and those who are cut off from it. Physically, it seems to take the form, in the first instance, of general, overall movement vague in outline, a kind of swimming of the arms and hands particularly, a groping, floating quality, curiously disembodied and unreal. In watching it you have the feeling that it is happening by itself, that no one or almost no one is there doing it. This is strange, too, because later, as the physical awareness grows, one is quite unable to say what has changed. Much of the movement is similar but it becomes indefinably real, three-dimensional and, somehow, in the body. These people are most at ease when allowed to improvise freely. They do not like form or pattern or any different timing than the one they habitually use and can only do a specific exercise at first if not required to be exact. In the early stages they seem to experience difficulty in connecting with any given part of the body – you have the impression that a message sent to the feet to move, for example, has to travel a long distance and that the foot responds like an alien thing, slowly, and with surprise at being asked.

At the other end of the scale are the people who cannot imagine a movement which they do not consciously initiate, on purpose, so to speak. They lay great emphasis on understanding exactly what they are doing and are happiest in exercises, patterns and forms. Sitting or lying quietly with their attention turned inward on their breathing affects them as boring and when they try to do it, their bodies jerk, their hands place and replace themselves, their shoulders twitch and they give the impression of being thoroughly miserable, restless and ill at ease. Freedom to move as they please terrifies them because they 'do not know what they are supposed to do' and even if they do move, they are apt to feel self-consciousness more than the movement.

When both kinds of people are in a group situation, it presents something of a challenge to the leader. The work has to include a given form for those who are unable to find a form of their own, at the same time that they need to be encouraged to find the feeling potential of any movement. This is usually done by description of what the movement is like, of the sensation that belongs to it, and, since no one image works for everyone, several must be tried. On the other hand, for the people who can only find the form through their feelings, descriptions of recognizable objects or actions provide a form into which the feeling can flow so that it takes an actual shape. Sometimes, when both needs are met, the room is suddenly full of real people doing real movement, fully focused and alive.

For the people to whom movement just happens, through whom it pours without any consciousness of the ego's part in it, the liberating experience would be the discovery that 'I am moving.' Not long ago a young woman arrived in a state of utter confusion, lostness and depression. She asked if she could talk and I suggested that if it came to her to say something while she moved, so that it was part of her movement, part of the ritual of moving for herself, and not a conversation with me, it would then be movement too. But it proved to be unnecessary. She went over and sat down on the rug. We used no music or other accompaniment. There followed what I can only describe as a quite miraculous birth of an actual body. There was a half-smile on her face, which appeared very near the beginning and lasted all the way through. She stretched, twisted, touched her own feet and legs, stood up from a sitting position easily and without uncertainty, and went on stretching and bending through all her limbs and torso, finally taking, for her, firm steps on the whole foot into the space around her. When it was over, she opened her eyes and looking at me with the most complete and joyous amazement, said: 'Do you know what happened? As I sat down, I thought – if I had a body – and then I did.'

For the people who are convinced that they do it all, the liberating experience would be the discovery that 'something moves me – I did not do it.' The members of a class were improvising one night, individually but all at the same time. Suddenly, one girl who had been working very close to the floor bounded to her feet and spun around with great rapidity. She was heavy and the movement was totally out of keeping with any I had ever seen her do – if I had asked her to turn in that way, she could not have done it. Afterward, she told me that it was one of the most shocking things that had ever happened to her, she was completely unprepared, she did not know how it happened nor have any image of its happening – 'it did it itself.'

A word about what this way of working with the body requires. There is necessarily an attitude of inner openness, a kind of capacity for listening to one's self that I would call honesty. It is made possible only by concentration and patience. In allowing the body to move in its way, not in a way that would look nice or that one thinks it should; in waiting patiently for the inner impulse, in letting the reactions come up exactly as they occur on any given evening – bear in mind that the reactions *are* the movement – new capacities appear, new modes of behavior are possible, and the awareness gained in the specialized situation goes over into a new sense of one's self driving the car or stooping with the vacuum cleaner or shaking hands with a friend. I know one woman who had never found it possible to talk back to her husband. As she discovered what it felt like to carry her body from the ground up, lifted in the middle, the legs firmly beneath her, instead of caved in, the shoulders and the head dropped forward to protect a retreating chest, she found she could no longer avoid speaking up for herself, even when it meant disagreement. She is not, incidentally, in analysis, so the connection is direct, without benefit of dreams.

It would take another paper to go into the question of dance – what it is and how these experiences are related to it – and still another to describe the use of movement as an adjunct to psychotherapy – where it becomes a method of active imagination in which there is the possibility of dancing a dream situation and finding out, directly and inescapably, since it happens in the real – that is, the physical – world, which is more primary than words and even than painting, a truth about that situation or a change in it or a further possibility that one had not known.

I am often asked whether what I am doing is therapy and, sometimes, whether this is psychology or body training or dance or what, and why don't I choose one and stick to it. To which I can only answer that any means to self-knowledge is therapy. If that is begging the question, I would be willing to say that I am engaged in professional therapy only insofar as my life, including my training, fits me to mediate experience which is therapeutic to the individual and not otherwise available to him. But it is not my experience and I do not do it. It is done in and by the body, strange as that sounds. As for the question of choice, the whole attempt is concerned with the connections between body and psyche or between physical movement which is outer and psychic events which are inner. I have ceased, very recently I must admit, plaguing myself with labels and explanations. I was enormously aided in this by two sentences from the foreword to the *I Ching*. There C.G. Jung (1949) says:

> Probably in no other field [psychotherapy] do we have to reckon with so many unknown quantities, and nowhere else do we become more accustomed to adopting methods that work even though for a long time we may not know why they work. [...] The irrational fullness of life has taught me never to discard anything, even when it goes against all our theories [...] or otherwise admits of no immediate explanation. (p.XXXIV)

There are many other questions which cannot be touched in this space. What is the difference, if any, in a man's experience of his body and a woman's? How much interpretation by the leader or observer is desirable or necessary? Can any correlation be made between the basic concepts of Jungian psychology (persona, ego, shadow, anima, animus, the self, the personal and the collective layer of the unconscious) and human movement? When an analysand is also working in movement, what exchange of information and material would be helpful and would this require at least an introductory experience of his own movement on the part of the analyst? These things and many others wait to be investigated. One cannot even guess at the answers but that there are answers I feel sure, and that they can help to increase our understanding of what man, in his totality, really is, seems equally certain.

And the Tao of the body? As an ancient sage said: 'Gravity is the root of lightness; and stillness is the ruler of movement.'

References

Jung, C.G. (1949) Foreword. In *I Ching* (translation by Richard Wilhelm) Bollingen Series (1967). Princeton: Princeton University Press.

CHAPTER 5

Physical Movement and Personality[1]

Mary Starks Whitehouse

Five years ago, at about this same time and before this same group, I attempted an introductory formulation of my work with physical movement, called, pretentiously enough, *The Tao of the Body*. Like all genuine efforts at clarification, its value lays as much or more in its effect on my own painfully forming attitudes and convictions as in anything it had to offer objectively. This is, for me, the second half of that other offering – the attempt to bring still more into focus the essential value and meaning of what has been inherent in the growth of my work as it happened to me. The title *The Tao of the Body* would still be appropriate, and perhaps less pretentious this time, since it has gained content and stands now for an established fact of experience in my own growth and in the realization of individuals for whom the work with the body has opened doors otherwise closed. I have chosen the heading 'Physical Movement and Personality' as a way of bringing to you a description of approaches to the psychophysical connections in movement.

We are accustomed to the idea that psychic changes, changes in personality, produce physical changes. When we speak of the change in a person produced by therapy, we are indicating, if not consciously pointing out, certain indefinable physical differences: a difference in the tempo and pitch of speech, a difference in the physical composure, a difference in the degree and kind of attention available. The attitude of the person toward himself and toward the world has changed and, with it, the body gestalt, outline and substance.

1   Paper presented at the Analytical Psychology Club of Los Angeles, 1963. Previously published in *Contact Quarterly*, Winter 1987.

But we are not accustomed to the idea that the conscious experience of physical movement produces changes in the psyche. The crux of the connection lies in the phrase 'conscious experience.' For most people, the tempo and pattern of all physical movement is habit formed, automatic, unconscious and, above all, organized toward a utilitarian end, toward an objective or goal. It is when the goal or the form of a purposeful action (reaching to get something, running to catch a bus, all the thousand-and-one acts packed into the day) is suspended in favor of movement as it happens that one can perceive the movement as an actual substance and begin to ask questions about what it reveals, what it says to the person moving about himself. And the awakening of the awareness of how one moves, in what manner, (slow or fast, heavy or light, restricted or easy) leads to a perception which carries over into a recognition of the character, also, of daily or habitual body usage.

For the wonderful thing is that the body is not and never will be a machine, no matter how much we treat it as such, and, therefore, body movement is not and never will be mechanical – it is always and forever expressive, simply because it is human. The body is the physical aspect of the personality and movement is the personality made visible. The distortions, tensions and restrictions are the distortions, tensions and restrictions within the personality. They are, at any given moment, the condition of the psyche. And the discovery of their factual existence, their physical existence, is the beginning of the process of what might be called psychosomatic recognition, for we are psychosomatic entities.

Where does movement come from? It originates in what Laban calls an inner effort – that is, a specific inner impulse having the quality of sensation. This impulse leads outward into space so that movement becomes visible as physical action. Following the inner sensation, allowing the impulse to take the form of physical action is active imagination in movement, just as following the visual image is active imagination in fantasy. It is here that the most dramatic psychophysical connections are made available to consciousness and it is this area I wish chiefly to describe.

Let me give an example of what I mean by following the sensation. Recently, I was invited to teach a class for the graduate dance majors at UCLA. They were interested not in performance but in dance as rehabilitation and therapy. I began by asking them in what way they would practice or work alone – that is, without teaching or being taught. There followed a charming display of industry. Some sat and stretched, some stood and stretched, all switched from one physical form to the next without any transition or connecting links. My impression was of a great deal of activity and movement but of nothing individual, reflective, discovered or spontaneous. It had all been learned. I asked them to sit with their legs crossed and to close their eyes. I described the open waiting, which is also a kind of listening to the body, an emptiness in which something can happen. You wait until you feel a change – the body sinks or begins to tip, the head slowly lowers forward or rolls to one side. As you feel it begin, you follow where it leads, like following a pathway that opens up before you as you step. One girl slowly fell backward and to the side until she was resting on her elbow. When she described what had happened, she used the words 'gravity pull.' I asked her why and she replied that gravity was a word often used but that she had never felt it before and had not known it had its own laws.

When one follows, one cannot at the same time lead. An early discovery in class or private work is that will power and effort impede movement. Gritting the teeth and trying inhibits the feel of the movement quality, its shape and weight, and ends up providing sore muscles and not much else. Whether it is a given exercise or free improvisation, one has to learn to 'let it happen,' as contrasted to 'doing it.' Since we are in general convinced that the body is our personal possession, an object, it feels strange to allow it, as subject, the independence of discovery. In this connection, the Taoist saying 'Non-action in action; action in non-action' becomes illuminating. The ego learns slowly an attitude toward what *wants* moving, not to act while the action is going on. Movement, to be experienced, has to be 'found' in the body, not put on like a dress or a coat. There is that in us which has moved from the very beginning: it is that which can liberate us.

A woman describes this experience:

Once, the first time I experienced 'being moved' rather than moving, I was sitting quietly cross-legged on the floor with my eyes shut. Mary had said that we should rise in the simplest, most direct way we could without overtones. I had only been working with her in classes for about six months and I had absolutely no muscle control or technical ability but I rose in one complete spiral movement, my legs unwinding me upward like a corkscrew. Physically, if I had been asked to do it, I could not have. 'It' moved me, I did nothing. It impressed me more than I can say – in retrospect, it seems to have been the beginning (despite a couple of years of analysis) of a new understanding of the autonomy of inner images. I had understood the concepts involved, but my stomach had never

believed them. I, and I alone, was responsible for the nice and the terrible
things I did. Suddenly this idea no longer held water.

The experience indicated always carries an element of surprise – it is
unexpected and seems to happen quite of itself. Again and again, the physical
action takes a form which would not be possible at will or which would take a
long time to learn by conscious intention. People balance incredibly without
knowing how to balance, twist or turn in a way quite out of keeping with
their normal rigidity, jump or run when they have long since forgotten how.
There is nothing magical about this. Shrunk to the size of the ego, movement
appears as inhibition, self-consciousness, poverty of gesture, deadness. The
openness of attitude allows the totality and, therefore, the body to function
freely, producing much more of the natural range of physical action, which is
the birthright of the human being.

Once the channel is open, experiences present themselves in the manner
of dreams – vivid, ephemeral, full of affect. Sometimes they are beginnings,
sometimes endings. I quote:

> Once I had a private lesson with Mary. I felt perfectly free and normal
> when we began. No big tensions bothering me. After five minutes or so
> of moving to music I had never heard before, I found myself in a position
> on the floor and with my arms folded in such a way that for a moment I
> thought I had a baby in them and was rocking and crooning to it. Had I
> been writing, I could have avoided what happened – I doubtless had
> many times. But now I broke into terrible, uncontrollable sobs of grief for
> the child that was not there. Up to that time I had not wanted a child; I
> felt guilty about that, but I didn't want one. Fear, selfishness, the refusal
> of commitment, not liking being a woman – a host of disagreeable
> unconscious material started to break through.

This is a beginning. The 'disagreeable unconscious material' has come into
consciousness to be looked at. The body attitude and the sobbing have
acquainted the one who moved with her actual feeling.

Many experiences are painful, but some bring a liberation and a reality
that is like a blessing. A woman sitting on the floor, groping forward with
hands and arms, suddenly confronted an earlier dream of hers in which the
ghost of a woman had the power to poison people and had at different times
killed one person and then four. The ghost was there in front of her and,
before she could think, she reached out and grabbed it, tipping over onto her
back and pushing, wrestling backward along the floor, holding on tightly,

the ghost on top. There came a prodigious push and the woman rolled over on top, at which point the ghost evaporated and the woman slowly sat up, beginning a passage of movement in which her hands wonderingly felt along her body – legs, hips, breasts, shoulders, arms – exploring, confirming, accepting. A week later, for the first time, she danced upright, stamping and slapping, a beginning in affirmation, the assertion of her right to be alive.

The movement can end an involvement as well as begin one. In one case, the improvisation took the form of a rocking of the body from the right toward the left. The left pulled at the body – whenever the woman yielded, turning into the space on the left side, feelings of despair and desperate grief overwhelmed her, a kind of drowning – as if an abyss had opened and she were being pulled into it. These feelings were connected with the death of a deeply loved man seven years before. She had never been able to separate from them and they remained the same. Frightened and repelled by the strength of the pull, she hung for a moment on the edge of choice then slowly, slowly turned away, climbed away, toward the right, turning her back. It was a definite separation; from that day her relationship to the personal loss changed. It became her loss and her love. It no longer overwhelmed and drowned her.

Sometimes, the movement is accompanied by images of what is happening. Pressed down by a black depression, a woman found herself moving easily and freely under water, rolling, swimming, opening and closing, mostly lying on her back, eyes closed, body relaxed. At length, the gathering energy turned her over and she pulled herself on her arms out of the water at the edge of the shore, her legs dragging behind her like a seal's tail, the upper body lifted. Then the eyes opened and she lay, still partly in the water, looking at the land before her. Only by going down under could she come up and out.

Another kind of experience is the sudden coming into consciousness of the emotions connected with past events. In Zürich, I had occasion to work with a young analyst-in-training. His left elbow had been badly injured when he was a child of five and the joint had been pinned together, resulting in a slight crippling which prevented the full straightening of the arm. Nevertheless, the left arm was the one with which he gestured when he talked, the one that led emotionally. In a series of appointments the actual limitation of the left arm became real to him – it felt more but could do less. At the end of an appointment he was reduced to tears, those tears that had never been shed by the little boy at the time of the accident because he had been so busy living up to his father's injunction to 'keep your chin up,' which, by the way, he also did. That night he went out to eat at a restaurant and sat at a table with other people whom he did not know. Looking across at him, an old man said 'Can I help you? Can I cut your meat for you?' and he suddenly realized that the left arm was lying crippled and helpless in his lap. There followed a developmental process in which he explored the relationship of the right arm to the left, finding the right arrogant and superior, with a tendency to prevent movement of the left, or, at the very best, to teach it what to do. It was a deep experience of equilibrium when he one day felt both arms together but separately and a passage of movement ended, as he put it, 'With me in the middle between two arms.'

This right-left polarity indicated in the two previous cases is a recurring motif for exploration in movement, just as up/down, open/closed seem to be. In a very recent case a girl who had danced all her life, but without this kind of awareness, was appalled to discover herself sitting on the floor with the right hand tightly grasping the left. As she turned her attention to this, the left hand doubled into a fist and tried to withdraw, but the right clutched tighter and tighter until the knuckles were white. During this time, she told me afterward, she was innerly screaming at the right: 'Let go, let go!' It would not. Finally, the left twisted free, still clenched, the right still hovering claw-like a few inches away. It was interesting that as soon as the left was free, she could no longer feel it, though she knew it was there but could only perceive the power drive of the right. Out of a series of experiments she was compelled to say: 'But my left side will not do anything I tell it to.'

You have undoubtedly noticed that, with one exception, the examples given are all of women. I believe there are two reasons why most men find their way so hesitantly to the movement experience. The first is cultural. It is a prejudice of Western civilization that dancing belongs to women, just as in some primitive societies it once belonged to men. Therefore, to participate in anything which is not a sport or not athletically oriented automatically opens the way to a suspicion of effeminacy. This is threatening enough but, even more basically, there is the unconscious fear of the body itself. There is an appropriate anxiety, an instinctive perception that emotions are rooted in the body.

In every woman there is the secret image of the dancer, of dancing as the meaning of the body. In addition, everything in her knows her own biological destiny. She creates out of the body. The movement which is created seems to her, no matter how surprising, somehow natural, belonging to her. But for a man, it is a submission, a discomfort and only gradually a reality.

You may be interested in a few comparisons of differences in the way men experience some of these things from the way women do. I have worked with barely one-fourth the number of men as women in the last nine years, so I cannot draw any conclusions. But it seems to be true, in an inner sense, that women feel as if the movement proceeds from something interior which pushed outward – toward form – while men express it as something which magnetizes the body, drawing it into space. One man said that he perceives a track, feels a pull from the space around him, which the body feels or follows. Again, women are most comfortable on or near the floor – the passivity and the weight are pleasant. Men have a tendency to feel irritable and restrained, therefore restless. For the woman, space is a fear; for the man, it is action and freedom. He likes shaping it. She likes swimming in it. Further experience would be needed to learn, from individual cases, what the general truth really is.

The experience related here must be seen not as the isolated happenings they appear to be but as points of revelation in a process of developing awareness. They are the speech of the total personality presenting itself to be heard – the inner process in physical form, having meaning which can be apprehended and value which can be received by the person moving. They are extremely compelling because the body is an immediate reality. One cannot evade the direct physical experience when it is direct and when it is physical. 'Making it up' and 'censoring,' both of which can easily happen with words, produce patent artificiality in the first case and stoppage of the movement in the second. One cannot even fly off on the wings of intuitive possibility, for the body exists in time and space and will not fly – it can only unfold movement a step at a time. So there one is, exactly where the movement is, exactly as unfree, exactly as conflicted, exactly as frightened. And the assimilation of this discovery strengthens and releases consciousness for growth, which is, I think, the basic meaning of personality.

CHAPTER 6

Reflections on a Metamorphosis[1]

Mary Starks Whitehouse

I am an ex-dancer, not only by virtue of the passage of time with all that means to strength, speed and flexibility, but by virtue of a slow metamorphosis, a gradually changing focus of interest. It is only now that I can sense the outline of all that has taken place in my journey from my dance years to the kind of work I am presently doing.

As I left dance, and I did leave it, it was not in order to do something else, find another profession, but in response to an urgent need to go beyond assumptions implicit in 'being a dancer.' It became a search for a different understanding of dance and of my commitment to it. I had outgrown that marvelous and simple-minded missionary zeal associated with an absolute conviction that dance, and modern dance in particular, would transform the world – that if everyone knew about and participated in dance, all the ills of Man could be healed. This conviction took the form of large and small concerts under varied conditions for various kinds of groups, of lecture demonstrations and master classes, in addition to regular studio teaching. It reminds me, now, of 'show and tell' in primary school, with its youthful amalgam of pride, enthusiasm and competition.

The war punctured the balloon of innocent ambition and dedication. With a husband overseas and two children to support, dance took on the dimensions of a job instead of a crusade. I made the transition into the relative calm and security of college teaching. But, as I looked at the modern dance of most concerts and classes in the late 1940s and early 1950s, it

1   Previously published in 'Impulse' 1969–1970 and reprinted in R. Head, R.E. Rothenberg and D. Wesley (eds) *A Well of Living Waters: Festschrift for Hilde Kirsch*. Los Angeles: C.G. Jung Institute, 1977.

seemed to me increasingly stereotyped in general content and form, increasingly skill-oriented. It had, in many ways, become an activity to be learned and I could perceive very little attempt to further its original impetus, which had consisted in the basic discovery that the dancer had something humanly significant to say.

It was an important day when I discovered that I did not teach Dance, I taught People. I did not know it but it was the beginning of a sea change, the stalk of an underwater attitude which would grow slowly to the surface over a period of years. What it meant, I could not really imagine, but it was accompanied by a feeling of relief and excitement. It indicated a possibility that my primary interest might have to do with process not results, that it might not be art I was after but another kind of human development. Perhaps there was something in people that danced, a natural impulse, unformed and, at first, even fugitive. If I could find ways of releasing it, if I could come to grips with what interfered with and prevented its expression, I might find the beginning of what my discovery meant.

Then it occurred to me to ask what it is that man does when he dances, not only as artist but as man. He expresses that which cannot be put into words; he gives voice to the ineffable, intangible meaning and condition of being alive; he puts himself in touch with forces beyond the purely personal and mundane; he swims in a river of movement that refreshes his spirit.

There was my clue: the meaning and condition of being alive. The degree of aliveness in people was the starting place. I had to be able to begin where people were, not where I thought they ought to be. I wanted, now, to help them explore and extend their aliveness. Together we had to suspend a specific image of dancing and of my teaching them to dance in favor of the discovery of their own bodily condition, their own attitudes, assumptions and feelings in the experience of themselves moving. Then came another clue: we needed to know the something in Man that dances. Dance does not belong to dancers, it belongs to Man – and always has. It was once the transpersonal stuff of his relation to his universe, and can be, even now. But now it begins with the personal, with ourselves as we find ourselves. For the dance to open out, for it to become more than ourselves in our little, difficult lives, we have to let ourselves be touched, moved. It is no accident that when we are touched we call it a 'moving experience'.

Gradually, I came to see that movement is one of the great laws of life. It is the primary medium of our aliveness, the flow of energy going on in us like a river all the time, awake or asleep, twenty-four hours a day. Our movement is our behavior; there is a direct connection between what we are like and how we move. Distortion, tension and deadness in our movement is distortion, tension and deadness in ourselves. As long as the body can be regarded as an object to be trained, controlled or manipulated, one need not experience these things; one is still doing something to it or with it. But when it is somehow myself, impelled by impulses, feelings and inward demands for action waiting to be perceived and allowed, I am suddenly aware of being differently alive, differently conscious of myself.

In sensing this, I found that I was involved with both an inner process of self-recognition and the possibility of inner growth. There is something incontrovertible in coming up against one's own body as it actually is, sluggish and resistant or floppy and yielding. As people begin to move in their own way, they are faced with feelings of surprise and delight and, often, of anxiety and embarrassment. Judgments, corrections and explanations are of no use. It is their movement and it happens just that way.

Change can happen and development can take place through the discovery of unused and previously unavailable qualities of movement. For instance, something as simple, but as basic, as large, strong, assertive action in a forward direction can be built up gradually from a walk and coaxed, not commanded, from the timid, self-apologetic ones. The experience of this new quality of movement provides a change in feeling, another dimension of the self. Change can also take place through the discovery of previously unavailable feelings. For the ones who move like bulldozers, the longing to experience themselves as yielding and delicate results in a changed quality of movement. So movement can lead to new feeling; feeling can lead to new movement. They are, in some way, one.

Nevertheless, for years I was still caught in that ancient conflict between form and content or between technique and improvisation that is an argument in all the arts. In dance it appears when people say: 'But before you can dance, you must train the body.' This is true, in a sense, for dancers, but for people who don't want to become dancers, it is the feeling of dancing that counts, not the discovery of what their bodies cannot do but of what they can do, of what is naturally available to them, of the joy and rhythm and energy that is their rightful heritage. As I let go of the materials of formal instruction, or used them differently, I saw that the deeper I could get into the sensation of how movement felt to the person doing it, the more expressive it became and the more clarity emerged.

The time came when I felt I could not continue with weekly classes. I still knew too little of what the individual inner development was, how it worked in movement. I was still too obligated to the group energy, timing, structure. Often, the impact of what happened to individuals had to be left hanging or was cut across by the democracy of the group reaction. I had begun, at intervals, to experiment with the difference between individual appointments and group sessions. It was not at all a question of doing alone, with special attention, the things done in class, it was a question of following myriad clues provided by that person, at that point in his or her life. Some of the clues lay in bodily limitations, physical usage, areas of blockage. Some lay in emotional reactions – involuntary tears or bursts of anger. Some showed up in verbal assumptions or judgments, points of view taken for granted as gospel truth and exhibiting an evaluative attitude not connected with the actual physical expression. It became a self-confrontation for both of us, a conscious integration of the not-before-known, with a consequent modification of the known.

But, satisfying as this new area of exploration was, it answered some needs only to activate others. People need people. It was not long before I found that there were those for whom moving alone in a large space while I watched was less rewarding than participating in a group. Something about the energy built up in common, the sense that everyone shared a similar struggle, the mutuality of giving and receiving, offered a more satisfying experience, a more illuminating development.

All the mystery and delight, all the anxiety and doubt of the I-Thou connection, immediately presents itself in the group. Questions of personal truth and individual impulse come up against different truths and different impulses – questions of how I can honor the reality of my own feeling without ignoring the reality of others, how I can be open to those others without over-adapting or over-assessing myself.

It was here in the passages of movement between two people that it became clear how much more immediate movement is than words. The physical situation, the actual movement communication, can be felt directly in the nerves and muscles, not glossed over by politeness or distorted by automatic agreement. I saw how some tend to lead and some to follow, some take the initiative and some hang back, how some want to give continuously and some wait to receive.

As the people became aware of themselves moving, we learned to take time to talk. After participating in each attempt to move together, they exchanged reactions, shared their feelings. Often, what one had 'heard' took on a different quality than another was conscious of offering. This necessitated self-questioning, an admission or a denial that opened up self-knowledge. Slowly they learned to let go of needs for leading or following, requirements for being generous or nice, inward assumptions of right and wrong. They learned that each contact was an existential moment in its own right, different from any other, that it consisted of I and Thou and a third element – that which is between us, that which is not mine, though I am in it, and not yours, though you are in it, but something more, something which contains us both and has its own feeling and its own development. When this third element is present, the movement takes on simplicity and inevitability, a rightness that is deeply rewarding to each because it comes out of a willingness to be there for what wants to happen. It is a paradox in which our differences meet and our sharing creates something new.

Experienced between two, this sharing can be extended gradually to include three, five, a larger group. Sometimes, there comes a wonderful moment in which a spontaneous rhythm or dynamic intensity gradually catches all the members of the group, lifting them into a leaderless whole, uniting them in a common action or common direction, a spontaneous order, a statement growing and expanding, swelling and changing until it comes to its own natural ending. From the outside, it has a quality of unpremeditated choreography. From the inside, it is an experience of participating in a totality made up of more than the sum of its parts but including each part equally.

It seems to me now that what I do is no longer dance, though it has moments of pure dance in it. It has turned into Tao, a way, a becoming. Movement, as I know it now, touches people in their lives. It opens up their individual sense of themselves and teaches them that they are humanly valuable to each other. It is the discovery of the growth process that is themselves becoming. The word 'becoming' moves, it is the movement aspect of eternity. Being is the essence; becoming is the movement of the essence.

After all, it is Life that dances.

CHAPTER 7

The Transference and Dance Therapy[1]

Mary Starks Whitehouse

C.G. Jung (1968) says that the transference is 'an awkward hanging on, an adhesive sort of relationship' (p.152). The more general term 'projection' includes objects, but in the transference the projection takes place between people. It is not voluntary. One never says to oneself: 'I will be transferred to my analyst' or 'I will have a transference relationship with this man or woman.' Since the transference is a projection of unconscious contents – something we do not know – we find it has simply happened. The only way it can 'unhappen' is for us to become conscious of what, belonging to us, has been transferred. Jung does not agree with Freud that the transference consists solely of erotic and infantile contents. He would say that the transference might involve anything in our world, that one can have a transference on a teacher, on a friend, on an acquaintance; it happens in many ways; its contents are varied.

All of us project certain qualities of our own onto people and objects, firmly believing that those qualities exist out there. We do not know that they exist in us; without help we have a hard time finding out. The facts attributed to the nature of the other person are, in reality, an illusion. We assume that what we are responding to exists objectively, separate from ourselves. This assumption is wiped out only when we find that what appears as objective really depends on our subjective view. If we can discover even a little bit of what seems to belong to the other person and recognize it for our own, by that much have we retrieved part of the contents projected, part of ourselves.

1   Previously published in *American Journal of Dance Therapy*, Vol. 1, no. 1, Spring/Summer 1977.

The transference is a special, intense kind of projection. Jung's lecture on the transference in *Analytical Psychology: Its Theory and Practice* (1968) is probably the most helpful and simple of his approaches to this subject. He describes the contents projected as having an emotional, compelling quality – in themselves overwhelming for the subject because they override any intention of feeling that way. They cling to the other person and he cannot get rid of them, he cannot get himself out of them. A bond is established that is quite unbreakable until the nature of the transference is at least partially understood. He goes on to say:

> Emotions are not detachable, like ideas or thoughts, because they are identical with certain physical conditions and thus deeply rooted in the heavy, heavy matter of the body. Therefore, the emotion of the projected contents always forms a link, a sort of dynamic relationship between the subject and the object – and that is the transference. Naturally, this emotional link or bridge or elastic string can be positive or negative...
> (pp.154–155)

The analyst, unlike the therapist, always works directly with the activated unconscious. Dreams forgotten (repressed, if you like clinical language), life experiences, images that seem to come from nowhere and unexpected behavior are all included. People who work with movement also work with this material. It is not a question of better or worse, it is a question of background and point of view. I discovered that I worked directly with the unconscious when I worked with the body. This must be called an approach, an orientation, and not a method, though I tried mightily to make it into one. Each teacher must have his or her own personal experience of the unconscious in order to guide in this way. Since no two people will have identical experiences, they will guide differently. My own experience was in analytical psychology, the analysis formulated as a method by Jung. I was experimenting with a familiar mode, dance/movement, and trying to see what it would look like in the light of a new mode, the reality of the unconscious.

The general psychological reason for projecting or transfering is always that the activated unconscious is seeking expression. I found myself able to allow the unconscious to express itself in movement. It became possible to support and encourage people on levels other than how-to and what-to. We gradually faced qualities and aspects, limits and gifts not known before and not confined to the physical body only. In private work, particularly, emphasis lay primarily on the relations within the person, intrapsychic contents, although the outer world was by no means excluded.

Picture someone coming to your studio who ordinarily would not interest you that much. They might not trust you that much either, there is room between you where work cannot take place. The gap is filled in by their projection onto you of those qualities that make them comfortable, make them feel you are necessary. You fall into it by responding to this, by providing the unconsciously demanded qualities. You even project feelings of your own into the relationship, unwittingly playing the asked-for role. Suddenly, the client is fascinating. This is called countertransference. It is valuable to ask yourself what you are doing in the relationship, how it is affecting you – it takes two for anything to happen! The client may be afraid of moving, of what you may ask for, so she finds in herself or creates a passionate feeling or a fantasy that will make her willing to do anything you suggest. This happens to people isolated from other people and the rest of the world. They come to you in despair, hoping that you can help but, underneath, convinced that you can't. They try to make it possible that you both succeed by projecting into the situation all the necessary feelings. For one client, for example, success might mean behaving like a good girl or knowing, in talk, everything that is wrong and why. In men such facilitation might take place in the form of infantile obedience or the most attractive expression of machismo possible.

Ordinary men and women may arrive because someone has recommended you – perhaps sent by a therapist because they exhibit hang-ups of a physical nature – or because they themselves want to come. Aware of bodily inhibitions, tensions, reluctance to express emotion, they arrive on your doorstep and mine, dutifully doing what we ask, or stubbornly refusing. It is the same thing. The bridge is again the transference, this time internalized and nearly invisible. You will have to deal with your feelings of failure and lack of success in contacting them while they struggle behind their walls with what is going on. You may realize that this interaction is neither good enough nor what is really needed. As Jung describes, the fire of emotion grows, it finally erupts, burning away the walls. Now you are faced with an intensity of emotion having very little to do with you personally. At this point you can let it flow over you, without accepting the idea that the way this person feels is your fault but also without retreating in the hope that you have nothing to do with it.

All this is both easier and harder in movement than in verbal therapy. It is easier because people are not talking but moving. It is harder because you may not realize that, even in movement, you can be adding to the possibility of a special relationship or transference. Transference is cured, as projections are cured, by becoming conscious. I came to see that movement could reveal what sort of material was coming out of the mover and, very likely, being projected around her. There was little chance, since it was not a verbal session, to discover where these contents were landing. I became convinced that if someone moved like a witch, for example, and I could link the witch quality back to the person, she could then ask questions about her life, about where or how she behaved like a witch. She might begin to understand that what she had assumed was attacking her was really herself attacking someone else.

Jung (1968) says:

> An analyst is not allowed to be too friendly, otherwise he will be caught by it; he will produce an affect which goes beyond him. He cannot pay the bill when it is presented, and he should not provoke something for which he is not willing to pay. (p.170)

This reminds me of the many times when my wanting to be all things to all people, together with a genuine belief that clients needed this, resulted in my appearing to hold out hopes for a relationship there was no possibility of having. Jung (1968) says: 'You cannot have affairs with eleven thousand virgins' (p.170). You cannot be personal friends with all your clients. There is a difference between the problems of personal friendship, the give-and-take of personal contact, and the problems of working with people, where you summon a concentration, generosity and conviction that is for their benefit. It is a neat trick to walk a chalk line between these two orientations, recognizing the difference, keeping yourself to yourself, while, at the same time, acknowledging that each mover teaches you that you have no need or right to arrogance or superiority. It is, if not a personal connection, a working relationship.

Generally, what is transferred are unconscious contents of varying degrees of value – the more valuable the contents, the more intense the transference. When the entire possibility of becoming individuated, the total potentiality, is projected onto the therapist, it is no wonder that the relationship becomes intense. As long as the projection lasts, the therapist seems to have all the emulated qualities and the client none. The projection has to be worked with somehow because it has to return to the client.

What form does the transference take in dance therapy? We have to arrive at an understanding of what to do about it and how to relate to it. We have to recognize the important differences in its manifestation when we work individually or with groups. I do not mean clusters of hospital patients, that is something else – neither do I mean classes. The teacher of regular dance classes usually catches the image of the performer and the members of the class react with 'oh' and 'ah.' However, when work with a group hits a certain level, unconscious elements may be projected onto the teacher by some individuals. But no substantive transference appears. What happens to the individual has to do with projection, not transference. It usually involves a discovery by a group member of her relation to an authority figure, derived from some unconscious feeling toward either parent.

In therapy this kind of projection often indicates quite innocent problems in the behavior of the therapist, which call forth unconscious feelings on the part of the client. I was astonished that one young woman, who had flown into town for infrequent private lessons and who always appeared at teacher's workshops, suddenly confronted herself and me with the fact that she thought I had favorites. This was news to me, it may or may not have been true. I felt so burdened by confusion and repudiation that I sought to express both in movement, not words. I let the comments, hers and those of others, sink in. Slowly, I lay face down on the floor in the circle of participants, arms stretched forward and head hidden. Moments later, there was a gasp from her: 'I see. The feelings I have toward you are the feelings I have toward my father. They are put on you. They are the expectations and rejections I have experienced with him'.

As you may well imagine, I sat right up. This was not a solution but it was a beginning. She could now carry responsibility for the fact that most of what she expected from me, she really expected from her father. I had not been able to draw this out of her because she did not know it herself; the feelings had to build up until she could say something. Movement sometimes prevents this kind of communication. You cannot move and talk at the same time. Sometimes, this means that problems that could be better handled in words are not even brought up in the movement. In this particular case, the two met.

Another teacher, in the same workshop, had already offered a comment. She had just come back from St Elizabeth's Hospital in Washington, DC, where she had trained to be a dance therapist. She had a Master's degree from the University of California at Los Angeles and had come to me as a dancer and stayed on as a client, finally going to verbal therapy on my recommendation. Said she: 'This isn't a group, is it? At least, not yet.' Being a creature of response to need, I considered whether there was enough clearing of the air, enough confrontation, enough openness between people for us to be a 'group' or whether the whole affair was too mysterious to everybody but me.

The impact of these two happenings resulted in a sequence of movement relationships for dyads that allowed us to find out how we actually felt toward each other. We sat in an irregular circle, spread out enough to make an empty place in the middle and also leave space outside. One person at a time would talk around the inside of the circle or step to the outside, passing each person in turn. When she came to someone with whom she felt tension, an electricity of connection, a need to explore further, she halted. The person sitting on the floor knew she had been chosen, not as in children's games, but for real. There was no rush into action because these people were experienced enough to realize that waiting would clarify what they were going to do. There followed two-by-two confrontations of a surprising nature. One person active, the other passive; two competing; two blending into each other – all sorts of connections.

When it came my turn to go around the circle, I found myself stopping by the woman from St Elizabeth's. We moved together, but in a way that led the group to point out: 'You chickened out, Mary.' They were all aware of the moment when it showed, physically, that I had decided not to oppose her, yielding to the imagined needs of another person instead of sticking to my own feelings. So we had to go on. This time I opposed her as strongly as I was able. At the end we braced forearms, her hands on my elbows, mine on hers, our legs in opposition, one knee bent forward, one leg straight back. We pushed hard against each other until we yielded to a downward pull that landed us on the floor. She looked at me with relief and surprise, almost in tears: 'But your power drive, your darkness and need to control are as great as mine.' I was familiar enough with that aspect of myself to be able to say: 'Of course.'

There is a huge difference between analysis and dance therapy. In dance therapy the transference is immensely complicated by the fact that people are involved physically with one another, that we touch another individual. The touching is both an asset and a danger. An analyst once said to me: 'Mary, don't forget that when you touch someone, you are touching the Self.' Over years of experience I have become aware of how true that is. Not only do you touch the physical body in front of you but, through the body, you touch the other layers of existence constituting the entire person. These are stirred up, penetrated, by being touched. It may seem that what you are doing is simply contacting the back, knees or shoulders of a client. Not at all: you are activating the flow of energies, positive and negative. And you touch more than just the ego, the center of consciousness that expects to control. When you touch, even to facilitate something so simple as a sensation, you touch the larger entity that we call, in Jungian language, the Self. This makes touching productive of transference: it calls up all the unconscious responses lying in wait, responses that the conscious mind is not aware of. It gives immediacy but it also opens Pandora's box. If you take on what is brought up by touch, without knowing what touch can produce, trouble may arise before you realize you are in deeper than you intended. This does not mean that you ought to be guarded, it only means that knowing something about what you are touching is essential. There is no such thing as not making mistakes; there is no such thing as doing it right; there is no such thing as being wise enough to avoid it. It is foolish of therapists, I think, to fend off the transference if it lands on them. It is just as foolish to seek it, regarding yourself as bigger because of it.

Not all movement clients produce transferences but the ones who come regularly to private sessions, especially if they are searching hard for themselves in the years under forty, are apt to find themselves in the middle of an embroilment, of being in love, of a magnetism that is both exhilarating and confusing. I was fortunate, depending on how you look at it, to draw down on myself mostly positive transferences. I carried for people a positive image of something they wanted, needed or felt I was like. Slowly, I learned what the opposite side of positive was. With one woman I noticed that more and more time was devoted to talking, less and less to movement. I could seem to do nothing but allow it. Nobody could receive as many gifts as she gave me, have that much done for her, be that looked out for, without carrying a larger-than-life value for the other person. In the steady work we did I was often baffled. One day I said: 'I wish you could love yourself as you love me.' This was apparently mind-boggling for her. It started her on an unforeseen train of questions about her own feelings. In the shower one morning she found herself thinking: 'I'm not Mary's daughter, why am I acting like it?' I must acknowledge my part of it. I had collaborated in her acting like my daughter by acting like her mother. I accepted the gifts, the errands, the admiration, only partly aware of what was going on. From the moment of her realization, a change took place in our relationship. As life would have it, we had to go on to the other side. Having found out that she was not my daughter, she was no longer allowing anything that she had accepted before from a positive, giving mother. We went through a time of blocking, hostility and arrogance on both our parts. Unable to see that she was acquiring a necessary balance within herself, I took unkindly to the change. Nevertheless, we persevered long enough for her to get off that hook: she was allowed to be the way she was. There are remnants, I'm sure, because I became ill at the time when we could consciously have worked on the negative aspects of the relationship.

Another case concerned a woman with a history of difficulty in other kinds of therapy. I found her scared, shy, awkward, appealing. Attracted, we became friends before I knew it, taking part in an obviously heightened electricity of relationship. I wanted the advantages, the luxury, the adulation and the involvement she offered, but, at the same time, I was unprepared to pay for it, as Jung says. Perhaps that is why she experienced me as slightly remote, though glittering with promise. I reminded her, she said, of an ocean liner steaming majestically along at night, all lights lit. But she also felt grateful that I did not turn away from her reactions, including anger, and that I took her fears seriously. Slowly, I learned to come out from hiding. At about the time I became strong enough to react as I felt without reference first to her feelings, she came up with a storm of abuse, anger and complaint. When she wanted to discontinue therapy, I had no available response but to let her. I was personally so wounded and taken aback that I had no resources of objectivity. We parted company. I see now that if I had been more real and less beglamorized all along, more able at the end to sustain a berating, helping her to sustain it, we might have come to some kind of balance.

It seems to me that the most important element in private movement sessions has to do with trust: the client's trust of you and your trust of yourself, and also your trust of the client and the client's trust of herself. Mutual trust allows both of you to say 'yes' or 'no' according to the way she really feels. This relationship is not transference, which is compelled by the unconscious. The more human – the more your actual self – you manage to be in your movement appointments, the less chance there is of confusion never resolved. This becomes possible by dealing with many different clients, by moving yourself, by being seen through as I was seen through by the group. It does not come easily or all at once.

Recently, a young professional asked me questions at the end of her appointment: 'Not everybody can trust you immediately. What ways do you begin, establishing trust at the same time?' One can provide reassurance, caring, approving, listening, directing, until safety has been established. The image of myself thus aroused in the client belongs not so much to me personally as to the needed quality of response, a response the person has felt missing from her life. Trust arises as soon as the individual feels there will be no betrayal, that it truly doesn't matter how much or how quickly she responds.

As for ways of beginning, there are many. My studio was large and cool, the amount of space could be frightening. I provided a warm rust-colored rug for sitting or lying. It constituted a kind of home base – people could leave it, moving into the larger space, and they could come back to it. Structured exercise, relaxation or guided sensation on the rug could come first. Since I had no method as such, I was free to experiment with what suggested itself. With practice, I could see whether what we did deeply involved the other person or not. Sometimes I started by giving a wide choice, like lying, sitting or standing, moving in space or being still, using music or not, being free to improvise or learning a form. My not choosing let the client determine the circumstances. When she chose, I already had something to go by, a clue to development, a beginning. One woman said that she would rather stand and move, so I asked her to walk around the studio observing everything in it, making friends with the space. She began the walk, became aware of its lack of focus and called: 'You mean I can do anything I want to?' I assented. Within minutes, still moving, she was talking about herself, the difference between being allowed to do anything she wanted and her memory of being taken out walking by her nurse when she was a little girl. Running away, falling down, going to investigate something were off-limit activities. Two things seemed evident from this: the walking itself needed to come under her domination, not that of another person, and she needed to feel free to break away at any time, to try the instruments at the music rack, to hide under the piano, to sit on the sofa. I would have to see what followed, the next thing could develop only out of that.

To go back to the larger-than-life image, if such an image is created and I get lost in it – in other words, if I identify with it – the other person may trust me but I am faced with a beginning transference. The trust is based on a perception of me coming up in the other person that is without objectivity. Allowing this can be intentional on my part. I can take the deliberate chance of not presenting myself in any way that I think would interrupt her process. I can wait and see. A question arises: when do you break into this image which you have helped to create? You have provided what is wanted – known or unknown. When do you begin to shift the client's expectation that you will provide to a realization that she herself must satisfy these needs?

There is no right answer: it is the question that is valuable.

References

Jung, C.G. (1968) *Analytical Psychology: Its Theory and Practice.* New York: Pantheon Books, Random House.

CHAPTER 8

C.G. Jung and Dance Therapy
Two Major Principles[1]

Mary Starks Whitehouse

Genesis

Odd, but I turned into a dance therapist without realizing it, simply because no such thing existed when I started. In teaching dance I was dimly aware of a different and new element. People would come up to me at the end of class and ask: 'What is this?' They would go on to elaborate that when friends heard they were going to 'dance class,' they felt what we were doing was short-changed. When they tried an explanation of it, they found no accurate words. I would ask: 'Well, what do you think it is – what do you get out of it?' The answer always had as much confusion as I had myself. It took a long time before our work together came to be accepted by us both as more, and less, than dance.

Please do realize that I am talking of the mid-1950s. Dance therapy was unknown, much less named. One evening I was sitting in my living room. Someone had sent me a medical journal containing pictures of Marian Chace doing work at St Elizabeth's Hospital, Washington, DC. I recognized that a dancer had made use of dance movement to reach people who had no intention of becoming dancers nor even of using dance purely as recreation. She had arrived at an understanding of what she was doing far ahead of my own. The fact that she was working in a hospital while I taught in a private studio deterred me not at all. I sent for reprints of her articles, eager to learn

1   Previously published in P.L. Bernstein (ed) (1979) *Eight Theoretical Approaches in Dance/Movement Therapy*. Dubuque, Iowa: Kendall/Hunt.

what she could say about her work. I found a point of view, a usage of dance that sounded familiar but unfamiliar.

Not surprisingly, the unfamiliarity existed in the places where her work was not like mine. No early experimenters could be said to be remotely alike. From the beginning it has seemed necessary to distinguish between therapists working in a hospital setting, therapists working under doctors in out-patient clinics and, especially, those working in studios. This chapter will be from the point of view of a teacher who worked largely in a studio. I started with dance as known material, going on to use it in ways, unsuspected before, that seemed to help people discover and deal with personal life problems. These people were functioning and what are called normal. Once, I was kidded by Bella Lewitsky when she felt that the term 'normal neurotics' was slightly funny. It is not slightly funny. Unfortunately, people have just as many, if not as flagrant, problems as people in hospitals. It is only that they manage their lives with 'quiet desperation,' instead of being markedly cut-off from the rest of the world.

From time to time, other articles reached me. I began to be aware of others who thought dance might be useful in a new way. Trudi Schoop and Jeri Salkin, formerly teaching at Camarillo Hospital, announced private appointments for using dance as an 'adjunctive therapy.' Charlotte Selver brought her work in Sensory Awareness to the West Coast. Something was stirring.

At about that time, two major things happened to me. One, my personal life fell into shambles that ended up in divorce and left me with two small children to support. The other, I became a candidate for analysis with a personal patient of C.G. Jung.

I had the traditional modern dance training of that time – from lessons in 'interpretive' dancing as a child to a diploma from the Mary Wigman Schule in Dresden, Germany. I had gone there because nothing in America allowed concentration on dance without falling into the category of physical education. I completely rejected basketball and tennis rackets as part of my preparation for teaching! The Wigman training prepared me for a particular approach, although I did not know it at the time. It made room for improvisation, placing value on the creativity of the people moving. It assumed that you would not be learning to dance if you had nothing to say. After the Wigman School, my education at home went on to include other teachers. I took Martha Graham's June courses for a good many years and went to Bennington Summer School of Dance before it moved to Connecticut College in New London. Through all of this I was, of course, teaching as well as performing. Since I lived in Boston, the New England area opened itself up, pristine and unaccustomed to modern dance. Practitioners were already there but I arrived full of zeal, fresh, young, ready to convert everyone to the fact that if they danced they would feel better. How right I was!

Making a living had become doubly important because of the divorce and the responsibility for my two children; dance became a practical means of supporting us. In depth analysis I slowly gained a new understanding of myself and a different view of the world; it made me wonder if the old way and the new way must be combined – they could not run parallel and I could not ignore one in favor of the other. Analysis does not put food in your mouth, it enables you to work in a characteristic outer way while you go on with this strange new inner work. My way was dance, yet I had to honor the new. The new would surely change the old.

Even without analysis, the break-up of my interest in dance had already begun. The 1950s and early 1960s saw a remarkably dull period. Early in the 1960s, John Martin, former dance critic of the *New York Times*, then at UCLA, remarked that modern dance was dead. I couldn't have agreed more. Without some kind of renewal, it seemed to me a sterile pursuit for further teaching. I hated the thought of going on with it year after year simply as a job – an injustice to it and to me.

Then analysis provided a different and larger meaning. Combining the artistic and the human meaning might bring together outside and inside; it might open the way I was to travel. Perhaps I even glimpsed that welding them together could result in a revitalization of what was now, at worst a trade and at best a familiar but slightly boring art.

Looking back, my beginning is hardly recognizable. I over-simplified of course, seeing new concepts and meanings too easily in the movement of people I taught, forcing everything I saw into a preconceived framework. If I then fell back on what I already knew, remembered things I had already learned, I also stumbled on pieces of genuine experiment, moments of movement that allowed people to discover something different for and about themselves, not because I taught it to them but because I made an opening for that discovery. I began to find a place for myself.

Don't think that I was clear about my aims or even my approach. As a matter of fact, I was clear only about the necessity. The reader needs to be aware that in talking about the mid-1950s, the beginnings of a new kind of work, the pioneer is the most in the dark of all. A theoretical model was not thought of, was not being sought – at least, I was not looking for it. I was desperately trying to become clear as to what was going on – that would be enough. In the early days there were times after classes when many of us went out to coffee to sit for a long time, discussing – valuable discussions that revealed reactions and brought up questions. There were some questions I could answer but more that I could not answer. They touched on issues I would have to face alone, as best I could. Often, I went home wondering what I was doing and why.

Whatever it was, we were traveling away from dance. I had to call it movement. In order to find what it was that truly moved people, I needed to give up images in them and in myself of what it meant to dance. There was another possibility: to dance surely meant the making of a product, finishing a piece of work to show. I was finding more and more that the things happening in classes allowed pieces of movement, not dances, and that it would be more directly descriptive to call what the people were doing movement until such time as they themselves wanted to make a dance.

The word 'therapy' was already creeping into dance language, from the medical and hospital model, I think. I had some resistance to it. It seemed to imply that I knew and that the person who came to me did not know. I had the feeling it could not possibly be true in my situation, even if it was true of other people.

For me, a theory of what is now called dance therapy came out of years of doing, of learning by action and experiment, rather than thinking, reading or being taught by other people. It came out of taking seriously the questions and needs of people along with what they produced in me. I learned to let go when people did not like me or my approach, admitting hurt but going ahead. When the announcement came of the Schoop-Salkin 'Adjunctive Therapy,' or I received word of Charlotte Selver's weekends with Sensing, I had to overcome an initial insecurity that wanted to say: 'Well, if they know what they are doing and they are doing it right, then I'm all wrong and might as well not be doing it.' My present conviction that 'it takes all kinds' was not available.

I have to be honest, presenting a polished theoretical model to students interested in dance therapy, without admitting that it is achieved in the first place alone with pain and struggle, may not be true for a second generation but needs to be known. If it is not, such a theoretical model can be easily learned without any reference to personal gifts or temperament. It can be adopted wholesale and imposed on patients, as clearly as any teacher of dance takes an acquired style and imposes it on her students.

Theoretical model

Can you believe how I resist the simple title 'Theoretical Model'? I associate it with an intellectual discipline, an organized rationality, that seems to me only one-half of a living process. Whatever theoretical model may be adopted, do not believe it is the whole. The whole can only be the whole person, the one teaching and the one moving in an atmosphere of mutual trust. A theoretical model that does not include this understanding is not complete.

For the sake of space, I should like to emphasize lesser known, less understood aspects of my own theoretical model. My background with C.G. Jung leads to certain emphases as the main spring of my approach. I wish to dwell on these emphases.

Depth analysis

When I refer to depth analysis, I am referring to certain clinical psychological processes. The client/patient co-operates with the analyst to enter the unconscious, a realm below that of daily consciousness. This is done by using dreams, being particularly sensitive to images and their associations, becoming familiar with what Jung (1961) called 'active imagination' and generally accepting a symbolic understanding of life events, inner or outer. The process itself is one of discovering the living reality of the unconscious.

There are many kinds of therapy, many approaches to the entity we call the person; there are not so many approaches to a complete, a whole human being, including what is not known of the self down to a level belonging to humankind, not to the individual. This factor has occasioned the naming of psychoanalysis and analytical psychology, as well as the Adlerian approach as 'depth psychologies.' I shall emphasize particularly the relations between the two people in the studio for private sessions, hoping these processes will be more clearly seen in an individual context.

'Self' and 'self'

Because of the depth analysis, I came to see and feel C.G. Jung's distinction between the many aspects of a human being, without his forgetting for a moment the wholeness of each one. It is a wholeness consisting of totality, completeness. Most people say 'self' using the small letter 's' to mean the ego, the individual, the personality. The world of the self is the world of the 'Me' and all its concerns.

Jung (1959) says 'Self' with a capital 'S' meaning also the world of the transpersonal, a world greater than the individual, more powerful than the ego. The Self is the totality of aliveness; it is wholeness, known and unknown, good and evil. If this idea lies at the bottom of dance teaching, then it becomes a primary value leading directly to another – that of self-knowledge. I use a wonderful quotation from Krishnamurti (1956) who says: 'Self-knowledge is not an ultimate end; it is the only opening wedge to the inexhaustible' (p.47). Let me paraphrase. The little self becomes the one that struggles with self-knowledge, taking the familiar structure of the personality apart and putting it together again with new elements, new understanding; but the inexhaustible is the big Self, the Unknowable, God.

Individuation process

The Self guides and directs the Me, once the process of becoming conscious starts. This is why a theoretical model must not be sided only in that which is reasonable. It must also include the irrational, illogical, unknown. Jung (1959) has said that the Self will make its experiment with each of us. The only real choice is whether we will be dragged by the hair or whether we will co-operate. Co-operation means the long journey toward what he calls Individuation – the unique and conscious development of potential in a particular person, the slow unfolding of a wholeness already there. Through self-knowledge, individuation puts the ego in the service of the Self, the whole. The growth of personality is only possible through inter-penetration of consciousness with the unconscious.

To say it another way, the personality can be enlarged by understanding that a theoretical model has only rational, abstract or intellectual content. It needs also to be brightened, lifted, differently ordered by the penetration of the irrational and the instinctive – unexpected thoughts, unfamiliar behaviors. If room is left for this second side, you cannot have a system of beliefs within which you safely function. If that is needed, you can help people only to a certain extent and in a certain way.

Since people are functioning wholes, a large part will be unknown to you both at any point that you are together. Self-knowledge and an introduction to the inexhaustible are what people come for, no matter what they consciously name as 'the problem.' They are people functioning as well as they can in their daily lives but feeling a lack of..., something missing.

It is my experience that individuals cannot be genuinely themselves doing their thing without a good deal of probing (not always pleasant) into their motives and limitations. This is not introspection and should not be understood that way. Instead, it is introversion, the necessary looking within that our age has successfully escaped for the most part. Individuals are accustomed to looking outward, gauging reactions and responses by a set of conditioned and acquired beliefs. They are not accustomed to finding a world within that also conditions – influences whether its forces are recognized or not.

Polarity

How do these ideas apply to a theory of movement/dance? To apply them involves concepts uniting already known versions of dance use with what is unknown – the unknown assuming a new importance and weight. A primary one, 'polarity,' is present in the physical body, through the personality, into all the pairs of opposites, including conscious and unconscious. Life is never either/or but always the paradox of both/and. This statement looks simple but it is not the way individuals live. Individuals live as if things were always a matter of either/or. They have but to choose and the opposite will go away. It is not true, is it? If you choose in life, you do not get rid of what you did not choose. There is no such thing as choosing only one end of the scale; the other end simply disappears from your awareness, exerting its heaviness, as in a seesaw, from below your consciousness. Black and white, day and night, masculine and feminine are familiar pairs in our daily experience. In the world of movement a dancer does not stop to think of curved/straight, closed/open, narrow/wide, up/down, heavy/light – there are myriad of pairs.

Applied physically, it is astonishing that no action can be accomplished without the operation of two sets of muscles – one contracting and one extending. This is already the presence of polarity inherent in the pattern of movement. Most are not aware of it in this form but it becomes recognizable in the act of walking. Normally, when there is no acquired distortion, the human being takes steps by opposing arms and legs – the right leg balances the left arm, the left leg opposes the right arm. Learning to change from the involuntary opposition of right and left to its conscious use is not at all easy, particularly in starting a forward motion. People have to see that they are freeing an arm and leg forward at the same time on opposite sides of the body. Once started, it is the powerful action of opposite weights on the two sides of the body that further lifts and carries us into the air. Leaps in a forward direction are a high, open extension of arm and leg against each other.

When the two complete sides of the body are opposed, left and right is learned – different but somehow mysteriously balancing. The opposites can balance but they do not always; sometimes one is more heavily weighted than the other. Left and right have many connotations, from the opposition of left arm to right leg to left and right sides. I remember I was struck by Martha Graham's description of the left as the 'sinister' side of the body.

The left has its own special quality as reflected in Nancy Ross's book title, *The Left Hand is the Dreamer* (1947). It is the left that is hidden, innocent, irrational, naïve – there are many names. In contrast, the right stands for conscious, familiar, controlled, active. They are physical and psychological opposites.

An exercise comes back to me. I ask groups of people, sitting on the floor, to concentrate on the right arm. Perhaps they can find a movement with it by taking time with their eyes closed. They can discover what sort of action the right arm is prepared to take, what movement it will make. Some people swing, some slash, some grab, some weave, snaking around their own bodies. This process increases in curiosity and intensity. To add, not to interrupt, I say softly: 'Without pausing to think, simply choose the first word that comes into your head. Allow yourself to be stuck with that word; it is the name of the right arm. Let the arm go on moving and say the name silently; don't change either the movement or the word.' This process is repeated with the left arm, taking long enough for a completely different experience to emerge, then choose a word, the name of the left arm. Afterwards, I ask the people to put these two words together silently, separating them by a hyphen, then to reflect on whether the two names represent qualities they already know or don't know of themselves. Sometimes, individual people give examples of their discoveries. They tell aloud what a shock the names are, carrying, as they seem to, a truth about themselves and their behavior. One man found that on his right, the word slash had occurred to him, on his left, the word 'swimming'.

Often, the two sides are not discussed aloud. Instead, I ask that both arms move at once to see what happens to each quality (remembered and named beforehand). What now takes place is of the utmost interest to the mover.

Sometimes, one arm wins over the other – the stronger over the weaker, of course, but, also, the less dominant, the one thought of as weaker can completely change the other. Rarely, one slightly influences the other and both come to an entirely new quality that must be named something different. At last, the group talks.

This right/left polarity is a recurring motif for exploration in movement, just as up/down, open/closed seem to be. A girl who has danced all her life, but without this kind of awareness, was appalled to discover herself sitting on the floor with the right hand tightly grasping the left. As she turned her attention to this, the left hand doubled into a fist and tried to withdraw but the right clutched tighter and tighter until the knuckles were white. During this time, she told me afterward, she was innerly screaming at the right: 'Let go, let go!' It would not. Finally, the left twisted free, still clenched, the right still hovering claw-like a few inches away. As soon as the left was free, she could no longer feel it although she knew it was there. She could only perceive the power drive of the right. Then, after a series of experiments, she was compelled to recognize: 'But my left side will not do anything I tell it to.'

Both these exercises bring us from the simple recognition of physical opposites into a larger framework, that of self-knowledge, a sense that the opposites mean more to us, individually, than mere physical conditions with which to work. A dancer usually has a stronger leg; she balances more easily on one leg than the other or it extends higher on one side. Dancers try to make the more limited side conform to the freer – they force the left foot to a point as hard as the right, thereby running the risk of injury. This is totally unnecessary for non-dancers. It leads, as a matter of fact, to the either/or attitude again. It presupposes something wrong with having two different sides – but they exist, and not only physically.

Authentic movement

Polarity leads into other forms of the same principle. I discovered in working that movement, especially in improvisation, acquired of itself words to describe it. When the movement was simple and inevitable, not to be changed no matter how limited or partial, it became what I called 'authentic' – it could be recognized as genuine, belonging to that person. Authentic was the only word I could think of that meant truth – truth of a kind unlearned but there to be seen at moments.

The opposite of authentic came to be 'invisible.' When one is helping people develop all the natural functions and capacities of their bodies – when one is encouraging them to become familiar with themselves – one quickly runs into their lack of awareness in certain areas. They have thrown whole parts of themselves away. These are the invisible parts – no matter how much movement takes place there is a queer effect, it does not show in a genuine way, it is invisible. Not until these areas are brought into conscious belonging can their movement become authentic and the invisibility disappear. We are faced with a pair of opposites again – authentic as opposed to invisible.

In the same way, 'I move' and 'I am moved' carry the same implication. Each is an act in itself, but a different act. 'I move' is the clear knowledge that I, personally, am moving. I choose to move, I exert some demand (not effort) on my physical organism to produce movement. The opposite of this is the sudden and astonishing moment when 'I am moved.' Dancers are terribly familiar with 'I move', they are accustomed to think they do it all, that they must exert will power and effort for each thing they want to have happen.

The moment when 'I am moved' happens is astonishing both to dancers and to people who have no intention of becoming dancers. It is a moment when the ego gives up control, stops choosing, stops exerting demands, allowing the self to take over moving the physical body as it will. It is a moment of unpremeditated surrender that cannot be explained, repeated exactly, sought for or tried out. If it is used as raw material for a dance, something is lost, but something has to be lost since that moment was an instant, a happening in and of itself – the structure needed for a lasting work of art is something else.

Once the mover has had the experience of being moved, he knows it is possible. He knows he does not do it all. At any time, without his choosing, a sensation of being moved can happen to him. This is humbling and freeing for the personality that demands perfection, control, conformity – all the ills of our social training.

I am especially interested in the moment when movers, including dancers, find themselves moved. A girl sat cross-legged on the floor in the studio; she was a dancer of great facility. On this particular morning she bowed her head and closed her eyes, taking a long time to move. We put on slow, rather innocuous music, without a strong rhythm. Her head sank lower and lower. She leaned further and further to the right until she toppled over, spread out and rolled at least a dozen times across the floor, all in one fluid movement. She sat up, white faced and trembling with shock. Her description came: 'I didn't know that would happen. I didn't do it.' In this case she meant I, the ego, did not assume control, did not produce the roll; her experience was of being moved.

Lastly, I want to describe the paradox in which the opposites are united; each becomes the other. This is the ideal – it is what is meant by 'both/and' instead of 'either/or.'

There is a saying that comes from Tao. It was not intended primarily for movement but it gives the whole of movement awareness a framework: 'Non-action in action; action in non-action.' Both pairs are in each half of the total saying. They cannot be opposed; they go together. For me, it means that in not doing anything, something is done. In taking no action there is already some action going on. The other half indicates a parallel possibility. In acting, in choosing, there is no action – the Me, the ego does not do anything, does not choose.

Experienced in many moments, many ways, a balance between action and non-action allows individuals to live from a different awareness. They come to the place where they can view everything, from a simple movement to the deepest and most poignant moments of their lives, with an element of detachment, having two qualities at the same time. It is not that they do not suffer but that they know suffering is not the only thing, its opposite is also there. It is not that they do not enjoy, they know there is suffering. Finally, if they are lucky, they can contain and be aware of both of these at once. Then something new is created. It is like the differing qualities of left and right; a third is found.

Active imagination

I mentioned 'active imagination'. It is Jung's term for a process in which, while consciousness looks on, participating but not directing, co-operating but not choosing, the unconscious is allowed to speak whatever and however it likes. Its language appears in the form of painted or verbal images that may change rapidly, biblical speech, poetry (even doggerel), sculpture and dance (Jung 1968). There is no limit and no guarantee of consistency. Images, inner voices, move suddenly from one thing to another. The levels they come from are not always personal levels; a universal human connection with something much deeper than the personal ego is represented.

Moments of insight, brought into focus by active imagination, have a natural effect on everyday life. They reveal a direction and show a development, acting as support and encouragement for what must be lived through, creating energy for a next step. The use of active imagination in movement is peculiarly valuable. Every possible way I could devise to involve people in their own fantasies and images, even moving out their dreams, provide raw material for understanding themselves.

A young woman stood at the edge of the big studio space. In front of her there seemed to be marshes – water lay everywhere but there was enough dry land to pass through. She crouched, carefully putting one foot in front of the other, proceeding out into the space. The water seemed to come up around her. She felt as if it engulfed her and said to herself: 'Oh, I must try to feel it, I must try to make friends with it.' She sat down, allowing the water all around her body but not her head. No matter how she played, the head took no part, staying well out of the water. At last she felt, 'no, no,' the water was becoming deeper. She stood up and walked away.

The next week everything had stopped – all her images, even her material in therapy. She didn't know what to do. I suggested that we go back to the water and the marshes, and she answered: 'You mean anything to do with water?' I nodded. So she went out on the floor and found water immediately. She lay flat this time, playing in it with her hands. It was very shallow, barely covering the ground and not going anywhere. Again came the feeling of the head resistance – still she could not allow herself to put her head down. Suddenly, she could not bear it anymore. She got up and walked away. This time she found herself in a burning desert. There was nothing, absolutely nothing but the heat – no water anywhere – no people – nothing. You could see her body begin to claw. She said that she was clawing in the sand to get at the water beneath the surface, longing to find it, somehow believing in its value now, despairing because it had disappeared. She couldn't get enough by digging for it; she couldn't get deep enough. It seemed cruel to leave her with that unfinished, incomplete experience, but we didn't disturb it. The refusal to allow her head, the thinking symbol, to become contaminated with water, a symbol for the reality of the unconscious, had led to the stoppage of images (already few and far between with her) and of spontaneous material in therapy, producing a depression. Her discovery of the close connection between refusal to allow her head to touch even shallow water and the proximity of dry, hot desert with nothing in it was spectacular in its results. Perhaps she needed to live with her despair, feeling herself digging for the life-giving water.

One reason that the movement form of active imagination is so valuable is that it is extremely difficult to censor. One moves before one knows what is happening. One can stop oneself from writing words and one can prohibit certain pictures in painting more easily than one can stop certain movements that come out of preceding ones. One cannot pick and choose from spontaneous movement the way one can from drawings and writing. Movement, like dreams, is ephemeral, one cannot will to repeat it exactly. Spontaneous movement, rehearsed and repeated, loses the very thing it shows: that inner processes take physical form and can be seen, their meaning apprehended, their value received by the person out of whose body the movement comes.

A student in a workshop stated:

Most important, though, was experiencing the way in which something long buried can be brought to the surface through movement; much less conscious than painting or writing, it is doubly valuable. Until a conflict becomes manifest in some way, nothing can be done with it; it will not paint itself or write itself. But the body moves constantly; it needs no tool, or time or place; it is always there, it needs only to be listened to. Presupposing a certain amount of honesty and desire for self-knowledge, it is the drum, the voice in the night that tells the hero where the battleground lies, so that he may go forth and rescue the maiden. So it is that an image wells up in the body and moves it in the same way an image springs up before the eyes and moves the heart, and again, the body, since there are often chemical and physical reactions to images – fear, trembling, sweating, blurred vision, accelerated heart beat – and if that's not the body, I don't know what is. What I want to say is that improvising is like active imagination, that it cannot be done endlessly in a vacuum but it must in some way be brought to a more conscious level. What Mary is trying to do is to show a method of getting at human action within a framework of personal movement.

Role of teacher/leader/mediator

Implementation of these central concepts of polarity and active imagination depends on certain attitudes in the teacher/leader/mediator and the student/client/patient. I purposely put all three possible names, since each aspect of the person is present in the private session. Relationships of leading and following, whether in dance studios or in the hospital setting, are as varied as the people concerned, but the necessary attitudes are permissiveness and allowance on both sides, acquired by practice. They cannot be present by talking, wanting or trying. The three names I have used already indicate three possibilities. One can teach something or lead something or be the mediator for something. All three happen at different times. The mover is sometimes a student of movement, a client who comes for help or, in the medical model, a patient.

A first and basic attitude of the teacher toward the mover is starting from where the other person is. This sounds axiomatic. Perhaps people will find it easier than I did. An analyst friend said to me: 'Of course you start where the person is.' I did not understand at all what she meant. I thought it a good idea, if possible, but I could not see how it was done. My head was a jumble of preconceived notions, learned devices. I must have thought the mover was blank. Over the years, I came to see that this is the single most important contribution of the experienced practitioner.

Starting where the client is can only mean willingness to be anonymously one's self in favor of observing, quickly and without barriers, what is available to that individual. When people first come, when we have been through whatever amenities we both feel necessary, I sometimes give an instantaneous choice for starting work. What would be most comfortable, easiest – lying, sitting, standing? The variety is amazing – some people lie, some sit and some stand, yet no two are alike. A starting point of this kind gives the client a chance to pick something of his own rather than being told to do a specific thing. Following what is picked, I find myself up against it since I then have to suggest the immediate next step – what to try. The queer part of it is that the client is both blank and innocent. However, there is a reaction, no matter how small, whether verbal or non-verbal. The job of the teacher is to see how the one who is moving feels.

In order to go on from the beginning, the teacher/leader has to be willing to use whatever she sees. It will be worthwhile to do successful things first; it allows the mover to find satisfaction in what is happening before strange or harder things are suggested. It is important that she does not correct directly but works indirectly to ask questions or make suggestions. She must never take away but always add something.

There are risks in doing it this way. One is not knowing what will happen and yet being able to stand it – this applies to both teacher and client. A second is that long silences are necessary to provide waiting, a quietness into which the mover can sink, find himself and then move. Waiting too long can be as destructive as not waiting long enough. If, with experience, one gains a sense of difficulty in the mover, it is possible to break up the immobile waiting with a suggestion to help the struggle. This does not interrupt: it is an additional suggestion given by a quiet, disembodied voice that offers help.

As important as the basic attitude of starting, the teacher must be willing to give up all preconceptions, all ideas of what would be good for the person, all assumptions of the importance of what she knows. When it comes right down to it, she doesn't know anything in this particular situation. Therefore, she has to follow her hunches. Intuition is no longer a dirty word; some years ago it was. Perhaps one was afraid of it because it was so irrational and illogical – a kind of interrupting faculty, apt to disturb our scientific approach to life. It would not allow itself to be catalogued and placed in a neat box.

Intuition tells one what to do and when to do it. In order to act on it, one has to be willing to make a mistake. The presence of what one calls a hunch in everyday language indicates a possibility that may or may not work. By acting on the things that come up within, by trusting, it is found that the more they are trusted, the more strongly they come. This gradually changes the work. It becomes not as logical a process but just as orderly; a different order than that of the controlling ego that grabs onto what it already knows, saying: 'I'll think it out. If this person can't do what I ask, then I must recommend the right thing next.' It may not be at all the right thing. Perhaps one wants the person to stand. The truth may be that standing will not come, spontaneously, for weeks. The mediator must ask: 'Why do I want the standing?' Another teacher's attitude might be called the willingness not to impose, to offer actions as suggestions. This carries an assumption that you may not be right or appropriate. I have known clients to pay no attention, to feel free to answer back or to vary a suggestion in a way I could not possibly have imagined. In the early stages I prefer to observe rather than to participate – the client can then become aware of beginning, of choosing. Since the process is a development of self-knowledge, the growth of individuation and conscious wholeness, there is no use in excessive verbal directions or explanations. Something being done will catch the attention forcibly and, after it, one can afford to say: 'Look, look: that was it. That's what you're looking for.' It may be a little thing, a moment of genuine giving in, a sudden ease of movement. Whatever it may be, it is the expression of where the client is. There is nothing else to go by. A chance is taken when seen, a chance that has to be taken or the development from that point cannot begin to be followed.

In turn, what attitudes does the client need for this journey, a journey formed by the observer's help and the mover's participation? The first discovery each can make is of the attitude already present – is there a predominant expectation, demand or need? The psychological approach to the dance therapist could be one of assuming that she knows or that she doesn't know. It could be wanting specific answers to specific questions or a feeling of having been sent – even a special sense of having come voluntarily, out of curiosity. The important moment comes when the client is what I call 'caught.' It is the moment when client and the teacher recognize and accept the client's beginning attitude without judging it. The cue is taken from you. The client is waiting to see what you will do or say to reactions presented. For instance, 'Isn't that silly?' is a common defensive reaction. If the dance therapist permits herself to be disturbed, to react by comforting and saying 'It's not silly,' if the observer does anything but preserve interest, sympathy and a waiting silence, the mover is apt to change to another attitude that might suit you better. This is not wanted. What is wanted is a genuine involvement. It is only from the involvement that the process itself can begin. Early interplay can come from the mover trying the observer out while she attempts to see whether she can get beneath barriers thrown to keep her from approaching. When the dance therapist does, the process starts. The client can be said to be 'in it,' however superficially. Earmarks of being caught are various. One is the client's complete self-permission for openness to what happens. Usually a first obstacle is 'monkey chatter' in the head, preventing the attention from settling into awareness of what is going on. Mental activity, voices that express goodness, badness, grace or clumsiness, value or lack of value, go on unmercifully. The cessation of these opinions cannot be expected simply by request. The monkey chatter must be accepted as it is, allowed to proceed with as little attention paid as possible, until it becomes less and less important, disappearing when something has taken its place. Permission without resistance, without judgement, proves stronger.

Permission like this is a sort of allowance, but one can give permission to one's self and then allow nothing further. A kind of deadness results. It takes the form either of no further action or the dutiful development of suggestions with no real interest. The first attitude has not led to its second half, allowing whatever happens to show, surprising or unsurprising. This is difficult to talk about and impossible to generalize, everyone operates at a different level. Working with a dancer, or a dance teacher familiar with movement, presents entirely different problems than working with those who have never for a moment considered their own physical reality.

The allowance described permits the client gradually to take over responsibility, accepting or rejecting the teacher's suggestions. I was working with a dancer and threw open the possibility of finding out what kind of day it was for her, not with words but in action. Why didn't she show it by moving rather than by telling me? Standing, she closed her eyes and dutifully waited to see what she would do. Then she opened them, saying: 'I can't. It's the most unstructured, awful beginning that you could ask of me.' We dropped it and moved on to another possibility. It is not necessary to analyze the whys and wherefores of the client's attitude. As a matter of fact, it gets in the way, fortifying and justifying resistance.

Permission to one's self, allowance of anything that happens, letting go – is the latter different? I think so. It does not mean what is usually called relaxation, a kind of collapsing, throwing away the energy to become limp, heavy, lethargic. It does mean mobilizing attention so that the energy can express itself. This attitude would be the act of attention, following what happens, concentrating on it. The movement leads and the mover follows.

Therapeutic process

Does that make any sense? It is an unaccustomed way of working. The impulse to move, however, is something in and of itself. If allowed, the observer and mover really do not know what comes next – they must follow it in order to find out. The impulse may go on through various stages, coming to a blank where it stops abruptly, or it may round itself out through an organic development to a natural ending. Such an ending must be recognized: the movement, this time, is finishing. Pushing it further would be padding. There has been no mental decision to structure or form it, to do it a certain way, to finish it. There has been only an authentic statement of followed intention – more simply, an authentic expression of the way it developed and the way it ended.

The mistake of assuming that all improvisation has no form cannot be made. A great deal of it does not include form and is not meant for that purpose but there comes a moment when the organic development of the movement problem takes on a form of its own, a natural form belonging to the movement itself. When I see it, I know that the movement has reached a level where the sticky, formless aspect of improvisation has been overcome. That in itself is a kind of progress. It should not, however, be desired before thoroughly indulging the other. As one psychologist said to me: 'We are, after all, adolescents in this area.'

Both people in the session can feel the moment when the movement becomes weighted on the side of the Self – of the new, not yet known. It is a moment telling both client and observer what is going on underneath. More is discovered than can be known by characteristics of time, dynamic, quality; more is found out than the conscious mind reveals. This happening is like a great iceberg – its top may have shown all the time, a peak above water – and one would think that there is more underneath. Then the iceberg tips over and the huge underpinnings are exposed, the buried parts, the two-thirds that have been out of sight.

This is one of the great values of Jung's concepts applied to movement. The client needs to learn patiently and slowly that this is so, there is no selling it to him. It has to happen in the experience itself. The teacher also must be familiar with it in her own life. The truth of the irrational has already manifested itself to each, perhaps, in slips of the tongue (what we call in everyday slang, 'Freudian slips'), in dreams, in moments of uncharacteristic behavior, different than the person usually known.

Irrational truth is not a truth of the logical mind, it is a truth of the deeper layers. It offers renewing life energy stored in levels not normally contacted. The quantity of verbalization – how many questions, how much linkage to the personal life – is a matter for individual decision. The life-giving quality of the irrational cannot be denied. Slowly, a positive attitude toward it is built up. Intuition is a good name because it is an irrational function. It covers understandable concepts which are not possible to elaborate here. Suffice it to say that the irrational is the side away from the logical, away from the incisively differentiated thinking a client is more likely used to simply because he lives in the kind of culture that he does. To let go the dominance of familiar functioning presents another form of the same attitude. Letting go is not only relaxing, it is giving up dearly held beliefs in favor of newly won convictions.

Setting and structure

Eventually, 'Movement-in-depth' became the name of my approach. It took various forms. Primarily, I worked with a private practice consisting of individual hour-long sessions with men and women. There were groups but no longer classes – I gave up classes because I found I could not follow, closely enough, what happened to individuals.

When I began group work again, I started it as weekend workshops for men and women. As far as possible, I tried to have even numbers of men and women. Even numbers allowed separation of men into a group by themselves, leaving the women to work alone. It also allowed work in couples, a man and woman together. Since not all weekends could be balanced in numbers, I found that two women and a man, or two men and a woman, not to mention two men or two women together, was something else again. The problems of sexuality, the difficulties with touching and being touched, the fear of self-exposure, all presented themselves.

From 1966 on, I gave what I liked to call teacher-training workshops. It is unfortunate for this approach that I did not stop to think that real teacher training would mean a sequential and logical development from beginning to end of whatever time we had. Teachers taking training courses could have begun where I thought training began, going on to different aspects of movement and ending with some small sense of the completion of a process. Instead, they found that I was doing what interested me at the time. Often, they received a natural impression, they 'know what Mary does.' They would elaborate at home what I had been experimenting on with them.

I had not set out to train them as teachers, I only thought I had. I remember a June workshop when I was impressed that only teachers were enrolled. I tried to do what could respectably be called training. After a time, I thought: 'Oh, to hell with it! I have to teach the way I usually do – reacting to what is needed and combining it with what I feel. We will make out of it whatever develops.'

What I was really doing was exposing experienced teachers to a new point of view. More often than not, it involved a discovery of themselves, something not hitherto recognized. These discoveries had nothing to do with telling them how or what to teach. The fact that they took away from them any of the exercises, reforming and using them, was incidental.

Mostly, teacher's groups were composed only of women – only once did I have a single man. His comments are worth repeating. He was an experienced leader himself and, accompanied by his new wife, had enough courage not to be intimidated by finding himself in a strange group of women only. Half-way through, we were talking one afternoon. He remarked that it was the first time he had ever felt completely outside a group, able to look at the woman's 'thing.' Apparently, the atmosphere of women together is a different strong and tangible reality. Although he was accepted, and, as he danced with single partners, could feel himself a man in relation to a woman, he remained outside the group. This demonstrated itself clearly when a number of the women took violent exception to his verbalizing the distinction: spontaneously, they surrounded him in a circle. The force of their movement brought him to his knees, then down to the floor. It looked as if the women were witches who had cast a spell over him, robbing him of power. He proved not to be helpless, however, and with a mighty effort, he pressed against the floor, brought himself to a crouch and slowly pushed himself to standing. Without touching the women, he moved to provide space and protection for himself.

Individual sessions and groups of any sort, whether classes, weekends, longer workshops are very different. The atmosphere in each setting varies – energy provided by several people meeting together enormously buoys and supports the single individual. Once the fear of being looked at and any sense of comparison is overcome, interplay and interdependence can be a joy and a delight. In a group you experience moments having to do with the outer-world relations to other people, attitudes toward objects, feelings toward atmospheres or circumstances. The reasons people come to individual work include their particular relation to being looked at – some feel unready, even unable, to be group members. These people trust the teacher figure far more than they do multiple strangers. Conversely, there are people who are not ready to be looked at by the teacher alone. They want to hide in the group, feeling their anonymity less penetrated by 'someone leading,' if they are one of many. They, themselves, change the format when they are ready.

In private work something may be learned about one's personal relation to someone, but mostly what is discovered is not a particular behavior within a group at that moment but life behavior acquired over the years, attitudes toward one's self and others, plus whatever is lying in wait to appear, if allowed. Even the times that seem blocked and meaningless turn out to be real discoveries. In one particular session a dancer wanted to work with an object in the studio – a box that was square, rigid and unyielding. No matter how she tried, she got nowhere, no life would start. She spent the whole session trying to find a working relationship to that box. Complete frustration was followed by giving up. In discussing it afterwards, she said without thinking: 'It's just as damn unyielding and rigid and ungiving as my relation to R...' This was a revelation to her. She had been dancing out the relationship without knowing it. Those same feelings in movement perfectly mirrored the agonies she constantly struggled with at that time.

The two forms of work, individual and group, have something in common. The top layers have to be distinguished before this commonality can be felt, but the underlying activity is an introduction to the reality of the unconscious, the other side of consciousness. This reality lives in each individual. It is the unknown balance of wholeness. It connects each person with the larger Self inhabiting everyone else and the surrounding world. The possibility of becoming deliberately acquainted with the known personality gives way to a discovery that something more needs recognition. The ego, center of consciousness, fights other patterns needing to be explored.

Each workshop contained a nearly equal number of technical exercises or actions, plus improvisations based on group or single explorations of specific situations. Images were given, pictorial beginnings, allowing members to find their own responses. For example, I would tell them they were in a cocoon, asking whether it was large or small, whether it was stiff or stretchy, unyielding or movable. I asked also what they were going to do about being enclosed in it. This meant I called for no action other than whatever they found available. Another image had to do with lying flat on the floor, right hand imagined as being tied down, even growing roots into the ground, it could not separate from the earth in any way. They were to establish the feeling of an immovable hand then explore their reactions to that condition. The hand could as well be the left or the right or either foot, the difference is instructive. These are random samples of specific images.

In groups people learned to encounter themselves and each other. Sometimes, a workshop would lean more heavily on one activity than on another, either because I cared particularly about exploring it or because their interest led me. Once, we sat in a circle. I asked them to become silently aware of the single person in the workshop whom they liked most and the single person whom they liked least. Then they were to draw lines (in their own minds) between themselves and the other two, making a triangle of a particular shape, depending on where each was sitting. Finally, they took turns standing up, calling the names of the others. From where they stood, all three began to move in any way possible. Perhaps an onlooker could guess who was the beloved and who the rejected from the way the movement took place.

Another time, sitting in a loose circle, each person had a chance to wander around inside the form. At length, there would be a stop beside or in front of one person. Everyone else watched the encounter between these two people. Sometimes, rivalry and competition appeared, sometimes two like natures. There were distinct differences in relationship. At times, one became weak, soft and helpless while the other became nurturing and caring. We saw sisters and daughters emerge, we saw fathers and sons emerge. There was a surprising honesty of connection between the two people who chose to become involved. Most people moved from an exploration of the 'Me' relating to an inner and outer world to glimpses of larger truth, a transpersonal area where all are subject to a larger Self and the experience of wholeness.

Two endings, each discovered by the doing of it, illustrate what I mean. When it was appropriate, I led the movers in single file. Gradually, we joined hands making a chain that curved all over the studio. When the time came, I doubled back, closely facing the second person in line. We slowed down as we walked and each person rounded the corner, coming eye to eye with every other person in the workshop. It took some time but was immensely worth doing, stimulating consciousness in each of us, not only of those who were there but of how we all seemed connected. When the last person had seen everyone else, a circle followed.

Many workshops end naturally in a circle, with or without the chain walk. We lift our hands together, palms closed in front of our breasts. In the language of certain religions this means: 'the God in me greets the God in you.' It is a statement for becoming aware again of our little personalities in contrast to the totality governing all of us.

Movement-in-depth, derived from my own experience of Jungian analysis, means 'Physical Movement as a revelation of the Self.'

Case study

Since the movement history of a person is implied in the title, I am taking liberties with the plan. I cannot bring myself to think of this approach as a method, which may be my own failing or it may be inherent in the approach itself. A primary characteristic, after all, is the unique dissimilarity of each teacher/therapist. The work has to become individually hers. Perhaps that keeps it from being a method. Examples are scattered throughout the text in places where I felt the material could not be understood without them. Perhaps this way of presenting a case study will further illustrate the values talked about.

The study is not of a person, it is of a process. It occurs to me to offer as complete a description as possible, beginning with simple technical functioning, including inner reactions that result from a given image connected with the physical preparation. This may allow more insight into my way of working. I intend to quote from various members of the same workshop concerning the same piece of work. Memories of mine are not involved, these are actual records from that time.

The process concentrates on the same idea in several different ways. Physically, work begins on the floor, focusing quickly on the opposites involved in up/down. Each is explored specifically, definitively. Everyone then goes on to discover the movement possibilities of the continuum on which up and down exist as two ends of a single scale. This brings a pair of opposites into contact with each other. The third stage takes an image, for 'The earth is my mother. The sky is my father.'

P... wrote me a note:

The work had its greatest flash on Wednesday after we had started on the floor, feeling the contact of parts of our bodies touching, even pressing into and out of the floor. The floor became a partner; the focus was on the up and the down. Up and down became mutually inter-dependent; they connected pushing into and away from the earth; they connected lifting and reaching with sinking into the floor.

For me, consciousness of extra meaning came when you developed the work already underway by saying, 'Now, the earth is my mother. The sky is my father.' It seemed so clear, pieces of difficulty I have experienced in feeling rootedness in the ground connected up my spine to the head in an erect posture. This has been something I have worked on ever since my first lab with you three years ago. I finally felt it growing through my spine, cat-like, onto my feet, even in standing and walking!

Those experiences came right into a sudden realization that I knew nothing of my father — up, the air and the sky; that I drew my own strength from the down — the earth, my mother to whom I have been very close. My father is unable to let his inner struggles out, to let others know his feelings. He is typically kind, gentle, and capable in many ways; but he works in an industry which frustrates and pressures him: television sound production. He has an alcoholic problem which I see as his means of coping or not coping with all of these things. What strikes me is the similarities I am now beginning to admit in myself to those I've known in my dance.

What came to me was that all my dependency needs are down, maternal; until now I had not consciously faced the realization that a blank side of me, a missing part, a large hunk of the unknown lay in my not knowing my father, maybe not admitting my father in me at all. Down felt strong and solid. Up felt vague, indefinite, intangible, uncontactable. I was deeply moved to know that I needed the up, my father; and that it (he) needs me too. I had been in tears the instant that you made the suggestion of the image. It seemed to be what I was already exploring without knowing why.

Three days later, she re-read the letter:

> As I re-read this letter, it all still makes sense. I think there is significance
> in the fact that we had been working from a familiar point, 'contact with
> the floor' up to that which has been more difficult for me to sustain, a
> connection inside from earth to sky. Never having focused on the
> continuum as the connection between mother and father, it pushed me
> into the realm of my own personal, family background – difficulties and
> vacancies yet unacknowledged.

I have included this letter in some detail because it mentions the entire
process much more clearly than the comments of others who picked out the
parts most important to themselves. The familiar being on the floor through
the development of an abstract up and down turned into an image of
up/down, father/mother and brought this person into contact with her own
immediate background.

Another member, E… wrote:

> The up/down images left me comfortable on the ground searching
> above me into the sky, looking out through the side of my face, arms dead
> and powerless, hanging weightless. But then, 'the sky is my father'
> brought a hurt, a nausea of tears; for a father as untouchable as the sky
> who had hurt me, toward whom I could reach only a little, always with
> fear of being hurt again. As I continue to work, it begins to fill the arms
> with strength, with a developing suddenly realized anger at his
> withdrawal. When the beating began, I glimpsed the power and extent
> of the anger – then it was over. Another day the masculine image came to
> be my father after several moments of no associations at all.

It is important to say here that up/down, sky/earth are linked with the
principles of feminine/masculine that are, in turn, included in the experience
of some people. She goes on to describe her personal father and then says:

> In writing about the father thing later, I realized how confused I am
> about it – him – it was full of discrepancies in father – Father. My own
> father seemed to have turned me over to God. My father was attempting
> to be that himself, a spiritual, ethereal man who never touched me, never
> felt about me at all as a human daughter. I felt I embarrassed him, he used
> to introduce me as his 'amazon.' So, I've been embarrassed about being
> that – as if people may be repulsed at the sight of me or I might upset
> them about themselves.

In this particular workshop we were emphasizing masculine/feminine, man/woman, up/down. In the beginning they were all separate opposites, later they formed two ends of a scale. The picture of the earth as mother and the sky as father was an image calling forth any available responses.

B... writes:

> When we worked again today, it was with stretching various approaches to being down on the floor with the earth as mother and the ceiling as father. I struggled with both, especially with the earth. I needed to get away from the earth, to go more to the sky but the sky was not strong enough to pull me up, and the earth holds on to me. I felt I had to take all that was available from both and find a way to reinforce, to integrate them in myself. I struggled to get up, even using the wall. At last I felt my own strength and knew I was standing on, above and below the earth but aware of the sky. I wanted to go further up and reach the father, but was ashamed with the mother there. This wasn't good enough, I needed to find more of my mother and father operating in me. This feels as if it needed support from the whole person in physical encounters, as well as in verbally expressing how I feel, whether kind and positive or angry and negative. Slowly I am able to allow a little more, still with anxiety, the feeling that I am bad and wrong, that they will not like me. But each day puts another brick in the foundation, and I begin to feel sure, comfortable with what I am like out there in the world.

Now I come to a different form of the same thing. To me, it is incredibly mysterious that each person, hearing the same image, can be affected so differently.

M... writes:

> I have to stay with the day that I cried. I don't remember ever crying like that, and I am not sure that I was finished when we stopped. I was not prepared for those words: 'the floor is your mother. The ceiling is your father.' I cried even harder when I tried to stand and realized I couldn't. The words I said as I went back down from trying and drove myself into a corner were, 'I can't stand it.' So the question is: what is it that I can't stand?

These are all impressions of individual experiences, internalized by one person without reference to the other members of the group. I want to include one form of group encounter between actual men and actual women at a different time. In this chapter I have given more weight to the private sessions – it is interesting that the quotes given have all, nevertheless, come from groups. Apparently, what goes on in groups can be individual. I do not think individual work can be group work. The kinds of questions, the kinds of talking that link it to the personal life are different in a private session and can be done on the spot. The quotes used are all in the form of personal letters written to me. They could only be individually followed up. I would not have known what the experience of beginning on the floor and following through the image occasioned in each person unless I had been told. In individual sessions I would probably have been told.

The group encounter described next presents my point of view, from the outside, in dealing with an actual man/woman situation. It comes from a movement session held in Bethel, Maine, for the National Training Laboratory and is part of the general work being done by a particular group with a particular 'trainer.' I was the movement leader for all groups so I saw each person in the workshop every day.

This particular group had come to, more or less, a dead halt. Men and women were at each others' throats. There was such a definite dislike that communication was stymied, nothing was happening. I was faced with this on the afternoon of a summer day, without the least idea of what to do. I record the actual happenings as best I can.

I took the break in relations seriously, to the point of asking the men to gather at one end of the big living room, leaving the women at the other end. I told the whole group that a closed wall shut them off from each other, separating the room into two halves. Within its own space, each group was free to do whatever felt natural. A long period of horse-play followed with many attempts at trying things, none serious or lengthy. Finally, something real began. At the men's end, some had gone off by themselves to exercise or simply to sit, reflectively, in corners. Two or three were engaged in playing games or persecuting each other – one fellow was forcibly dragged between two others to a satisfactory position and made to hold it. The five or six women were having an even harder job concentrating than the men. They were not satisfied until they got hold of several pillows they could throw at each other. This created a kind of game. They smiled and looked more pleased with themselves. They paid no attention to the imaginary wall. The pillow tossing yielded to approaching each other until they were all down on the floor in a circle, heads on the pillow toward the center, feet out, like little girls telling secrets.

It seemed to me that the two groups were ready for a recognition of someone else in the room. I announced softly that the wall had been lowered to shoulder height. It was now a fence that could be seen through. The men gave up their games, everything they were doing, and focused in the direction of the fence, drawing nearer and nearer to it as they watched the women, who paid no attention, continuing to giggle and laugh in their circle, occasionally changing places. The circle had hardly any movement but it did provide involvement – relationship among themselves if not toward the men.

After a few minutes, I encouraged the men to reach under the wire toward the women, making their presence known, asking for attention. One or two moved up to the borderline, reaching under and through, their hands spread out on the rug. The tension of their longing was obvious in their bodies, although they voiced no need nor any claim. By this time, the women had gotten to their knees or feet, slightly loosening and breaking the circle. One or two looked in the direction of the dividing line.

I remarked aloud that the fence had opened and the men could crawl through. At the same time, I gave a soft warning, conveying that sudden movement, or an assault, might drive the women further away. The approach might need to be gentle, even tender. This provided an influence. Their approach was slow, in most cases on the belly and the knees. The women, separated now, were lying or sitting all over their own space. One man led the way, giving the others courage. He crawled up beside one of the girls and sat for a while stroking her hair. Since there were not enough women to equal the number of men, some found themselves with a man at the head and another by the feet.

A friend of mine, an analyst, once said that a place exists where men and women do not communicate, cannot exchange their ideas or feelings. This group seemed to have reached that place. When they were put in physical touch with each other, the door opened and, somehow, the log jam moved, so slowly that it took many minutes. There followed a gradual growth of trust between men and women, between the sexes. They could accept each other again.

It was striking that the trust included getting to the feet. In some cases the woman swayed in the middle, facing a man, with another man behind her. In other cases a woman and a man rocked together, arms around each other, or the man stood behind the woman while she leaned on him as they moved. There were many different ways of coming to a slow and reflective movement. It was impressive to look at, having, as it did, a quality of resolving something. I remember feeling humbled by my experience of not knowing ahead of time what to do or how to do it. For a long time I had no idea what would happen next. Eventually, it seemed to me that enough had taken place for then to go on, they could give up their defensiveness and begin work, they could communicate again. When the session was over, people stood around, talking more than usual but also more slowly than usual. The man who had first led detailed his experience of dancing with a man and a woman at the same time. This opened up other couples, other threesomes, to describe their own experiences. The whole group shared itself with itself. Gradually, one by one, they disappeared to find their trainer waiting in the hall. They approached him, faces more open than when they had begun. He breathed a sigh of relief and they all went into a room to work.

This is a different kind of group work than the other, which yielded individual examples. It took place within the framework of Encounter groups (T-groups) and limited itself to the here and now situation. There was no hint of linking it to the personal life or to inner experiences outside the moment when the encounter was taking place. Yet it presented the same kind of involvement and development in dealing with the man/woman opposition.

The reality of the opposites, polarity, is not limited to any familiar pair that can be thought of. It is a principle inherent in the way life is lived. What interests many now is how widely separated the function of men and women has become. Could the present attempt to equalize the sexes mean that the woman in the man and the man in the woman be liberated?

References

Brooks, C.V.W. (1974) *Sensory Awareness*. New York: Viking.

Durckheim, K.G. (1970) *The Vital Centre of Man*. New York: Fern Hill Books.

Frey-Rohn, L. (1974) *From Freud to Jung*. New York: C.G. Jung Foundation.

Ghiselin, B. (1952) *The Creative Process*. New York: New American Library.

Herrigel, E. (1971) *Zen in the Art of Archery*. New York: Random.

Jung, C.G. (1959) *The Undiscovered Self*. New York: Dutton.

Jung, C.G. (1961) *Memories, Dreams, Reflections*. New York: Vintage Books, Random House.

Jung, C.G. (1964) *Man and His Symbols*. New York: Doubleday.

Jung, C.G. (1968) *Analytical Psychology: Its Theory and Practice*. New York: Pantheon Books, Random House.

Krishnamurti, J. (1956) *Commentaries on Living*. Series I. Wheaton, IL: Quest Books.

Lao Tzu (English translation by Jane English, 1972). *Tao Te Ching*. New York: Random.

McGlashan, A. (1967) *The Savage and Beautiful Country.* Boston: Houghton & Mifflin.

Progoff, I. (1973) *The Symbolic and the Real.* New York: McGraw-Hill Book Company.

Richards, M.C. (1969) *Centering in Pottery, Poetry and the Person.* Hanover, NH: Wesleyan University Press.

Ross, N.W. (1947) *The Left Hand is the Dreamer.* New York: William Sloane.

Sorell, W. (1970) *The Duality of Vision.* Indianapolis: The Bobbs-Merrill Company.

van der Post, L. (1955) *The Dark Eye in Africa.* New York: Morrow.

Janet Adler

Janet Adler's Papers

It is a privilege to imagine my own experiences and thoughts bound between the words of my deeply gifted teacher, Mary Starks Whitehouse, and my treasured friend and colleague, Joan Chodorow. When Joan and I first met twenty-five years ago, I recognized then her integrity and her extraordinary capacity for clear thinking. It was thrilling to learn that she, too, had been a student of Mary's because I already knew that Mary's presence, Mary's way, had entered and irrevocably changed the unfolding of my life, of my work.

Participation in preparing these papers for publication has been an invitation to see more clearly the evolution of my work, my questions concerning the development of conscious embodiment in moving and witnessing. Patrizia's work as editor has been central to this query. I have chosen, in this extremely humbling process, to make revisions but primarily to preserve the original language and context of each paper, thus hoping to clarify the actual historical development of the discipline of Authentic Movement.

All but one of my papers developed as public presentations to colleagues and students. My first paper, 'Integrity of Body and Psyche: Some Notes on Work in Process', written in 1972, after a decade of work with disturbed children, reflects my need to better understand my experience of Mary's teaching in relationship to developmental psychology. In 1976, as my studies of developmental movement deepened, I felt it necessary to address the fact of libido in the experience of embodiment in my paper 'Authentic Movement and Sexuality in the Therapeutic Experience'. As I look back now, I see that those first two papers, written from my perspective as a movement therapist, appeared during the time in which I became a mother of two sons. My experiences as a mother with a child and as a therapist with a client must have simultaneously grounded, in a very direct way, my growing interest in better understanding the relationship between mover and witness.

'Who is the Witness? A Description of Authentic Movement', written in 1985, the only paper occurring purely because I needed to clarify my own thinking, marks the end of an initiatory experience chronicled in my book *Arching Backward*. Perhaps this paper, drawn from the richness of my experience of my students at The Mary Starks Whitehouse Institute, was a bridge between my understanding of the embodiment of personal history and the direct experience of the numinous. As our family then moved from the East Coast to the West Coast, I also moved from a therapeutic practice toward a teaching practice.

In 1991, I further explored my questions concerning the relationship between the practice of Authentic Movement and mystical practice in my paper 'Body and Soul'. This work, leading me into a deeper inquiry into the relationship between the embodiment of personal consciousness and the embodiment of collective consciousness, is expressed in my paper 'The Collective Body' written in 1994.

Currently, I am writing a book about my experience of the organic evolution of the discipline of Authentic Movement within the last thirty years. In this writing process, paradox becomes more vivid – as the awareness of each embodied moment within the development of mover and witness consciousness clarifies, the mysteries of this way of work become more luminous. My commitment to continued study and practice of this discipline expands as my experience of this paradox deepens, both with individuals choosing the discipline as their primary teaching practice as well as those choosing to enter the form of Authentic Movement as a mystical practice.

Janet Adler
January 1998

CHAPTER 9

An Interview with Janet Adler[1]

Neala Haze and Tina Stromsted

Janet Adler, PhD, ADTR, has been a dance/movement therapist since 1963 when she trained with Marian Chace at St Elizabeth's Hospital in Washington, D.C. She documented her work with autistic children in the award winning film *Looking For Me* in 1968. A student of Mary Starks Whitehouse, the first person to describe authentic movement in the presence of a witness, Janet further developed the work, and, in 1981, founded and directed the Mary Starks Whitehouse Institute, the first school in which the discipline of Authentic Movement was studied and practised. Since moving to Northern California in 1985, she has been leading groups in the study and practice of the discipline of Authentic Movement. In 1988 she created a film about Authentic Movement called *Still Looking* and completed her doctoral degree in mystical studies in 1992. Author of the book *Arching Backward: The Mystical Initiation of a Contemporary Woman*, she currently lectures and offers groups in the United States and Europe. She is part of the faculty of the Authentic Movement Institute in the San Francisco Bay Area.

Janet's early work stresses the development of a psychological under-standing of the therapeutic relationship in the mover/witness dyad. As her work develops, her understanding of the role of the witness deepens and the spiritual aspect of the practice expands. Janet brings a remarkable capacity for seeing, listening and reflecting her students' experience, as well as a willingness to take important and creative risks in further developing her work. Her warmth and clarity of presence have been a gift to colleagues and

1   Revised interview, previously published in the *American Journal of Dance Therapy*, Vol. 16, no. 2, Fall/Winter 1994.

students alike. Her respect for life's mysteries and courage in following her vision are sources of inspiration to many.

On a beautiful spring day, the three of us gathered under a canopy of roses in the garden outside of Janet's studio in Bodega, California. She had prepared a beautiful array of fruits, nuts and cheeses held in a woven basket. We sat chatting, eating and sipping tea. After many years of advanced training in the form of Authentic Movement, we felt it was time to document the development of Janet's contribution to this work. And so we began...

I: 'What childhood experiences influenced your becoming a dance/movement therapist?'

JA: 'I loved to move. Dancing lessons throughout my childhood offered not only great pleasure in just the sensation of moving but also, I can see in retrospect, a form within which my energy could expand, become visible and be contained. Those lessons fed my imagination as a small child, my need for mastery in latency and my love of beauty as an adolescent. When I was old enough, my parents arranged for me to travel alone on the bus to the city and study privately with a prominent dancer in the Sadler Wells Ballet Company'.

I: 'What was that like?'

JA: 'I lived for those lessons, yet left each one wondering "when will she let me dance?" Each time I arrived for a lesson, no one was there. Once inside the old building, I walked up the many wooden steps in a narrow, cold and gray stairwell. I waited at the top of the steps on an uncomfortable, wooden bench outside the studio. Eventually, my heart would leap as the door opened downstairs and I could hear her pink spike heels lightly touching each step as she came closer. After her silent, stern nod of acknowledgment, I followed her into the studio'.

I: 'Not exactly a warm nurturing environment. Ballet has been traditionally seen by our culture as the ultimate feminine form, yet in this situation a major aspect of the feminine principle seems to have been absent'.

JA: 'Yes, and one day, just before I followed my teacher into the studio, I saw an image out of the corner of my eye, to my right. I saw a girl, exactly my size. She was completely white, yet transparent. She had no weight or density. She was reaching away from me, up toward her right, her arms extended. Once in the studio, we began to work near the mirror, under a row of large windows on the left. I remember the light felt muted, without focus or shine. My teacher showed me a simple series of steps and told me to do it. I couldn't, or maybe I wouldn't. Nothing came, absolutely nothing. I felt hollow, sensing an acute absence of color and sound. I vividly remember feeling without myself, a specific sensation that I came to recognize in certain situations for years to come. Perhaps I had seen an image of my "spirit," the very source of my passion for dancing, exit as I entered the room, clearly marking, making visible, the split that the classical ballet training created in me. Though I have no memory of deciding at the time, 'this is the end!,' my life changed. I made no more Saturday trips to the city on the bus. The magic and power of the archetype – of the twirling ballerina inside my jewelry box, of the pink toe shoes – was diffused. So ended my dream of becoming a professional dancer'.

I: 'How did that loss get translated into your exploration of dance therapy?'

JA: 'Somehow, having been released from a form that did not hold my body and soul, I was free to explore that relationship from another perspective. Thus began my journeys, with my blue record player and drum, in orphanages, mental hospitals and homes for crippled children. I needed to dance with feeling with children who maybe needed to do the same thing. Though I didn't really know what I was doing, in retrospect, I believe that I must have been searching for direct expression from unconscious realms. Relentlessly guided by my intuition, I danced more and more with psychotic children'.

I: 'What was your educational preparation?'

JA: 'Because in the early 1960s psychology departments at the universities were mostly experimental, rat lab programs, I chose a back door into the more formal study of the disturbed child. Between 1959 and 1963, while I was earning a Bachelor of Arts degree in Speech and Language Therapy, my mother sent me an article about Marian Chace, one of the first dance therapists. I contacted her and she became my first mentor'.

I: 'What do you remember in particular about those early days working with Marian Chace at St Elizabeth's hospital?'

JA: 'I remember that the spacious, manicured hospital grounds felt so different from the inner life contained within the structure of the giant, square, red brick buildings. Marian worked in a basement room next to the boiler room, an indication of the lack of respect that the administrators had for dance therapy at that time. She also visited many back wards each day, working there with people too ill to leave their floor. She looked like Mrs Santa Claus to me – thin white hair piled on top of her head, dancing slippers and usually donned in cotton flowered skirts. When we did leave her room, my job was to push the RCA Victor phonograph from ward to ward. I remember it was incredibly heavy, but I didn't mind. I was so thrilled to have such an important job!'

I: 'Could you describe some of your impressions as you worked with the patients?'

JA: 'The nurses unlocked us into back ward after back ward until we arrived at the home of the most seriously disturbed people. Many were not clothed, most did not speak. They leaned against walls in unusual positions, totally absorbed in their own realities. And then Marian would say to me "waltz" or "polka" and I would run to the phonograph and choose the record while she would magically gather these individuals up and into a circle. Slowly, people would stamp, clap, sway. We would find a common rhythm, sound or feeling and the shouting or crying would begin. I remember the time when a woman passionately raised her fist and repeatedly asked:

"Why?" Her plea echoed in the voices and bodies of those around her. When our thirty minutes were over, the nurses unlocked us back out into a series of other wards. As we left, I remember seeing people, as if in slow motion, quietly returning to shapes awaiting them, silently slipping back into the walls, into the familiar inner worlds where they had been living for decades'.

I: 'What was Marian's most significant contribution to your development?'

JA: 'Marian taught me about the power of the unconscious and how it lives in the body. She knew about this force and how it could be contained and embodied in the circle, an ancient and universal aspect of ritual. I wanted to understand what everything meant, how the movements and statements that patients made related to their lives. I remember Marian insisting that what mattered was the movement expression itself. Now, thirty years later, her insistence on direct experience intrigues me. It wasn't enough for me then. I had to first leave the realm of the collective unconscious and study how personal consciousness evolves from it and in relationship to it, in the body. Having made such an excursion into the development of the self, in recent years I have chosen to return to the study of direct experience, but this time with more conscious awareness'.

I: 'One of your early contributions to our field was the award winning film *Looking For Me*, which was the first film made about dance/movement therapy. Can you describe your work with autistic children and how it led to your film?'

JA: 'I felt compelled to encounter the most disturbed child who was out of this world and to bring her back. I began dancing with such children in a huge room on the 11th floor of the Psychiatric Institute and Clinic at the University of Pittsburgh Medical School. The walls were institution green and there were bars on the windows. This was in 1967, as I was earning a Masters of Science degree in Child Development at that school. I loved the amount of external space and what felt like an invitation to explore the vastness of internal space. I loved being alone in it with those little beings not yet here'.

I: 'What did you do with them?'

JA: 'I would rock with them, not looking, looking, shifting – I needed to be near a child whose tiny limited world was intensely physical. I did whatever the child did, bringing all of me to those interactions. I am sure Marian Chace's work with psychotic adults deeply influenced my choice to try to mirror the gestures of these children. I loved mirroring the self-stimulating movements and soon I was not just mirroring, I was in them more and more fully. I was descending in the presence of these children, who maybe were descending in my presence. My memory is of searching more and more deeply. We discovered relationship with each other, based on the sharing of the ritualistic movements of the child'.

I: 'It sounds like you were intensely involved in your work in those years and on a path of self-discovery as well'.

JA: 'Yes. In retrospect I realize that those little beings knew things I needed to know. First, they knew about a pre-conscious realm that I recognized in my bones but didn't know how to access. This was my first extensive experience as an ally within altered time and space, before ego, before words, before consciousness. What was important was not only my longing to join them in the realm of the unconscious but also my longing to track our way back across a thin membrane, a boundary into consciousness, toward the language of my time and space. Eventually, by mirroring my world, they each, in their own way, crossed that boundary with me. It was very mysterious moving back and forth across that line between ordinary and non-ordinary realities. This was another gift. I needed to have direct experience of that interface and these children were my guides'.

I: 'In those early days of dance therapy there was little documentation of the impact that movement could have in working with people. How did your film come about?'

JA: 'So all of this material first became the stuff of my thesis. Working in the linguistic-kinesic laboratory at the Institute with two of Professor Ray Birdwhistle's protégés, and using the natural history approach, I learned to study movement on film at 24 and 48 frames per second. It was through the exhaustive study of film segments of me moving with individual children that I became conscious of what had been mostly intuitive work, an extremely significant time in my development personally and professionally. *Looking For Me* became an extension of that graduate work, a surprise project based on meeting a man at a cocktail party, who, as director of a foundation, happened to have a discretionary fund of $4500 which had to be spent immediately because the calendar said so!'

I: 'As therapists, we are often drawn to working with others as a part of our own healing process. How do you understand the strength and passion of working with autistic children in terms of your own developmental history?'

JA: 'One reason I needed to learn about the pre-conscious realm was because I was hospitalized at 13 months due to serious digestive problems and not allowed to see my mother or to have any transitional objects for six weeks. My body has told me that I developed 'autistic-like' behavior at that time. Such a connection between my early trauma and the autistic children in the Institute was completely unconscious when I was a young adult. Yet I know my need to relive that trauma and thus free energy still bound in that experience was guiding me. The autistic children took me exactly where I needed to go. It is not a coincidence that I found them. Since, I have understood that often my most intensively directed work in the outer world is primarily chosen to bring balance to my personal development in my inner world, even though it is always enriched by the hope of helping others in the process'.

I: 'How does the work you did with autistic children connect to the work you've been doing the last twenty-three years in Authentic Movement?'

JA: 'My experience of merging in the symbiotic realm with the
        children and then moving with them toward the beginnings
        of discovery of two separate beings freed me to next explore
        the development of personal consciousness. I needed a terrain
        in which I could study separateness and boundaries. I
        remember soon after *Looking For Me* was finished, standing in
        the center of my kitchen, spinning bare-footed, wondering
        what was next. The phone rang and I was invited to be a
        member of a Personal Growth Group at the National Training
        Laboratory in Maine. They were short on women and
        someone suggested my name. I had never been in a group and
        I knew nothing about leading groups, so this seemed like a
        good way to learn'.

I: 'What form did this take?'

JA: 'Well, my next teacher, John Weir, led the group. Josi Taylor,
        one of Mary Whitehouse's students, was teaching the
        movement part because Mary couldn't be there as she had
        been the year before. I had never heard of any of these people
        but the first morning, when Josi said to us "lie down, listen,
        wait for impulse, then move", I had an extraordinary
        experience and in that moment fell in love with authentic
        movement. Josi and John introduced me to Mary on the phone
        the next day and I knew I would go to her as soon as
        possible'.

I: 'This sounds like a most auspicious time! How did this
        training influence your thinking?'

JA: 'That workshop was a milestone. Not only did I meet Mary
        because of it but I met John, Josi and the rest of his staff. I
        learned about leading groups. (He is a master at that.) Most
        importantly, he taught me about "percept language." In this
        language individuals are asked to own their experience by
        using the words "I saw" or "I felt" rather than projecting or
        interpreting or judging other people's experience'.

I: 'Not easy to do!'

JA: 'Right, and speaking it religiously for two weeks in the lab
        opened me to a whole new way of understanding experience

in relationship to another human being. This learning became incorporated into my own understanding and subsequent teaching of the discipline of Authentic Movement in the most central way as my study of the form deepened. That practice is the source of my work with the witness in regards to the awareness of projection, judgment and interpretation which John called "self-ownership."'

I: 'Yes, learning how to conceptualize one's experience has been a vital contribution to the verbal aspect of the form as we have learned it from you. How did your work with Mary begin?'

JA: 'She had just learned that she had multiple sclerosis when we began planning how and when I would come to her. Because of the news of her illness, it was difficult for her to know how to plan our work together. Essentially, I closed my life in Pittsburgh and flew to Los Angeles to apprentice with her. I remember walking into the studio for the first time. The space felt vast, infinite. Permission was given. I fell into my body on the empty floor. Movement came through me as if it had been waiting for centuries. Boundless energy which had been withheld and compressed was released. There were no obstacles. There was impulse and, simultaneously, my body, creating order, received and shaped the energy, offering a clear vessel. Finally, I felt I was truly allowed to dance'.

I: 'Could you elaborate more on how you experienced yourself physically?'

JA: 'The impulse to move felt very far in – in the center of me. The minute I closed my eyes it was like coming home. I recognized myself. And Mary, as my witness, saw me seeing myself. My movement was an expression of unformed, unconscious material. As I spoke about my experiences with her, consciousness evolved in an organic way, a way that was completely meaningful to me and endlessly fascinating'.

I: 'Depending on when people studied with Mary, they learned different things. What did you receive that contributed to your work?'

JA: 'Most importantly, I received the structure of the form itself.
        Mary was the first person to describe authentic movement –
        what it is, how it can occur in the presence of a witness. Her
        background as a Wigman and then a Graham dancer gave her
        a strong embodied base for the movement aspect of the form.
        Her studies in Jungian analysis became the foundation on
        which she used a symbolic perspective in exploring the
        movers' and witness' inner images. This brief but unusually
        intense five months I studied with her was my introduction to
        authentic movement in the presence of a witness, the
        beginning of my own study, practice and teaching of the
        relationship between moving and witnessing'.

I: 'How would you describe the differences between Mary's
        work and yours?'

JA: 'Mary gave me so many seeds with which I have since been
        working. Maybe, my teaching style is different. In general,
        perhaps Mary was more often directive than I am in
        relationship to the mover. Also, her interest in symbol was a
        strong aspect of her work. I have tended to be increasingly
        interested in movement before and after symbol. Perhaps, my
        work has developed in those different ways. As I look back, I
        realize I have been especially concerned with the inner
        experience of the witness and how that experience was
        offered to the mover within the dyadic relationship. Even now,
        as we are talking, I can see how I continue to be drawn to the
        mysterious and compelling role of the witness as the form
        expands'.

I: 'What did you and Mary actually do together?'

JA: 'I saw her almost every day, twice a week in her studio
        privately, once a week in a group, and then, often, we met for
        a meal or with the specific intention of dialoguing about the
        work. We tried taping her speaking about the work or just
        talking as I sat at her feet taking notes, dreaming about what
        was next in the teaching of the work or sharing personal lives.
        I spent time with her family and her close friends. For some

blessed reason, our relationship felt wonderfully free as it developed'.

I: 'Sounds like she was an inspiration to you on a number of levels. Could you say more about what touched you personally?'

JA: 'The freedom she gave me to MOVE, her trust in me as her student, her constant reaching toward new understanding, her non-attachment to what she knew, her self-doubt in my presence, her eyes when she spoke of her own personal history and her will to stay in intimate relationship to her body as she became increasingly ill – she gave me many, many gifts. Another very important one: when I came to her, I was full of all of my personality intensity and she kept gently reminding me that there is more to us than personal history. In that way, though I wasn't quite ready, I became conscious of the idea of the numinous, through her teaching based on Jungian thought. I am profoundly grateful for her presence in my life and all that she offered me'.

I: 'How has the archetypal realm, the numinous aspect become more consciously a part of your work?'

JA: 'The autistic children, my first teachers about the numinous, allowed me to participate in the arrival of spirit into body as they journeyed into conscious time and space from another, pre-egoic, time and space. But without the following years of primary commitment to the study and practice of the development of embodied personal consciousness, I could not have allowed myself to step more openly toward my questions of the numinous within the discipline of Authentic Movement. This is because I feel so strongly about mystical experience not being misused or misunderstood in relationship to the essential work regarding healthy egoic development. As is now commonly understood, it is not safe to "transcend" an ego that is not developmentally secure'.

I: 'Why did you close your private practice?'

JA: 'In 1981, still fiercely focused on the moving body, I opened the Mary Stark Whitehouse Institute in Northampton,

Massachusetts. It was there that my own conceptual framework of the discipline of Authentic Movement was "in labor." I needed to step out of the role of the therapist and into the role of the teacher, so that I could be free to look more carefully at my questions about the form, especially about the inner experience of the witness. With all of my conscious work energy directed toward the beginning of this new little school, I was suddenly hurled into the realm of the numinous'.

I: 'You have told us some about that time of transition and the great changes that occurred within you'.

JA: 'Yes, it does not feel appropriate to say too much more about that time now. I can say that it was one of the most challenging experiences of my life and my gratitude continues to be indescribable. My experiences within those four-and-a-half years irrevocably altered my perception of reality. During this time a specific energy entered my system spontaneously. In this process of what I now understand as an initiatory experience, I reawakened to the sacred, directly experiencing the numinous as physical sensation in my body rather than channeled through my mind or emotions. Perhaps the ten years of such intense study and practice of the discipline of Authentic Movement after leaving Mary were a preparation, though I had no conscious interest in experience of the spirit in those years'.

I: 'It is important to hear you speak of direct experience in this particular way. The ramifications of your initiation have been, and continue to be, vividly apparent in our work together in the studio'.

JA: 'In the studio my questions that emerge increasingly about moving and about witnessing are reflections of wonder about direct experience. The unmet longing to be without interference, density, duality, the longing to be whole, in union in the presence of another, as mover or as witness, with oneself, with another, with one's God, seems to be at the root of our despair and suffering in this contemporary world'.

I: 'Yes, the compassion that can develop in both mover and witness carries the lifeblood that heals the individual and the collective. Can you say more about direct experience in relationship to your studio work and writing about the collective body? In your second film, *Still Looking*, the concept of the collective consciousness was striking'.

JA: 'Yes. The film was an attempt, in 1988, to make a summary statement about my own understanding of the discipline of Authentic Movement. It marks a time in my experience of the development of the discipline when the language systems of psychology, with the dyadic format as ground, were opening to include the question of collective consciousness or the collective body. Maybe the simplest way to say it is that mystical experience is direct experience and one cannot have a mystical experience without receiving a cellular glimpse of the whole. My initiation taught me more than I can say about the importance of finding our way from the privilege of individuation, developed consciousness of the self, into membership in collective consciousness'.

I: 'Was this the reason for your doctoral studies in mysticism?'

JA: 'Yes. I had to know what had happened to me, I needed a context, but I needed years of recovery, rest and integration first. Once strong enough, two tasks became essential aspects of my return. I needed to find the correct form in which to communicate or translate my initiation experience so that it could be offered back and I needed to correctly place these experiences within the cross-cultural context of the history of mysticism. Both pieces of work became my dissertation'.

I: 'Will your dissertation be published?'

JA: 'The first half, *Arching Backward*, the phenomenological part, will be published in 1995 by Inner Traditions'.

I: 'How did your initiation influence the development of your theoretical framework in the discipline of Authentic Movement?'

JA: 'The discipline of Authentic Movement continues to be the
        very large and mysterious vessel which safely and
        appropriately holds my personal and professional development
        in terms of my need to know about the relationship between
        the unconscious and consciousness. In the process I learned
        about impeccability, surrender and will. My initiation
        indescribably widens and deepens my practice. The form
        expands to include more of the human experience, spirit as
        well as personal history. In my work with long-term training
        groups in the last eight years here in Northern California
        (which, by the way, have felt like the birth of my own
        conceptual framework after the labor at the Whitehouse
        Institute) we have been studying the issue of timing – in
        relationship to merging, separation and union between mover
        and witness as well as within the intrapsychic process of both
        mover and witness. Though we always try to be conscious of
        the psychological process of projection and the embodied
        aspects of transference and countertransference, we are
        working increasingly with circles of external, conscious
        witnesses who can hold so much more than an individual
        witness in the presence of a mover who is engaged in direct
        experience. We are participating in the organic evolution of
        ritual. All of these changes in the manifestation of the
        discipline reflect the great possibility of increased
        understanding of the collective body as it becomes more
        visible in Authentic Movement'.

I: 'Thank you for articulating the evolution of your work. Your
        responses invite a deepening of our own questions and an
        appreciation for the capacity of this form to embrace such a
        full range of human experience'.

CHAPTER 10

Integrity of Body and Psyche
Some Notes on Work in Process[1]

Janet Adler

For many years I worked with people, mostly children, who were swimming in the realm of the unconscious. With movement as the medium, I tried to give them a taste of the conscious world and a hint at the joy of the power of choice between these two worlds. Recently, I find myself working, still primarily through movement, with adults, men and women, who want very much to release their constrained consciousness and know more deeply the life within themselves. They seek a freedom of commerce between the two worlds. And so my work changes, as a reflection, I'm sure, of my own personal growth. I grew from being a young woman primarily unconscious of my inner world to becoming a woman with a developing consciousness of myself and the way in which I grow. As my own consciousness evolves, I feel more capable of being with others as they journey into their unconscious lives and back to a clearer and fuller sense of themselves as conscious adults.

In these last few years I have been exploring a particular way of movement work which I experienced with my teacher, Mary Whitehouse. As I integrate some of what I learned from Mary, I realize that the mover can make deep and transformative journeys which can be appropriately understood within a psychological framework.

As I work with people in their search for connection between body and psyche, I have discovered some clear similarities between the process of movement therapy as I experience it now and the processes described in

1   Revised paper, previously published in the *Proceedings of the Seventh Annual American Dance Therapy Association Conference*, Santa Monica, California, 1972, from a presentation at the same conference.

verbal psychotherapy. I am going to briefly and simply try to identify some emerging parallels within a progression of five stages of development. Although I describe them as distinct stages, in actual experience the boundaries are fluid.

I will be speaking about this particular kind of movement therapy and verbal psychotherapy for people who are not mentally ill – people just like us who are searching for a way to live well – to live better by learning how to allow themselves fuller access to the complexities of their individual development. I speak of a *process* called movement therapy, not a cure. My clients are each in his or her own way choosing to listen to and to speak from their inner lives with care. Some of them are also students of dance/movement therapy, of psychology, of the arts.

The search for authentic movement

In my work the first stage in movement therapy with an individual in a one-to-one setting is the client's search for authentic movement. Authentic movement, as Mary Whitehouse (1970) used to describe it, is movement that is natural to a particular person, not learned like ballet or calisthenics, not purposeful or intellectualized as 'this is the way I should move' to be pleasing, to be powerful, to be beautiful or graceful. Authentic movement is an immediate expression of how the client feels at any given moment. The spontaneous urge to move or not to move is not checked, judged, criticized or weighed by the conscious mind.

Gradually, as a client becomes comfortable with authentic movement and can recognize when she is experiencing it and when she is not, the true discipline of this sort of work emerges. She can move completely freely, with less inhibition, and yet she is conscious of what she is doing, as if she is watching herself move but not interfering, not even commenting. She is allowing herself access to her unconscious and, as her unconscious speaks through her movement, she can become conscious of what she is doing. This is what I learned in Mary's presence. Freedom to stumble upon authentic movement and then to slowly bring such experience in relationship to one's will is not unlike the natural development of a small child. Mary often, and beautifully, spoke of this important parallel.

In psychotherapy there is a similar beginning. The client tries to sort out and disentangle authentic from 'adopted' feelings. He is also seeking an experience in which he can speak freely from his heart, without his mind judging and criticizing that which he says. It sometimes can be more difficult to find one's authentic nature through speaking, as it seems to me that the body lives much closer to the unconscious aspects of the mind than the conscious aspects. And it is the realm of the unconscious which I believe holds our most important and powerful secrets. Growing closer to oneself means knowing, and then owning, these secrets as they are freed from hiding and allowed to be integrated with one's conscious reality.

The expression of authentic movement

Again, in my work, the second stage in movement therapy is the open expression of authentic movement. Once it is discovered, time is needed to learn to trust, to live with, to enjoy and explore the new discovery. Clients in this stage always experience the freedom to move with great joy. Some of my richest experiences in my work with Mary were imbued with such freedom.

In psychotherapy the corollary would be freely and continuously talking of one's true feelings, an experience that is strikingly rare and precious. Often during this stage in both types of therapy, the individual learns that she has permission to move in any way that she wants or say anything she wants to say. An awareness of freedom develops as the underlying ground of trust – in herself and in her therapist – becomes firm and reliable.

The recognition of an emerging repertoire

The third stage in movement therapy is recognition by the client and therapist of a slowly emerging repertoire: the same movement patterns continually reappear. The client finds herself moving again and again in the same ways. Authentic movement seems to have powerful and self-imposed limits and such limits often come to the client as an unwelcome surprise. In psychotherapy a similar phenomenon begins to appear – the client speaks repeatedly of the same themes or the same person, of the same behavior patterns.

The exploration of themes: focusing

The fourth stage begins the real work for most of my clients. In response to recognition of repetitive behavior, they begin to experiment with ways to focus on a specific theme, to get to know more about it, to go with it, to exaggerate it, to confront it. In psychotherapy, it seems to me, the very same thing occurs: the client begins to explore, dissect and work with the recurring themes in his repertoire. It is at this stage in both movement therapy and psychotherapy that different therapists guide the client in remarkably different ways in an effort to help them come into fuller awareness of the problem and its modes of resolution.

The experience of resolution

The fifth stage is in the experience of resolution. My teacher, John Weir (1969), speaks so very clearly when he says: 'The only way out is in and through.' In the fourth stage the client is going in and through the feelings that need to be experienced. The fifth stage is the coming out, emerging with freed energy for continued growth. The deeper and more authentic the fourth stage, the more powerful and clear is the resolution. Thus the fifth stage embodies feelings such as relief, amazement, clarity, peace – all of the good and deserved aspects of self-love.

In movement therapy this stage is often more verbal than the previous ones. It is a time to collect, synthesize, organize and digest the process in which unconscious material has been experienced in the body and subsequently made conscious. The experience of resolution in psychotherapy is very similar to the same experience in movement therapy. In the fifth stage of psychotherapy the client also experiences clarity and relief as the pieces of his puzzle finally fit together and make sense as a whole.

A case study: Heather

I have referred briefly to these similar stages of work and want now to describe the illustrative journey of a movement therapy client whom I shall call Heather. My interest here is in providing an example, drawn from my own experience as a movement therapist, of a client's progression through the stages described above. I am not attempting an exhaustive account of the therapeutic process. I will address only a few aspects of Heather's work.

In discussing a client's work it is difficult to speak consistently of the therapist's behavior and to speak certainly of the relationship between the client and the therapist. Therefore, before describing Heather's journey, I want to say something of my behavior as a therapist with people like Heather who are not mentally ill.

The typical pattern of a movement session is as follows. Like Mary once did with me, I begin by asking my client if she wants a 'movement problem' or if she wants to move freely. If she wants a 'problem' to help her get started (this is often the case in the early sessions), I suggest a simple one which may lead to or stimulate an authentic movement. These 'problems,' usually related to the exploration of polarities, were a central aspect of Mary's work. For example, I say: 'Move, with your eyes closed, from a standing position toward the floor. Let the gravity pull you down. When you are down as far as you want to be, begin to move up. And when you are up as far as you want, begin again to move down. Continue to explore the cycle between the earth and the sky in this way'.

Often, a client gives me a clue, like 'I feel depressed,' and then asks for a 'problem.' I might then suggest finding a way to move in which her body can feel heavy and move downward. After the client moves, we talk together about her experience and sometimes about my experience as an observer. Mary always invited discussion with me after I moved.

As Mary was to me, I am primarily a guide to my client as she explores her feelings through movement. I suggest going with, staying with, exaggerating, waiting and, most importantly, I encourage her to trust where she is – to trust herself – and to force nothing. I find I increasingly trust the natural process of growth. Learning to give ourselves what we need, as much as we need, means satiation, and satiation means free energy for more growth. As I learned first in my work with autistic children, there is great power in regression to unfinished periods of development. Reliving, re-experiencing unconscious material frees the client to bring that material into consciousness, to talk about it in a way that makes sense to her. When it feels appropriate, I selectively share personal experiences with my client as I too am 'in process' and therefore do not represent a 'finished product' in the client's eyes. Also, I feel more real, more present, when I can be honestly responsive.

I will speak about a series of twenty-eight sessions that cover approximately a three-and-one-half month period, with an average of two one-hour sessions per week. Heather and I first spoke together because she wanted to become a movement therapist and therefore had many questions about preparation for such a profession. I talked about psychology and dance but I also mentioned the critical importance of her own inner work. I insisted that those of us who want to truly help another person realize himself more fully must first begin to realize and awaken to our own psychodynamics.

Heather understood and wanted to begin working at once on her own personal growth in movement therapy. I learned that she was nineteen years old and lived at home in the New York area with her parents. She was an only child. Her parents owned and together operated a toy store. She was not seeing friends, not going to school, not taking dance classes (she had been a dance student for years) and she was sleeping and eating a great deal. She felt immobilized: she couldn't leave her parents' home but she hated staying.

At the start of work with a client I rarely have more information than that with which I began in Heather's case. I find that I trust the client and come to know her best, in the beginning especially, through her movement. There are times, however, as the work progresses, that I explicitly ask for material from the client's personal history.

Heather moved quickly through the first stage of experience, in which she discovered authentic movement with little difficulty. Her only distraction was danced movement, which she gave up completely by the third session. As she then moved into the second stage, into free exploration of her authentic movement, there was great fullness, variety and enthusiasm in her work. When Heather moved, she was 'all there,' moving almost always from an unconscious source. This gift of accessible unconscious movement is rare; its cost can be a tenuous grip on self-management. In the beginning she had little or no memory for her movement and little concern for clarifying, organizing or verbalizing her experience. Heather simply had an insatiable need to move and, once she discovered the freedom with which she worked, she moved consistently with a sense of herself as free and newly found.

In the third stage I experience the themes in a client's repertoire emerging on three different levels: specific body parts emerge as more or less available and energized; culturally symptomatic movements become apparent; and idiosyncratic movements become visible. Heather's hands are the best example of specific body parts invested with energy.

In the very first session her hands were obviously more tense than the rest of her body. She wrote in her journal: 'What was interesting was the more I tried to relax them, the tenser they got.' In the second session, when her hands were again exceptionally tense, I suggested she focus on them, let them go where they wanted to go, not try to make them relax. She was able to do this easily and soon her hands clasped tightly together, her entire body sank and her face looked very sad. At the end of the experience she spoke briefly of a feeling of sadness. By the fifth session, Heather's hands were clawing at herself and she became aware of anger welling up beneath the sadness.

Heather was repeatedly shrugging her shoulders back and pushing away from her torso with her hands and arms during the first five sessions. These gestures might culturally be read as 'get off' or 'go away.' When exaggerated, that gesture pattern might commonly suggest claustrophobia. Indeed, her verbal response after experiencing this pattern during the sixth session was: 'I've always been very claustrophobic.'

Idiosyncratic movements are most powerfully expressive of the less conscious aspects of the personality. They seem to have no meaning to anyone else and appear unrelated to anyone else's movement patterns. Of its very nature, then, it is difficult to identify an idiosyncratic pattern as such until it is repeated so many times that it becomes clear. Even then, I seldom have the slightest idea what it means or where its source lies. These movement patterns or qualities truly reflect the uniqueness and the enormously complicated nature of the individual.

An idiosyncratic movement pattern developed in Heather's work while she was lying on her side. She lifted one leg straight up and then put it down, bent, foot flat on the floor in front of her other leg. She then pushed against the floor with her bent leg, pivoting her body around ninety degrees. As early as the fourth session this pattern evolved into consecutive quarter turns until she was into a tantrum. It was very brief and very frightening to her. She wrote in her journal: 'It's amazing how my body had remembered that motion where my mind had forgotten about it.' After this experience she told me that she had temper tantrums frequently during latency between the ages of nine and twelve. This characteristic leg lifting and pushing reappeared in fragments consistently throughout the sessions until she experienced a resolution which I will describe in some detail later.

A second example of Heather's idiosyncratic movements was unusually slow movement. She appeared to be moving in slow motion. This quality of movement began to emerge around the eighth session and gradually became predominant in her work. I will also describe more of this later.

I have mentioned some of the themes: specific body parts, movement patterns and qualities of movement of which Heather and I gradually became aware. I will now briefly sketch the way she worked these themes and thus developed a richer understanding of herself.

As we focused on her hands in the early sessions, they increasingly embodied feelings of anger. The feeling tone of the short tantrum was clearly anger. The more she lifted and pushed her leg, the more she stopped or changed this movement. She vaguely associated it with the tantrum but repeatedly stopped herself, rarely conscious of the stopping but very conscious of her fear. This is the kind of moment at which I urge my client to be aware of what she is doing – not stopping what she is doing but simply noticing. As Heather became conscious of the ways in which she was blocking her leg lifting and pushing movement, she experienced more and more frustration. I then suggested that she try to learn more about the movement by staying with it a little longer. As she did so her fear increased, as did the concomitant feeling of knowing she was getting closer to 'something.' Heather never chose to work on this pattern. It simply kept reappearing out of free movement. More and more time was spent in the sessions with this pattern and the variety of unconscious ways she blocked it.

During the thirteenth session she was violently stamping, covering the entire room. She appeared proud and, when she stopped, looking very satisfied, she said: 'I stamped them out.' She did not know to whom 'them' referred. I asked her if she was finished and she decided she was not. She proceeded in pantomime to collect the remains of 'them', burned them, smashed the ashes with a huge imaginary stone and then suddenly noticed a tiny flower growing out of the ashes. This embodiment of a fantasy is a rich example of the power of imagery and its relationship to authentic movement. After the release of anger through the stamping, the fantasy extended the experience of aggression. When it seemed that 'they' were totally and completely destroyed, new life freely grew from the ashes.

After the thirteenth session, when Heather's fantasy occurred, she began to talk openly of anger towards her parents, a feeling of which she could not remember being conscious before. There was also less self-directed anger in her movement after that session. The work with her hands, the gradual awareness of the leg lifting and pushing, and many other movement experiences in the first thirteen sessions seemed to be expressive of unconscious material related to feelings of anger. The expressive movement brought the feelings into consciousness, which, in turn, allowed Heather to examine them, own them and accept them.

Heather felt less tense, relieved, with a clearer sense of herself and her situation at home. And then, slowly, during the following weeks, she became depressed. During the nineteenth session she reported feeling a little better. Then suddenly, in the midst of free movement, her leg went up and down in the obvious pattern of beginning the quarter turn push and, this time, unlike the very first brief tantrum, she did not stop. She was fully into a wild tantrum, her entire body deeply engaged in the expression of rage. The instant the tantrum concluded, much to my surprise, Heather became immobilized. She 'could not move.' Her breathing quickened. She looked pale. In a few minutes she sat up and spoke of a 'film' that covered her the instant the tantrum felt finished.

And so came the resolution of one theme – she went into and through the rage – and, at the same time, came the beginning of a new theme. As we talked, it became clear that Heather had experienced the tantrums as a child as a fight against the 'film.' She said she felt claustrophobic and unhappy during much of her childhood. Some force was keeping her from being the 'real Heather.' The tantrum had been a successful way of keeping the 'film' – the force – from overwhelming her. Perhaps because of the full expression of her anger toward her parents, her energy was now freed to address directly the threat of the 'film.' The film, represented by a slow motion in Heather's movements, was the new 'enemy.'

Again, becoming familiar with this made it less of an unknown and, therefore, less frightening, so that confrontation was gradually possible. After the twentieth session she wrote in her journal:

I had an image of a greasy, grey film coming from the kitchen of our house. Before I could get to it, it engulfed me, coming very quickly towards me in swirls. I wanted to move but couldn't. It was so powerful, more powerful than my own will. At one point, one of the swirls turned into a face, looked at me and laughed, as if to say: 'you idiot, move.'

After the twenty-first session she wrote:

I got the image again and still couldn't move. My body didn't mind because I didn't seem to panic. All my concentration was going towards the film. I started getting really dizzy. I seem to get dizzy when I get near to something.

During the twenty-second session the film seemed to her to be pulling her apart by encircling her legs and arms. She wrote again after the twenty-third session:

For the first time the film made a clearing (I didn't make it, the film did on its own accord). It made a tunnel but at the end of the tunnel a person was standing there in red, calling me to go through the tunnel. I couldn't move.

By the twenty-fourth session Heather was experiencing extreme frustration and exhaustion. She was trying anything to get more information about the 'film', wanting so much to be freed of it. She tried cutting it but it bounced back. She tried becoming the film and realized: 'I was my own prison.' This realization was an important turning point in Heather's owning and taking responsibility for her own experience. She had to encounter the film repeatedly, letting her unconscious emerge in her own time, before she could understand or fully accommodate the feeling and the roots of her immobilization.

During the last two weeks of this stage of her work, the 'film' surrounded her frequently outside the movement sessions as well as dominating the sessions themselves. 'All my feelings and movements are death-like,' she wrote in her journal. On occasion, in the sessions, she would fall over and not catch herself responsibly. I told her that I would not catch her, that she had to catch herself. She then moved as if she had understood: she was responsible for her own work.

Feelings of fear increased as she remained in the immobilized state for longer and longer periods of time. Finally, during the twenty-seventh session, she lay 'death-like' with rapid breathing, pale face and tremendous fear for perhaps five minutes. When she sat up she said she felt like a huge block of cement was falling on her. I encouraged her to lie down again and to go with that fantasy. She did, and the odyssey that followed, taking her through life and death passages, was indeed extraordinary, full of vivid imagery reflecting her struggle at that moment with the life and death issue of the 'real Heather.' She ended, in the personage of a bird, by climbing out of a horrible dark prison, out into the sky and the sunshine, growing new feathers as she climbed.

I think Heather had experienced what always had been most threatening and frightening to her: no self, no 'real Heather.' In reaching for her own identity as separate from her parents, her work brought her to the inevitable but very frightening choice to live as herself and let aspects of her experience of the parents within her begin to die or to let her 'real self' die and live only the reflection of her experience of her parents.

Conclusion

Heather worked through to resolution two closely related themes. Her movement released anger at a body level. Through consciousness of her frustration and fear, and acceptance of her anger, she was able to relive fully the tantrum that her body knew so well from childhood. The second theme had to do with fear of immobilization, which first was expressed through the experience of the 'film' enclosing her. Again, as consciousness and ownership developed in relation to the 'film,' she was able to allow herself the feelings of immobilization and, finally, to let those feelings possess her. She then experienced a kind of death. Aspects of the internalized parents died, an archetypal occurrence in the experience of adolescence. And, as always, the psychic experience of death allowed a rebirth. More of the 'real Heather' was available for living. Heather returned the next session announcing that she had applied to college. She said she felt much better. She soon moved out of her parents' house into a dormitory and fully into the experience of college.

Heather followed several problems through to resolution, two of which I have described in detail. The first stage of her work concerned her discovery of authentic movement. In the second stage she hungrily enjoyed expression of herself through the free movement. Conscious awareness of the meaning of the movement was irrelevant for her at that stage. In the third stage we watched specific themes emerge – through her hands as specific body parts highly invested with energy, through her culturally described claustrophobic movements and, most powerfully, through her idiosyncratic movements, like her leg lifting and pushing pattern, and her slow motion movement. The bulk of these notes is concerned with how these idiosyncratic patterns were trusted and followed. Heather was able to confront each of them and thus experience the joy of resolving these problems with clarity and intelligence in the fifth stage.

Heather continues to work with me in movement therapy and has circled back at times on some of the themes, but the struggle is less intense and often of a slightly different nature. Her work continues to be rich with imagery. New themes appear and old themes slowly disappear as she grows towards a deeper consciousness of self.

References

Weir, J. (1969) Personal communication.

Whitehouse, M.S. (1970) Personal communication.

Whitehouse, M.S. (1979) 'C.G. Jung and dance therapy'. In P. Lewis Bernstein (ed) *Eight Theroretical Approaches in Dance/Movement Therapy*, pp.51–70. Dubuque, IA: Kendall/Hunt.

CHAPTER 11

Authentic Movement and Sexuality in the Therapeutic Experience[1]

Janet Adler

For years, when I was introduced at cocktail parties as a movement therapist, others invariably responded with embarrassment and great curiosity. They would then say 'a-ha' or 'we know what that means,' clearly inferring that my work carried sexual overtones. As a budding movement therapist, I felt challenged by such assumptions and insisted upon appropriate corrections. Now, I am sobered by those brief, but important, exchanges. My work as a movement therapist is related to sexual energy. It is time to clarify that reality. The medium is actively, inextricably connected to libidinal energy.

I want to explore the perhaps unconscious ways in which we teach our movement therapy students not to be sexually provocative with patients. I'd like to clarify the sexual implications in the therapeutic experience, rather than discuss response or treatment for specific sexual problems that movement therapy might offer.

I turn first to our heritage. Dance is an ancient symbol of physical, spiritual and social expression. It has always given shape to the personal and collective events of a lifetime and of a culture. Historically, dance has been an avenue for expression of feelings, an invitation to emotional experience. From the beginning of time, dance has been an instinctive and essential step in the mating game of so many species: insects, animals, people, even flowers with the help of the wind. Dance invites and embodies sexual energy.

---

1   Revised paper, previously presented at the American Dance Therapy Association Conference, Washington, DC, 1976.

Now we find dance as a significant source for therapy, possessing the potential to lead, to open us toward the deeper realms of the psyche. We have learned much about these unconscious places from Sigmund Freud. Whether or not we accept his general interpretive schema of life, many of us have come to accept as natural wisdom some of this man's teaching – his bringing shape to a place called the unconscious, his attention to fantasy and dream life, his descriptions of phenomena such as transference, countertransference and the oral, anal and oedipal stages of development of the small child. I am currently studying his descriptions of libidinal energy and his early insistence on the 'special chemistry of the sexual function', as distinct from other psychical instinctual forces.

If libido is a critical presence in the process of any therapeutic encounter and is also a critical source of physical movement, sexual energy then doubly enters the arena of movement therapy. In essence, we are not only engaged in a process – therapy – that would guide people toward discovery and clarification of their feelings about themselves, about their bodies, but we are offering a medium that by its very nature literally heightens awareness for the client and the therapist of the bodies of both. I am not talking *per se* about sexual arousal within a therapy session but about the fact that movement itself grounds, makes concrete, embodies the sexual person. From this perspective, the client is not only talking about sexual feelings of yesterday, he *is*, through his movement, the sexual person now.

I am increasingly aware of the number of people who do not choose dance or movement therapy as a way of self-exploration because of imagined fears of sexual feelings based on an understanding of the very physicalness of the type of therapy. And, conversely, there are many people, perhaps, choosing the medium because of hopes for sexual arousal. Either of these positions can prevent or inhibit valuable work.

I recently asked a Freudian psychoanalyst friend how he would feel about a client primarily working with authentic movement in his presence rather than free association as the basic framework for analysis. He responded with amazement: 'You mean watching someone physically enacting their feelings? It's one thing to listen to someone unravel the threads of their psychosexual development but it would be quite another to watch a person go through that process by moving!'

Isn't that, more or less, what we're doing? We are either inviting people to move together or with us or to move while we watch. Each situation invariably complicates the therapeutic process because of a more conscious threat and/or promise of sexual feelings.

People who are mentally ill often need the immediate presence of another person moving with them. Whether this person is another patient or a therapist, the very invitation to move together suggests the strong possibility of sexual tension for the patient in the form of anticipatory excitement and/or anticipatory fear. With the understanding that sexuality is one of many issues, let me give you an example – in which, for the purpose of making my point, I highlight it.

A pretty female dance therapist approaches Mr Herron, a subdued gentleman living for several decades on a back ward of a state mental hospital. The therapist smiles, extends her hands, bounces rhythmically to the background music and says: 'Hello Mr Herron, come and dance with us.' She conveys energy and enthusiasm about dancing together. This may present a conflict for Mr Herron. If he rejects her offer, he may give up hope for feeling sexually stimulated. If he accepts, his fears of sexual arousal while dancing could be overwhelming.

This bind must often exist within the total personal and social psychodynamics of the dance therapy situation. It is a dramatic bind that feels essential to our understanding of our patients. What is the therapist offering to the patient by inviting him to dance? Dancing is a form of social intimacy. Maybe sexual tension of this nature is a necessary and even a helpful ingredient in growth. Maybe sexual tension cannot be tolerated by the patient, or the patient and therapist together, and thus inhibits growth.

I would like to turn my attention now to the phenomenon of sexuality within the context of my private practice. I invite my clients to explore a kind of movement which my teacher, Mary Whitehouse, called 'authentic'. As individuals discover this kind of movement in my presence, I am seeing how the psychological complexes soon find shape in repeated physical movements. Some of these themes are specifically related to sexuality. A client's sexual feelings can occur in relation to another client in his or her group, in relation to the movement itself and/or in relation to the therapist. I want to share the following stories with you as examples of these occurrences in an effort to further clarify questions that might guide us to a richer understanding of sexual expression and sexual tension in the arena of movement therapy. All of the people in these stories are well-functioning professional adults.

Eva and James

My first story reflects the complexity of interaction between two people in a group, who are powerfully drawn to each other. The structure of my group is as follows. After a brief warm-up, people find a comfortable place and position in the room, close their eyes and wait for an impulse to move. Though they cannot see each other, they are increasingly aware of each other through sound and general kinesthetic and tactile sensation. After moving alone and/or with others for approximately 20–45 minutes, they meet together to talk of their experiences. They then move again and talk again. My role is to watch the movement and to lead the discussion.

A woman and a man, whom I shall call Eva and James, were in a group of six young adults meeting once a week for two-hour sessions. Eva, born of Russian immigrant parents and reared in Manhattan, was a musician. James, an identical twin, grew up in a farming family in mid-west America and became an architect. For four months Eva's movement was generally the same: she lay on her side with her legs curled up and her finger in her mouth. Usually, she entered this position quickly and she rarely left it. She refers to this posture as her infantile place.

All of the time that Eva was deeply immersed in experience of her infancy, James, too, was powerfully working in relationship to a very early time and place in his history. He usually sat with his legs relaxed in front of him, his face released and open, and his lips especially full. His face looked to me like that of a small child in its innocence and vulnerability. As the weeks passed, his fingers, slightly shaking, constantly touched his lips. Slowly, over the months that followed, James began to move around the room, scooting backwards in his sitting position and then scooting flat on his back, leading backwards with his head. Once, he blindly bumped into Eva in her infantile place, paused and went on. This was their first meeting.

Always when he made contact with another person, he used the back of his head and shoulders. He did not face another person and rarely left the floor. Early in the fourth month of work, quite suddenly, he scooted to the wall and pounded it with his fist several times, yelling in anger. He then wept. Eva immediately stood up out of her infantile place and slowly walked toward him. When she arrived, she knelt behind him and barely touched him as her arms dropped over his shoulders and back. She placed the side of her face on his back. They remained motionless in that position for a long time. This was the second time Eva and James met.

Soon, James was confronting people head on, standing up more and increasingly feeling power in his hands, which he often held up, palms out, as he walked around the room. He reported having images of his older sister, who had reared him, as his angry feelings followed his increasingly aggressive movement.

Slowly, over the months, Eva found her way to the wall, which she pushed against with anger, accompanied by fantasies of her father. She told us about his power and her anger and fear in relationship to him. One time, when Eva was audibly pushing against the wall, James was howling like a wolf, expressing an incredible amount of masculine energy on the opposite side of the room. Suddenly, he stalked over to Eva, picked her up, threw her over his shoulder and stomped around the room. Eva screamed in protest, hitting James on his back with her fists as if she wanted down. When he put her down they began to fight. As the fighting intensified, she tried to pull him on top of her. He resisted, continuing to fight. Eva became limp and the fight was over. This battle between them was repeated many times over a period of two months. When they talked after moving together, they became aware of some of the feelings around the struggle.

They learned that a strong sexual attraction between them was a constant source of energy for their work together. Had such an attraction not been there, perhaps, energy would not have been available to either person for such an extended and critical exchange.

Eva learned how she consistently replaced anger toward James with sexual feelings. As James moved into the embodiment of his strength in relation to Eva, he learned how he consistently repressed sexual feelings and eagerly pursued confrontation. James carried the pursuit and readiness for battle. Eva told us how she needed, wanted and feared that. Eva carried the capacity to express sexual feelings. James told us how he needed, wanted and feared that.

The detail of Eva's and James' developing awareness of the complicated relationship between sex and anger, how such complexity can be rooted in early parent-child relationships, and how it is evident in their present lives (James' girlfriend goes limp at crucial points of fighting), is beyond the scope of this paper. I have learned that all encounters which carry strong sexual attraction deserve careful attention as they unfold. They are complex and profoundly significant to the growth struggles that need resolution in a therapeutic experience. Because in a movement therapy group people are constantly coming in touch with the physical reality of others, sexual feelings are frequently a primary aspect of encounter, thus heightening the difficulty and the importance of understanding the dynamics.

Pamela

I would like to tell you now of two different sessions with a client in private one-to-one therapy, whose work reflects examples of sexual feelings evolving from the movement itself. A forty-two year old woman, whom I shall call Pamela, is married, a mother of three children and active in a successful career of social work.

In her movement therapy work, which extended over a three-year period, fantasy was richly apparent and reliably helpful as an extension of her movement. Image can often serve as a grounding, a bridge between movement and understanding. Her experiences beautifully reflect such a relationship.

Pamela's movement most directly evoked her sexual feelings at a time in her life when she was exploring her relationship to her husband, whom I shall call Andrew. She came to a session very distraught and quickly moved into a position on her back in which her pelvis was completely lifted and her weight was held up by spread bent legs, feet flat on the ground. Her arms were extended straight back over her ears. In this position, raging, she had the following fantasy: Andrew was standing at her feet, looming above her, huge and powerful. He was smiling sardonically as he gently worked a yoyo, which was attached to her pubis, up and down. She felt unable to escape. She had no feeling in her body except in her arms, which were reaching.

She was encouraged to focus on and follow the movement of her arms, which she did. Her hands grasped as if on a life-line and towed her to an imagined figure of a woman sitting cross-legged behind her head. The woman's embrace quickly became a self-embrace and her hands quietly began finding and re-finding her face, her body. Very soon, she experienced sexual feelings throughout her body and allowed herself the sensuality of organic pelvic movement.

At another point in Pamela's work, when her mother was visiting her home, her movement in the studio brought her again in touch with her sexuality. She was on her knees, bending forward, pounding her hands on the floor. This movement spontaneously evoked feelings of anger toward her mother. Suddenly, she had the following image: inside her vagina, looking out toward the opening, was the face of her mother, distorted and forbidding. Pamela was horrified and very surprised to learn that the internalized power of her mother was interfering with her sexual experiences.

I have chosen Pamela's stories not only because of their vividness but because she lives on the other end of the spectrum from Mr Herron. Because of her sophistication in the world of psychology, because of her rich fantasies and her unusually physical sense of herself, she was very able to follow her body's lead, which repeatedly guided her toward significant experience.

Steven and his movement therapist

I would like now to describe Steven's story, which suggests some of the complexities in movement therapy of a client's sexual feelings about the therapist.

Steven was a married man in his forties, a professor of sociology, who worked privately with me in movement therapy for two years. His mother had been an invalid since he was seven years old. Because his father was not at home during the day, Steven, an only child, physically cared for his mother most of the time when he was growing up. He often bathed, dressed and fed her. When Steven's father was at home, however, he forbade Steven to physically care for his wife.

Steven's movement themes were primarily concerned with his feelings about each parent. The first year of our work together, countless times, he rolled from side to side on the floor, primarily on his back, covering his face and whimpering, sometimes crying. This movement gradually was accompanied by fantasies of his father yelling at him and pushing him and his utter sense of helplessness. In these images his mother often was present, watching, unable to stop her husband. Interspersed with these struggles with his father, Steven spoke a lot with me about his ambivalence as a younger man in separating from his mother.

My work that first year with Steven was almost entirely one of support and nurture. My awareness of the complexities of transference issues increased as I noticed an assumption on his part that I knew what was best for him. By Spring of the first year, on three different occasions, he said he could not move with me watching. He decided that I should try turning my back. I did so and though his movement reportedly was not changed, the third time he put his hands in the middle of my back and pushed me away from him. This experience was slowly followed over the weeks by his efforts to persuade me that he needed to move with me. He enthusiastically felt that having a chance to literally struggle with me would help him. I declined his offers.

By the time we were into the second year of work, Steven's side-to-side roll on the floor was gaining momentum. Each turn to the left was accompanied by a fierce slap of his right hand onto the floor and an impassioned 'NO!' Often, he would suddenly jump to his feet after such an experience and prowl around the studio, slamming his right fist into his left hand. He spoke later of looking for a man to fight.

Steven gained an increasing ability to feel and express anger toward both of his parents. He grew from a helpless victim, in relationship to them both, toward standing on his own two feet. Perhaps this newly earned strength laid the foundation that was necessary for the next level of work which standing up invited – his sexuality. He began reporting dreams that reflected deep anxiety and confusion about himself as an interloper in sexual liaisons.

He told me one day about a dream (one of many) in which he was with me and my husband caught us together. In the dream he fled in great despair and shame. We spoke about his feelings about me, about my marriage and about his parents' marriage. He was especially interested in my feelings about his dream. The next session he urged me to accept a copy of his dream that he had especially typed for me. I did not. I insisted that it did not belong to me, it was not my dream.

I had watched Steven move hundreds of times. Over a period of two years I experienced his movement as passive, powerful, sexual, energized, fascinating, self-stimulating, angry, beautiful, soft, surprising, etc. I paid close attention to his many fantasies about me that accompanied his movement – what he thought, wished, assumed I was thinking and feeling while watching him move. Because the countertransference, or my own feelings, in this situation were free from sexual tension, I could comfortably and freely watch and listen.

All verbal therapies invite the possibility of sexual attraction between client and therapist. Steven's story, in that sense, is not at all unusual. What is unusual is the immediacy of the sexually provocative material evoked from the movement within the therapy session. In this specific realm, as movement therapist and client, we have no classical models.

Because authentic movement can invite such fullness of embodiment, the work not only encourages successful expression and resolution of sexual experiences but also could encourage some masking of feelings for both the client and the therapist. Sadly, but understandably, if and when this happens, essential material could be left unexplored, challenging resolution of transference and countertransference. This question must be studied further.

I believe that, as individuals, our sexuality most anciently and instinctively reflects and encounters our mothers' and fathers' sexuality. If, as therapists, we cannot help but find ourselves in the role of substitute parents, the power of our sexuality is obvious. The dangers of our own libidinal energy, as well as the gifts of that same energy, though very often largely unexplored and unconscious, are at the same time critical to the impact of our therapeutic work. It is then our choice as individual movement therapists to work toward our own consciousness, including an in-depth exploration of our own sexual feelings in relationship to our clients.

Finally, I wonder if a young profession like ours, growing toward greater consciousness, cannot be likened to an individual struggling to become increasingly aware of what blocks his or her capacity to use and enjoy inherent beauty and power. Perhaps the dark mystery of the ancient and intimate qualities of sexuality both inhibit and inspire us in fully embracing the great and authentic powers of the medium we have chosen.

CHAPTER 12

Who is the Witness?

A Description of Authentic Movement[1]

Janet Adler

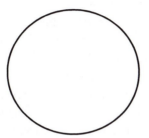

Like the river,
Return to the source.
(Tao Te Ching)

The Mary Starks Whitehouse Institute

In November of 1969 I closed my life in Pittsburgh and flew to Los Angeles to study with Mary Whitehouse, the first person to describe authentic movement in the presence of another. I went directly to Mary's studio, which was closed. Three doors down the block I found a motel room and settled there. Getting through to Mary by phone was impossible. Though we had not yet met, I knew she had just learned that she had multiple sclerosis and she knew I was coming. So I waited, mostly in the room, in case she returned my call. I ate popcorn and watched television for seven days. At the end of that preparation, we met and began work immediately. I came to her every day for either individual work, group work, theoretical work, breakfast, lunch or dinner. We met at many levels during those five exceedingly rich months. Among the many things I learned from Mary, most importantly, she taught me about consciousness.

---

1   Revised paper, previously published in *Contact Quarterly*, Winter, 1987.

By mid-March of 1970 I had returned to the East Coast. I invited my first client to explore authentic movement in an old and beautiful light blue loft in Amherst, Massachusetts. For the following eleven years I sat in the corner of studios, in the presence of people descending toward themselves as we together learned about seeing and being seen.

In the Fall of 1981, two-and-a-half years after Mary's death, I was ready to try to objectively study the phenomenon of authentic movement in the presence of another without the complicating responsibilities of being a therapist. Because I learned the form, the basic structure of the work, from Mary, I named the center which I then founded 'The Mary Starks Whitehouse Institute'. Eight post-graduate students were invited to come for a nine-month intensive excursion into an infinitely mysterious process.

The outer form of this work is simple: one person moves in the presence of another. It was at this time at the Whitehouse Institute that I began to use, without realizing it, the term 'witness' to describe the person whom Mary called the 'observer' or 'teacher.' I imagine I learned of this word 'witness' while working with my teacher, John Weir, a Master psychologist, in 1969.

The witness, especially in the beginning, carries a larger responsibility for consciousness as she sits to the side of the movement space. She is not 'looking at' the person moving, she is witnessing, listening, bringing a specific quality of attention or presence to the experience of the mover. The mover works with eyes closed in order to expand her experience of listening to the deeper levels of her kinesthetic reality. Her task is to respond to a sensation, to an inner impulse, to energy coming from the personal unconscious, the collective unconscious, or what Wilber (1980) calls the 'superconscious'. Her response to this energy creates movement that can be visible or invisible to the witness. As the work deepens, the movement becomes organized in specific patterns, in specific body parts, within specific rhythmic and spatial forms. In a broader context, it often becomes most readily organized within the dominant function of the personality – that is, guided more by emotion than intuition, or sensation rather than thinking.

After the mover moves, the mover and the witness usually speak together about the material that has emerged during the movement time, thus bringing formerly unconscious processes into consciousness. Though the mover's work, especially initially, is the primary focus of both the mover and the witness, the inner reality of the witness appears to be as vast, as complex, and as essential to the process as the inner world of the mover. With the movement of one as catalyst, the witness and the mover work together, over time, each refining her capacity to integrate her experience of formless material into form.

Before the Institute was established, I had some understanding of the relationship between the mover and the witness in the realm of therapy. In the preceding ten years I had been learning about the witness as a therapist and the mover as a client. In the dance world I was intrigued by some of the parallels between the therapist–client relationship and that of audience–dancer. By 1981 I wanted to be able to articulate what actually happened to the two people, before the movement or the witnessing carried specific meaning for the psyche, before symbol. I needed to describe the process.

As a mover, I knew in my bones about the relationship between surrender and will. Mary explained the experience of authentic movement as one of 'being moved and moving' at the same time (Whitehouse 1963). As this balance becomes manifest, one begins to lose the illusion that one is anything other than one's body. In so doing, what is ultimately affirmed is the body, not the knowledge of the body.

Even though I had been a witness for a decade, because the witness does not move, I did not fully understand the relationship between surrender and will in that experience. There are two major reasons why it is more difficult. First, the witness is responsible for seeing her mover as well as her self. Second, the witness does not enact or engage in her own experience, she witnesses it. Thus the Institute was created to gain a deeper understanding of the experience of the witness and of the relationship between the witness and the mover.

Each week in the Institute, the interns and I met for a theoretical seminar, for a group training experience and for training experiences in dyads. They also met weekly with my deeply gifted colleague, Edith Sullwold, for a seminar focused on the emergence of creative forms. The first task was to teach the experience of moving authentically. Then, because, by definition, learning to be a mover must precede learning to be a witness, the interns were asked to be silent witnesses for the first three months of training. Finally, when we began to explore and share actively our inner realities as witnesses, those experiences became visibly more complex.

Several months after beginning the Institute, I repeatedly saw the following shape in my mind:

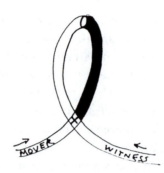

I began to see the dynamics of the two parties as inseparably linked. This is how the process might be described when it is working well. The witness (the light curve) is witnessing the mover (the dark curve) move. Suddenly, the mover becomes immersed in material that engages her totally (marked by the X). In the intensity of her experience she has seemingly forgotten her witness and lost her self-consciousness. Her movement is more dominant than her mental image of her witness. She might be feeling, repressing or expressing anger, joy, confusion, sadness. She might be seeing images, hearing sounds, immersed in a memory or thinking a particular thought. She might be simply experiencing the kinesthetic sensation of the movement. Any or all of this is happening between the X and the O.

Simultaneously, at the moment of the X, something is awakened in the witness by the particular movement quality or form of the mover. Now both people have embarked on their own individual path. The witness is having her own active internal experience: image, sound, feeling, idea, memory, kinesthetic sensation. Because of this awakening, there has been a shift in the quality of the presence of the witness. In some ways, though the empty space between them in the drawing symbolizes how powerfully they are connected, the witness and the mover are separate. When the witness is fully alive to the mover, she is, paradoxically, completely present in relation to her own inner experience. They meet again, in dialogue (at the O), where new consciousness and insight can become apparent, possibly shared and even expanded.

Another, and, perhaps, more authentic, representation of this process would be a shape that reflects not only the passage of time but the fact of sequential places of meeting and not meeting. It might look something like this:

As the work develops and the discipline of the mover becomes refined, she learns to internalize the witness. This seems to happen exactly the way the infant, with no sense of self, gradually develops one, because he internalizes the mother. Thus the mover learns consciously to witness her own unconscious material as it finds form through her movement. As this begins to happen, the same experiential loop or loops in the drawings can represent the process of one person rather than two.

For the mover, the dark curve represents the process of moving and the light curve now represents the process of internal self-witness. Here, too, in the beginning (before the X), there is a self-conscious awareness of witnessing oneself. When the mover and the internal witness meet (at the X), they lose their sense of distinctiveness. She can 'see' herself as she is. Insight can follow at the O.

But for the witness, the same drawing appears to be incomplete. Though the dark curve can represent the process of her own internal activity, it also must somehow represent the movement she sees in her mover. Similarly, the light curve must represent not only her internal self-witness but her continuous and dominant process of witnessing the mover. Her loop, one of double vision, then, could look like this:

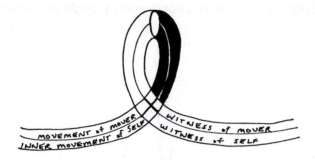

Authentic movement and psychoanalytic work

By the end of the first year, with the skeletal map described above, I began to understand this developing relationship between moving and witnessing as a discipline. Somehow, I named the discipline 'Authentic Movement', based on Mary's phrase, which describes a specific kind of movement. But, without realizing it, I began to use these words to speak of not only the experience of the mover but of the witness and of the developing relationship between the mover and the witness.

We continued to primarily carry our consciousness of the discipline within a psychoanalytic framework. When the witness enters the work within the perspective of psychodynamic process, she is a trained therapist with a strong background in the psychology of movement, developmental psychology and psychoanalytic theory. Such knowledge rides immediately behind and informs her intuitive capacity to know, to see and to hear the presence of her own body and the body of her mover.

There are many similarities between psychoanalytic treatment and Authentic Movement. The client in psychoanalysis lies on a couch so that he cannot see the analyst sitting behind him. In Authentic Movement the mover also cannot see the witness because her eyes are closed. This fact seems to be of paramount importance in both traditions. Such a format invites surrender to the process that ensues – that of free association. The client in psychoanalysis is encouraged primarily to develop and use the mode of free association. Similarly, the mover, in developing the discipline of Authentic Movement, is engaged from the beginning in a free associative process, but at a non-verbal level.

Both disciplines require long-term work because 'regression in the service of the ego' is not possible otherwise. Because of the natural wisdom of the body and its capacity to store every memory at a seemingly 'bone level', Authentic Movement is particularly helpful to people who have experienced early, especially pre-verbal, trauma. Transference and countertransference are thus inherent and central forces in both ways of work. The clientele for both is also similar. Both disciplines are most helpful to adults who have a strong enough ego structure to choose and to sustain extensive exploration of the unconscious. When a client enters either analysis or Authentic Movement for treatment, there is an assumed end to the work. The major difference between the two ways is that the analytic client usually lies still and the mover actively embodies the material. In so doing, the experience of being 'seen' is somehow heightened and elongated.

Within this psychoanalytic framework of Authentic Movement, the mover actually feels bound to her personal body. The qualities of time, space and weight are specific to, and in direct relationship to, her experience of her body. Her body is her ego. The attitude of the witness toward the mover is nurturing, protective, empathic and parental at times. The witness honors the mover's dependency on her and understands its value. Talking together after the movement clarifies and slowly organizes the material within the language of psychodynamic theory. This sharing can reduce tension and expand the understanding of both people, and it is almost certain to develop a deep bond between them.

Authentic Movement and meditative practice

As the first group of interns – therapists and artists – brought their intensive training to a close, my own experience of reality was undergoing unsolicited and terrific change. Perhaps, because the laws of nature have a tendency toward balance, my extreme concentration on the personality was irrevocably shifted to an awakened awareness of transpersonal energies. These energies imply experiences that are not related to personality or to personal history. Witnessing myself surrendering to this impersonal force brought me toward a new understanding of the relationship between surrender and will as a witness. Related to my work with John Weir, we have made the assumption that the mover can only go as far as her witness has gone. Consciousness of transpersonal energy in the experience of the witness automatically expands the potential experience of the mover.

By the time the second group of interns – again artists and therapists – came the following Fall of 1982, this new consciousness created new questions. For example, we began to notice that there were times when the mover did not seem bound to her personal body. Her energy was not contained there and the qualities of time, space and weight were not specific. Those qualities were not felt in relation to the body ego.

When this transpersonal energy was apparent, we realized that the attitude of the witness toward the mover was quite different. Because in these situations the material with which the mover is working is not about her personality, the witness is seeing from a place not circumscribed by her personality.

It seemed that under these circumstances the dynamics of transference and countertransference, as we have come to understand them in therapeutic work, are less central, less binding and, somehow, expanded. The witness can experience herself beyond the boundaries of her personality as she shares the same energy field with the mover. She is seeing with much less projection, judgement and involvement in content. Talking afterwards is often not helpful. There is not the same need to sort, organize and understand the material within the language of psychodynamic theory. At these times there is an experience of no edges, no boundaries. There is a sense of clarity, within and without, a feeling literally of no density, no obstruction, no place in the body through which light cannot move. In these situations the body becomes a vessel through which energy or light can pass unobstructed.

The psychoanalytic framework began to feel limited, as if we needed a larger form within which we might understand the process. It began to be apparent that the roots of the discipline stretched more broadly than originally conceived. Psychodynamic theories of the ego structure were only one root system. Though much less familiar to me, meditative practice and its roots in Eastern philosophy was another. We have just begun to articulate some of the similarities and differences between Authentic Movement and meditation.

In both disciplines there is a primary focus on the relationship between observation and action. However, in meditation both the witness and the activity are internal. Usually, the meditator is not actively moving his body although his experience of his body is a very active aspect of this process. He learns to be an undistracted observer of his body and of his mind. The activity in meditation is that of the active mind, which automatically includes the sensed body.

The discipline of Authentic Movement, at the basic level, is about the relationship between two people, the witness and the mover. Initially, one carries the role of the one who sees and the other the role of the one who is seen. Yet, as the work develops, a conscious witness emerges within the mind of the mover and, concomitantly, unconscious activity surfaces within the experience of the witness. Increasingly, like the meditator, both mover and witness carry the tension and the union between these polarities within themselves.

In both the discipline of Authentic Movement and meditation there is a continuous effort to witness the conscious mind as it habitually interferes with the deep listening encouraged in both practices. In both ways of work several years of commitment are necessary for a continuous development of the process, which can bring experiences of balance, clarity and wholeness. The major difference between these two disciplines is that meditation usually requires specific body posture. In Authentic Movement the 'right way' is defined through the movement itself, not specific body shape or form but only the shape that awakens or is awakened by the psyche, the spirit or the Self.

People who seriously practice meditation or Authentic Movement are similar in that they have an established body ego structure. They are people with a self-awareness, an ability to concentrate, a curiosity about the unknown. The longer both of these disciplines are practiced, the more developed is the witnessing mind. Such development produces a sense of clarity in relation to one's own behavior, enacted or internal. A long-term commitment to either way of work can occasionally generate an intense experience of spiritual rebirth.

Beginning to understand Authentic Movement as a spiritual as well as a therapeutic discipline offered new perspectives on the work. By the end of the second year of the Institute it was clear that through Authentic Movement a broad developmental spectrum of energy can be manifested from pre-verbal to trans-verbal, pre-egoic to trans-egoic, from sub-conscious to 'super-conscious.' We have come to believe, as does Wilber (1980), that people need not be prisoners of their history but are impelled to transcend it.

The relationship between personal and transpersonal experience in Authentic Movement

I would like to offer here three examples of Authentic Movement work which concern the relationship between personal and transpersonal experience: one in which the witness, Julia, consciously chose to respond to the mover's personal material from a transpersonal perspective; one in which the witness, Gail, consciously chose to respond to the mover's transpersonal material from a personal position; and one in which the mover, Lila, worked with both personal and transpersonal energy while her witness was synchronous with her throughout the experience.

In Julia's case the mover was talking about her need to be near Julia, to be held by Julia, to be nurtured. In her movement she repeatedly moved close to Julia, touching her and struggling with her need to climb into Julia's lap. Finally, she forcefully rolled into Julia and began crying as she lay face down in front of her. Julia felt a pull to gather her up and rock her. While debating within herself how to respond to the situation, she realized she had shifted to sitting on her knees, had placed her right hand on the mover's back and heard herself saying inside: 'Protect this woman. Let her remain in this position, as she is now, as long as she needs to. May she learn to be patient, to allow time to experience her pain and to know when to get up.' Julia had moved from a pull to be the woman's 'mother' to another pull to be her 'spiritual mother.' When the mover finally got up, she reported a feeling of great peace. She said that the experience felt 'just right,' though she did not understand what, if anything, had happened.

In Gail's case the mover was sitting with legs crossed, rocking in a deep but sharp rhythm, with a 'beatific' expression on her face. Her hands were crossed over her heart. When she finished moving and began speaking, she talked of white light encircling her heart, opening it and then radiating throughout the room. Gail, in response, spoke of her images and feelings as she watched the movement. She felt as though she was in the presence of a fifteen-month-old baby who was all alone, rocking, maybe to soothe herself, and 'looking like' she was detached or not related to what her body was doing. Gail felt deep sadness and wanted to rock her baby. When hearing this, the mover began to cry and talk of early abandonment and her attraction to 'religious' experiences as the only way to forget about her loss and pain.

We have found, as Mary did, that a witness must learn the very subtle differences between being quiet and letting the experience stand alone and speaking about it. She must further learn, as the preceding vignettes reveal, discernment regarding the differences between personal and transpersonal experiences in her body as she witnesses, as well as what she chooses to share with her mover.

In the following description, as the witness, I continually responded to the mover's work out of a similar energy source from which she seemed to be moving. In this case, Lila's movement work was both personal and trans-personal in one session. In this particular session there is a clear sequential order, with the movement originating continually from a deep and unconscious impulse. Although she had done extensive work as an intern in the

Institute over a period of time preceding this session, the breadth of material within one session is unusual.

What follows is my experience as the witness of Lila's work. She begins lying against a wall, as an infant, with deep pleasure in her own sounds, her skin sensation, her non-differentiated movement. Her fingers look and act like those of a baby as they explore her mouth and her skin. I feel peaceful, soft and content. Now, with no apparent line of demarcation, the same fingers become those of a young girl, of a pre-adolescent. They are tentative, not lingering, and are moving under what might be a self-conscious eye. Now Lila shows clear signs of distress as if she is actually in physical pain. Her hands eventually pull herself into a sitting position. I feel anxious, a bit confused and wanting to help.

As this phase of the work progresses, her arms cross. Her left hand is delicate and exposed, her right hand grows large and strong. Now she begins to look like a woman. She seems grounded as she stands up, reflecting a quality of firmness as she leads with her right hand. It is as though the space between her head and her pelvis fills up, fills in, becomes solid and mobile. I feel relief, wonder and met in the presence of this woman.

Again, with no recognizable transition, Lila changes, this time into a woman with great strength and clarity but, at the same time, with less and less form. The quality of her movement is larger than her physical form. It is as though a figure has arrived from the inside of her form but now extends, in its expression, vastly beyond her form. She stands much taller than her usual self, her head turned to the left as her fingers and face reflect a very ephemeral quality. Her face actually appears radiant as this quality sustains itself. Her 'Lady' has appeared, an archetypal guide and teacher familiar to her from earlier work. My body becomes warmer and slowly my awareness of my weight and form diffuses. I experience wholeness, within myself and with Lila.

In this one session Lila traversed and embodied a time span that included moments of resolved and unresolved personality work as well as a moment beyond her ego structure in which the pain and pleasure of her personal history and present reality were transcended.

New questions

Enlarging the perspective of Authentic Movement work to include the spiritual as well as the psychological not only enriches the work in significant ways but also creates new questions. Using Lila's work as a base, it seems appropriate here to explore some of the questions.

Is it useful to see the spectrum as developmental?

That is, should personal work precede transpersonal work? It is clear that the stronger the body-psyche connection, the more the body can contain, withstand and ground the spirit. A well-developed ego structure helps an individual not to identify with material from the transpersonal realm. In Lila's case, because there is still work to be done with the shadow at the time of adolescence, encounters with the shadow in the transpersonal realm could be premature.

On the other hand, though the logic of personal work preceding transpersonal work seems convincing, could the opposite also be true? Can transpersonal energy guide and direct personal growth? The answer must have something to do with timing. In Lila's case it seemed as though the Lady was instructing the less developed aspects of the adolescent Lila, helping her to grow up: 'By example, by the Lady being in my body, I could know by experience how to be in my body as a woman instead of an adolescent.'

In Lila's case transpersonal energy was helpful and, perhaps, no more helpful than a psychological exploration would have been. It seems to me that there are times when this energy is the only source of help and, ultimately perhaps, an essential source in order to perceive this world as a whole. Continual effort to see all experience within the framework of the ego structure can dramatically limit an individual's capacity to see oneself. On the other hand, as in the case of Gail's mover, transpersonal energy can distract, confuse, seduce, enchant, inflate a mover so that essential developmental work within the ego system is avoided or even betrayed.

Is it necessary for the witness to offer the mover a form, beyond the body itself, within which she can bring her experience to consciousness?

First, is it essential for the mover to talk after moving, make associations or consciously remember personal history? We know that movement followed by talking can expand the experience, especially when the material concerns personal history. Words as symbols are often a natural way to respond to the movement work, a common language for the witness and mover. Sometimes, images as symbols are deeply connected to the material. If images are dominant and/or there is little specific emotional content, making a drawing, a piece of sculpture or creating a dance or story are vivid and rich ways of bringing form to and further enhancing the energy that has been awakened. When strong emotional content or transpersonal energy first infuse the movement, it can often be overwhelming in its newness and power. When this happens, or when significant transitions occur, verbal response from the witness seems helpful.

Are there times when any response, verbal or other, from the witness or mover is unnecessary? Logically, it seems that as long as we live in the human form, at some level our need for form exists. Some movers report that when the experience is trans-egoic, sometimes there is not a need for form other than the form of the body itself to either contain the energy or release the energy into an experience of no form, no boundaries. Can the body be the container, the form, in relationship to the energy? Is it possible that the movement witnessed over a long period of time can be intrinsically transformative, whether the energy source is personal or transpersonal? Can this process, without the overlay of Western psychological theory, be in itself a cohesive and sufficient way of knowing?

As a witness of Lila's work, I felt as though I had nothing to say in response, though I often spoke in response to work that preceded this session when both personal and transpersonal work were the center. This time it was as though her body was a sufficient container, a form that could completely hold and sustain her energy at any point along the spectrum of work as it developed. The work resolved itself. As witness of this work, it seemed unnecessary to offer anything beyond my presence, which felt synchronous with her experience.

Can one ever do Authentic Movement without a witness?

Certainly, within a therapeutic context, by definition, a witness is essential. As long as the mover is developing a 'good enough' internal witness and as long as the phenomenon of tension, which is a primary seed for growth, is apparent, the presence of an external witness is critical. When the unknown is being explored through the arrival of and encounter with unconscious activity, there is often the element of fear and/or awe. The presence of another in either case can be a response to the human need for safety, containment or balance.

However, when fear and/or awe are not experienced as overwhelming, it becomes less and less clear why a mover working, especially with trans-personal energy, needs a designated witness. Would Lila have been able to move through the energy layers as she did in the session being discussed if she had been alone? Moving toward the answer to this question first concerns the idiosyncrasies of Lila and this particular session: Lila's familiarity with the personal aspects of the work, her tolerance for and understanding of the pain around the unresolved adolescent work, whether or not the Lady had appeared before and the quality of energy radiating from the Lady. But, most important, was her non-attachment to her ego — to the self needing to be seen — so established that the intrinsic power of her internal witness could carry the intensity and clarity of the experience?

Relative to this question, there is a larger context. One of the very first experiences of life is that of being seen. The parent witnesses the infant. The infant, as it grows into childhood and adulthood, moves through endless experiences of being seen and seeing oneself. This could be one way of describing the development of the self. It is interesting to notice in our movement work so far that being seen inevitably precedes seeing oneself: 'I can't see myself here. First you see me as I am in this unknown place, then I begin to witness myself anew.'

Witnessing oneself in Authentic Movement can thus only be developed through extensive experience, first as a mover being seen by a witness. Because of being witnessed, the mover is automatically developing an internal witness, which is, in turn, preparing her to witness another. (It never, of course, is so neatly developmental in practice). It is at this point, mastering the witnessing of another — loving another — that the next essential step occurs. For no matter how well and objectively one can witness oneself, that self-witnessing is transformed after truly seeing another as she is. It is as though there is now a reversal. In the same way that being seen by another originally enabled me to see myself as I am, in a further sweep of the spiral, seeing another as she is — loving her — enables me to see myself as I am. This is a different seeing myself as I am because it is no longer birthed by another — the mother, therapist, witness or lover.

This seeing myself as I am is birthed by myself and is it not then a birth of humility? It somehow miraculously evolves from loving rather than being loved. The deepest longing now has shifted from being seen as I am by another to seeing another as she is, others as they are, my universe anew. And so the cycle continues to recreate itself, each time expanding consciousness. Increasingly, the concern is about seeing and loving. Being seen by another gradually becomes irrelevant and uninteresting. Now who is the witness? A synopsis of this spiral could be:

I long to be seen (narcissism)

I feel seen (trust)

I long to see myself (ego)

I see myself (healthy ego)

I long to see another (love)

I see another (compassion)

I see us both as one (union)

Did Lila's body actually look different when the personal energy was active than when the transpersonal energy was manifest? If so how?

As mentioned earlier, we have been trying to learn to see how the body itself is different, literally, when moving from a transpersonal source of energy rather than a personal source of energy. The Japanese word '*koshi*' means 'essence of the body.' It refers to the pelvic bone. In my opinion, this is the first, and continues to be the most important, place in which there is a difference. As the Lady entered Lila's body, her pelvis held her in a very specific way, a way which I sadly cannot yet articulate. As the interns worked, especially in the first two years, I witnessed some of them, sometimes, 'drop' into the essence of the body, the pelvis. As this happened, the work inevitably shifted toward a greater capacity to contain larger amounts of energy.

When the pelvis is free from unresolved developmental issues, when the psyche's energy can ride in the pelvis unblocked, and when the legs and the feet can ground the pelvis, then transpersonal energy can be ignited from the 'ground' up, as in the rise of the kundalini, which can begin at the base of the spine. This grounding can sometimes assure a safer and, possibly, more integrated spiritual journey.

Another place in Lila's body in which a distinct difference was obvious was in her wrists, hands and fingers. When the Lady arrived, the quality of this area of her body became heightened, as if her hands were almost shaping mudras in the most organic and unconscious way. Two associations come immediately to mind. First, there are the autistic, auto-erotic children whose wrists, hands and fingers are so distinctly expressive. Having never bonded, these children live at the beginning of the spiral of human development in a pre-egoic state. They spin, they rock, they can seem 'out of this world.' Second, there are the people found in the expanded sweeps of the same spiral, whose wrists, hands and fingers, in the form of mudras, reflect a trans-egoic state. Some of these people, as messengers between God and man, spin, rock and sway. They too can seem 'out of this world.' The autistic child can be as focused, as passionately engaged in repetitive spinning, as is the whirling dervish. Though one is pre-egoic and the other trans-egoic, we cannot help to ask: 'What is the relationship between these two kinds of people? How do they know one another? Where do they meet or have they met within the mandala of life?'

To come back toward the center, whether the energy source is personal or transpersonal, whether the experience is one of regression or egression, underneath the differences the basic ground is always the same in Authentic Movement. With an increasing capacity to concentrate, to listen to inner impulse, the mover learns to recognize the channel within which the creative or authentic energy flows. In so doing, each movement, no matter how small, becomes impeccably ordered, placed or sensed. Her honoring that knowledge holds the transformative power of this work. In both personal and transpersonal work the mover learns to allow and accept the early experience of chaos, of irrational forms embodied or imagined, of not knowing.

In both ways of work the witness must honor her developing awareness in exactly the same way as the mover, but she contains her experience rather than actively expressing it. She learns to begin a session with no expectations, no plans, no directions to her mover. The witness strives to bear, to contain, to embrace her experience of the early chaos within her mover, the irrational and idiosyncratic patterns that emerge, the unknown that is explored in her presence. She is also open to the messages from her own unconscious and is responsible for a growing consciousness of them. She is highly selective in choosing what to share with her mover of her own internal process.

Death, loss, and suffering are integral aspects of both ways. Though here, especially, it seems artificial to make a separation in the personal work, encounters with the shadow within the frame of transference and countertransference bring death of old patterns, old ways in which the ego developed in its need for survival. In the transpersonal work there is also the possibility of a death, death of the self as it was known prior to a spiritual rebirth:

> In the beginning, there was not the word, but rather there was the symbolic action, a union of body and psyche. In the beginning, dance was the sacred language through which we communicated with the vast unknown. In these earliest times, the dancer was at the same time healer

and priest. Then, through the centuries, in the name of progress and civilization, mind and body were split apart. (Chodorow 1984, p. 39)

The collective unconscious was 'the beginning.' The personal unconscious evolved from it. From that came personal consciousness. Now our task, and our longing, still in an effort to heal a split, is to bring our consciousness as individuals into a conscious collective. Though the collective unconscious informs and instructs us in this task, there is no way back. Trans-egoic is completely different from pre-egoic.

It is interesting to note a parallel, admittedly a general one, in the evolution of Authentic Movement. Often, the first format is a group of people moving with a single witness. The first task of the witness is to begin to distinguish elements of the collective unconscious from elements of the individual or personal unconscious. Next, the experience of an individual moving usually deepens when she is witnessed alone, the result often being an opportunity for strengthening the development of her individual consciousness. In this year, the fourth year of the Institute, we have found ourselves working within a form that might reflect a part of the next step. One individual, after many months of being witnessed by one person, moves alone in the middle of a circle of eight witnesses. These eight people, a conscious collective, help to carry, contain and strengthen the mover as well as themselves. Each witness, then, one by one, creates and strengthens the experience of the mover as well as the other witnesses.

To bring this discussion of the evolutionary process in the Authentic Movement work toward completion, we are finding that after years of sitting still as witnesses, the individuals forming the circle around the mover are beginning to join the mover, to move again themselves, but this time as personally conscious individuals dancing together. At this point, sacred dance is revealed as the true source of the work. Marian Chace (Chaiklin 1975), in her original dance therapy groups, from my perspective, offered a way to embody the collective unconscious. Mary Whitehouse (1963, 1958) offered a way to explore the relationship between the personal unconscious and personal consciousness. Now these two traditions begin to unfold into the manifestation of the conscious collective.

Conclusion

Whether challenged by the unknown within the embodiment of personal or collective consciousness, the evolutionary process that we are each living, as clients, therapists, artists and seekers, is about the transformative power of suffering. The task of locating, listening to and then trusting the guide within is always, by definition, hard work. Much of the work in Authentic Movement is difficult, painful, redundant and frustrating. It involves hiding, risking, premature insight and paralysis, as well as reward. When it works, as when a piece of art works, the clarity and simplicity – the gift of wholeness – is stunning.

Inherent in being a person in the cultures of the West is the longing for a witness. We want, deeply want, to be seen as we are by another. We want to be witnessed. Ultimately, we want to witness, to love, another. Jung (1954) speaks of the phenomenon of the witness:

> Thus the underlying idea of the psyche proves it to be a half bodily, half spiritual substance, an *anima media natura*, as the alchemists call it, an hermaphroditic being capable of uniting the opposites, but who is never complete in the individual unless related to another individual. The unrelated human being lacks wholeness, for he can achieve wholeness only through the soul, and the soul cannot exist without its other side, which is always found in a 'You'. (p.243)

Traditionally, people expect such a blessing in relationship to a parent, a mate, a child, a friend or a god. We are given or not given, find or don't find, create or destroy that 'other', or the potential for that 'other', as we move through our lives. Whether the other is another individual, God or the god within, our developing relationship with that other is one of our greatest tasks, one of our greatest opportunities. Archetypally, we experience this in images of loving parents, of their union with each other, of their union with us. We live always in relationship to these archetypes, though as we grow they evolve and deepen into the union of Earth and Spirit. Authentic Movement is one more way – Mary Whitehouse (1958) called it the 'Tao' of the body – a way that can lead to union and wholeness, whatever the source or shape of energy, as it infuses the time and space of our lives.

References

Chaiklin, H. (ed) (1975) *Marian Chace: Her Papers*. Columbia, MD: American Dance Therapy Association.

Chodorow, J. (1984) 'To move and be moved'. *Quadrant 17*, 2, 39–48.

Jung, C.G. (1954) 'Psychology of the transference'. In *The Collected Works of C.G. Jung (Vol. 16)*. London: Routledge & Kegan Paul.

Whitehouse, M. (1958) 'The Tao of the body'. In D.H. Johnson (ed) *Bone, Breath and Gesture: Practices of Embodiment*. Berkeley, CA: North Atlantic Books, 1995, pp.241–251.

Whitehouse, M. (1963) 'Physical movement and personality'. *Contact Quarterly*, Winter 1987, 16–19.

Wilber, K. (1980) *The Atman Project*. Wheaton, IL: The Theosophical Publishing House.

CHAPTER 13

Body and Soul[1]

Janet Adler

There is no body without soul, no body that is not itself a form of soul.

(Sri Aurobindo, Satprem 1984, p.172)

The human heart can go to the lengths of God.
Dark and cold we may be, but this
Is no winter now. The frozen misery
Of centuries breaks, cracks, begins to move,
The thunder is the thunder of the foes,
The thaw, the flood, the upstart Spring.
Thank God our time is now when wrong
Comes up to face us everywhere,
Never to leave us till we take
The longest stride of soul man ever took.
Affairs are now soul size
The enterprise
Is exploration into God.
Where are you making for? It takes
So many thousand years to wake,
But will you wake for pity's sake?

(Christopher Fry, from *A Sleep of Prisoners* (1985), p.253)

---

1   Revised version of a paper previously published in *American Journal of Dance Therapy 14*, 2, 1992, and presented as one of four keynote speeches at the 26th Annual American Dance Therapy Conference, *Shadow and light: Moving toward wholeness*, San Francisco, 1991.

Introduction

Once long ago, when there was a great and terrible problem demanding resolution, a rabbi went to a certain place in the forest, lit a fire and prayed, and the problem was solved. Generations later, when another rabbi was faced with a very difficult task, he went to the same place in the forest and prayed, but he no longer could light the fire. Regardless, his wish was granted. Again, after hundreds of years, a rabbi went to the specific place in the forest because he and his people encountered a great problem. While there, he said: 'We can no longer light a fire, nor do we know the secret meditations belonging to the prayer, but we do know the place in the woods to which it all belongs – and that must be sufficient'; and sufficient it was. But when another rabbi many generations later was confronted with a great and difficult task, he simply sat down and said: 'We cannot light the fire, we cannot speak the prayers, we do not know the place, but we can tell the story of how it was done.' And that was sufficient, so the story goes (Scholem 1961, p.350).

The only thing which is left of the great mysteries is the 'tale.' Is this sufficient? Our current search for the mysteries, the depth of our longing, suggests that the story is not enough. Because of ego-consciousness, we cannot go back to that place in the forest, light that fire and say those prayers. How can we rediscover spirit if we don't know where to go, how to kindle the light, or what to say?

A recent spiritual leader in India, The Mother, speaks of the pioneering necessary to proceed: 'You don't know whether this or that experience is part of the way or not, you don't even know if you are progressing or not, because if you knew you were progressing, it would mean that you know the way – but there is no way! No one has ever been there!' (Satprem 1984, p.333).

A contemporary mystic, Satprem (1984), explains:

It was probably necessary to preach heaven to us, to draw us out of our initial evolutionary sclerosis – but this is only a first stage of evolution, which we have turned into an ultimate and rigid end. And now this end is turning against us. We have denied the Divinity in Matter, to confine it instead in our holy places, and now Matter is taking its revenge… As long as we tolerate this Imbalance, there is no hope for the earth… We need both the vigor of Matter and the fresh waters of the Spirit… We have lost the Password, such is the bottom line of our era. We have replaced true power with devices, and true wisdom with dogmas. (pp.371–372)

In search of the password, we gather repeatedly in our particular collectives, among our colleagues, in an effort to listen and to speak together about the evolution of our work, our efforts to better understand the evolution of our own consciousness within the different language systems of our study of human development.

In pursuit of this study, the development of each collective is a microcosm of the development of the human psyche, of the history of religions, of civilizations. We tenaciously adhere to the unfolding of the unconscious into consciousness. Satprem (1984) writes that 'Becoming conscious is the very meaning of evolution' (p.102) and that 'This physical life in this physical body therefore assumes special prominence among all our modes of existence, because it is here that we can become conscious – this is where the work takes place' (p.127). The Mother insists: 'Salvation is physical' (Satprem 1982, p.60). Satprem (1984) explains: 'The whole story of the ascent of consciousness is the story of an opening of the aperture, the passage from a linear and contradictory consciousness to a global consciousness' (p.208).

Another story comes to mind, also from the richness of the Hassidic tradition: Once there was a great force called the universe and it became too big and much too hot. When it exploded, the trillions of moments of light fell everywhere, each becoming the source for new life…a salmon, a violet, a baby dove or person, a stone, an alligator. So all of us, including the tomatoes and the giraffes, have within us at our cores, a little light, a divine spark, a piece of the great light energy that is called life (Buber 1958).

Satprem (1984) writes: 'the world and every atom in the world are divine' (p.281) and '…the external veneer of a person usually has nothing in common with that tiny vibrating reality' (p.72). A Buddhist scholar in Tokyo, Nukariya, speaks of our source similarly: '…when our inmost pure and godly wisdom…is fully awakened, we are able to understand that each one of us is identical in spirit, in being and in nature with universal life' (Suzuki 1949, p.10).

At the very center of our differences, this light which we could call spirit or soul, radiating within each tiny newborn, reflects our sameness. The Buddhist most responsible for bringing Zen to the Western world, D.T. Suzuki, speaks of this phenomenon: 'Each individual reality, besides being itself, reflects in it something of the universal, and at the same time it is itself because of other individuals' (Unno 1984, p.12). Within a lifetime, or within generations of lifetimes, this oneness of spirit among us is usually threatened as it comes into relationship with power and economics represented by the structures of religion. Satprem (1984) tells us that the psychic being '…is appropriated by churches, countless churches, which put it into articles of faith and dogma' (p.94).

How did this happen? Gershom Scholem (1961) writes lucidly about the history of religion. Originally, nature was the scene of the individual's relationship to God. There was no abyss between men and women and their God. Then the 'break-through' of religion occurred and created an abyss. God's voice directed people with his laws and demands across the vast chasm. People's voices responded in prayer, in longing, in fear, in love. The infinite distance was created. But, as Satprem (1984) explains, 'Through this separation we have become conscious. We are still incompletely conscious: and we suffer, we suffer, we suffer from being separated – separated from others, separated from ourselves, separated from things and from everything because we are outside the one point where everything joins together' (p.174).

The individual is lost from a direct connection with his or her God. Scholem (1961) describes the effort then 'to transform the God whom it encounters in the peculiar religious consciousness of its own social environment from an object of dogmatic knowledge into a novel and living experience and intuition' (p.10). The human psyche inevitably demands to experience direct relationship with spirit, to know the sacred.

Grof (1985) calls it transpersonal, Wilber (1980) calls it the superconscious, Otto (1923) calls it the numinous, the Huichols (Meyerhoff 1974) call it Tatawari. The rebirth of spirituality within the New Age culture suggests the growing hunger for direct experience of god. It reflects the longing for a new container for the soul, for a new god. The urgency of this longing is also apparent in the search, signaled by some as a lack of connectedness, an escape, confusion and illusion. Unquestionably, the desire is to return to the old unity, but on a new plane. It has been the mystic, within religious traditions, who has lived most closely in relationship to this quest.

Is there a relationship between mystical practice and the practice of Authentic Movement?

Authentic Movement

Exploration of mystical practices reveals some similarities to the practice of Authentic Movement. Useful therapeutically, meditatively or within any creative process, the discipline of Authentic Movement is defined by the relationship between a person moving and a person witnessing that movement. Inherent in being a person in the cultures of the West is the deep longing to be seen as we are by another. We want to be witnessed, without judgement, projection or interpretation. Ultimately, we want to witness, to see another (Adler 1987).

In this discipline movers work with eyes closed, slowly bringing their attention inward as their movement becomes highly specific to their own nature and history. Witnesses are invited to focus not only on what the mover is doing but on their own inner experience in the presence of the mover. As the witness owns projections, judgements and interpretations, the mover is increasingly free to risk honoring the deepening need to follow movement impulses which are born out of the unconscious. As the body finds form for the expression of what is at first formless material, personal consciousness evolves.

As movers hone their awareness of their developing internal witness and witnesses become aware of their internal mover, movers work within a circle of witnesses, which creates a deepening possibility for collective consciousness. The experience of the mover, the witness and the relationship between the two occurs on many levels, creating a complexity that spans the realms of the unconscious, consciousness and what Wilber (1980) calls the 'superconscious.'

In this chapter discussion of the discipline of Authentic Movement is a reflection of only one perspective on this way of working, which is currently being studied and practiced from many different and rich vantage points. The bare bones of this evolving form – the structure – is the common denominator. Content that emerges from the skeletal framework can be understood in many ways – ways that are not necessarily mutually exclusive.

There is a need now for a different way of describing what increasingly happens in the practice of Authentic Movement. We are learning that immersion in this practice means immersion in a developmental process in which personal history, as most clearly understood within psychological theory, slowly becomes integrated into the evolution of the psyche, taking its place within a larger self. There is more to us than, at best, highly developed, healthy ego structures. As we bring this developing ego consciousness toward the reawakening of the spirit, the discipline of Authentic Movement expands to include experiences that occur outside of personality and to include a language system within which to place these experiences.

Mystical practices

Because of the vast number of mystical practices, it is important to limit this discussion of mysticism to traditions which appear to be most germane to our lives at this time: Judaism, Christianity, Buddhism, Shamanism, and a few voices from Hinduism because of the particular way in which these individuals in that ancient tradition speak to the great spiritual questions of this time.

There are four specific aspects of mystical practice which will be discussed: direct experience of one's god, the impossibility of describing it, it's profound effect on the body and the emotions, and the evolution of such experience developmentally. The primary focus in this chapter, which is concerned with the relationship between Authentic Movement and mystical practice, will be on the mover because the mover initiates the process of Authentic Movement and is always at its center. The witness, as much as the mover, can find herself experiencing the numinous, but we must take one step at a time.

DIRECT EXPERIENCE

In the texts of most religions mysticism can be described as one's experience of God and religion can be described as one's relationship to, or one's belief in, God. These two perspectives are not necessarily mutually exclusive. Gershom Scholem (1961) says that mysticism is a definite stage in the historical development of religion, a certain stage of religious consciousness which has always been incompatible with the other stages. The Christian mystic, Rufus Jones, writes that mysticism is 'religion in its most acute, intense, and living stage' (Scholem 1961, p.4).

A foremost authority on the phenomenon of shamanism, Mircea Eliade (1964), explains: '...it would be more correct to class shamanism among the mysticisms than with what is commonly called a religion' (p.8). A contemporary anthropologist who has made significant contribution to her field through her study of shamanism, Joan Halifax (1982), says that 'the shaman acquires direct knowledge from direct experience' (p.10). Richard Katz (1982) writes: 'The !Kung speak of the gods directly, not of their beliefs about the gods' (p.29).

The author of a classic text in Christian mysticism, Evelyn Underhill (1911), suggests that mystics are people who 'not merely have reasoned about the mystical experiences of others' (p.83) but instead are doers, not thinkers, and each person ventures for himself. It is said of St Theresa: 'What others believed, she experienced in herself' (Merton 1968, p.26).

A priest and trappist monk who was an ardent student of Zen Buddhism, Thomas Merton (1968), writes: 'Personal experience thus seems to be the foundation of Buddhist philosophy...the chief characteristic of Zen is that it rejects...systematic elaborations in order to get back, as far as possible, to the pure unarticulated and unexplained ground of direct experience' (pp.36–37). Zen is direct experience. Merton (1968) continues: 'The whole aim of Zen is not to make foolproof statements about experience, but to come to direct grips with reality without the mediation of logical verbalizing' (p.37). D.T. Suzuki (1949) insists: 'Personal experience...is everything in Zen' (p.33).

A distinguished philosopher of religion, William James (1982), suggests that direct experience is '...something more like a sensation than an intellectual operation' (p.64). Sensation is what the body perceives. It can be experienced as perception of an image, of light, a sound or a kinesthetic sensation. In mystical experience sensation is perception through any or all of the five senses plus another sense which is nameless.

Direct experience can be of form or of no form. It can be the experience of nothingness. In mystical experience the power and richness of symbol often expands into the realm of emptiness. An ancient Jewish scholar, Rabbi Akiva, insists: 'Man must therefore dispense with the mental ideas, or image of God, and by transforming himself, experience Him' (Epstein 1988, p.36). The great and heretical Christian mystic, Eckhart (Merton 1968), discusses the mystical experience as non-symbolic, urging the destruction of the symbols of nature's nakedness.

For many mystics, stepping aside from the archetype of God, or moving through it, leads them into what they describe as direct experience of an energy field in which no form or boundary exists. Description of such a space can be found within many mystical practices.

DIRECT EXPERIENCE IS INDESCRIBABLE

Like the mystic, the individual who practices Authentic Movement is often challenged by what can be a very disturbing conflict. There is a knowing that says to contain the experience until it is complete, concomitant with a longing to share it. The longing is inextricably linked to the knowledge ahead of time, that it is impossible to describe.

For some, this longing seems to be in relationship to completing the experience, as if the verbal or visual description would bring it more clearly into consciousness. For others, describing it brings hope of being seen, understood or reducing the loneliness that such experiences inherently create. But, often, once this is attempted, the mystic reports a sense of self betrayal or an excruciating sense that what was once so vivid and profound has been reduced, limited and incorrectly described. 'He does not want it misunderstood or altered in any way in the act of revelation' (Larsen 1976, p.109).

In relation to this question, James Hillman writes in his commentary on Gopi Krishna's story of his kundalini experience: '...there is something in the nature of mystical experience that demands secrecy, as if the archetype behind the events which are in process needs a certain tension in order for it to be fulfilled. The alchemists envisioned this secrecy in their image of the closed vessel. In many fairy tales the hero or heroine is ordered not to say anything until the ordeal is over.' (Krishna 1971, p.131).

An articulate and distinguished shaman, Black Elk tells us: 'I saw more than I can tell and I understood more than I saw' (Neihardt 1979, p.43) and 'When the part of me that talks would try to make words for the meaning, it would be like fog and get away from me' (Larsen 1976, p.108). The Bible says: 'To attain to this spiritual wisdom, one must first be liberated from servile dependence on the wisdom of speech' (Cor. 1:17). Scholem (1961) writes: 'How is it possible to give lingual expression to mystical knowledge, which by its very nature is related to a sphere where speech and expression are excluded?' (p.14).

A woman who has made a remarkable contribution to the understanding of medieval woman's visionary literature, Elizabeth Petroff (1986), speaks of the illnesses of these women as a manifestation of a conflict related to writing about their experiences: 'They are fearful about what they expect to be negative responses to their writing' (p.42). Fear of response can drastically alter a description. Margery Kempe, one of the 14th century mystics discussed by Petroff (1986), said: '...I began to consider within myself how difficult and even impossible it would be to find thoughts and words capable of explaining these things to the human intellect without scandal' (p.43).

Merton (1968) says that Zen 'resists any temptation to be easily communicable' (p.46). He insists that one wishes 'to grasp the naked reality of experience' but 'grasps a form of words instead...' (p.37). A contemporary Buddhist scholar, Bancroft (1979), discusses this challenge: 'Words are essential but...when we rely too much on words we begin to substitute a world of indirect knowledge – knowledge about – for the immediate intense impact of what is actually there before thoughts and words arise' (p.7).

An ancient Zen teacher and scholar, Ch'an Master Hui Hai (1972), writes: 'To comprehend (real) meanings, we should go beyond unsteady words: to awaken to the fundamental law, we should leap beyond writings' (p.123). Suzuki (1949) explains: '...the human tongue is not an adequate organ for expressing the deepest truths of Zen... They are to be experienced in the inmost soul...' (p.33).

The great poets know much about this dilemma. Ryokan (Unno 1984), a late 18th century Japanese poet, writes:

> Looking at this scene, limitless emotions,
> But not one word. (p.7)

And the extraordinary Persian mystical poet, Rumi (Moyne and Barks 1984), expresses the impossibility of this task:

— In these pages many mysteries are hinted at.
   What if you come to understand one of them? (p.v)
— If I could wake completely, I would say without speaking
   Why I'm ashamed of using words. (p.41)
— Why can't we hear thought? (p.79)

MYSTICAL EXPERIENCE AND THE BODY

A universal and completely central part of mystical experience is its direct affect on the body, which is visibly altered. Transformation of consciousness means transformation of the body. The Mother (Satprem 1982) writes vividly about this: 'To transform, you need to go down into the body, and that's terrible... Otherwise nothing will ever change, it will remain the same.' She continues: '...I seek my way downward – that's what I can't find. The way I am seeking is always descending, descending – it's never going up, it's always descending, descending. Oh! I have no idea when it will be over' (p.60).

The Mother's contributions to this area of inquiry are dramatic as she worked entirely phenomenologically: '...One never really understands unless one understands with one's body' (Satprem 1984, p.240). 'I have had a unique experience. The supramental light entered my body directly, without going through the inner or higher planes of consciousness. It was the first time. It entered through the feet...' (Satprem 1982, p.163).

R. H. Blyth (1960) tells us that 'Zen means thinking with the body' (p.28). A great Jewish mystic, Abulafia, who was not unlike a Zen master, assigned each letter of the Hebrew alphabet to a corresponding body part. Focusing on a body part as an expression of a holy letter increased the aspirant's possibility of reaching God (Epstein 1988). What follows is a description of what can happen:

> After much movement and concentration on the letters, the hair on your head will stand on end...your blood will begin to vibrate...and all your body will begin to tremble, and a shuddering will fall on all your limbs, and...you will feel an additional spirit within yourself...strengthening you, passing through your entire body...[like] fragrant oil, annointing you from head to foot. (p.84)

Stephen Katz (1983) writes:

> The concrete meetings of mystic and beloved in Christian tradition, moreover, are almost always with the Christ whose physical body and wounds...are seen and felt by the Christian initiate. Indeed, this feeling of sharing in Christ's wounds is a striking feature of many Christian mystical occasions... Yearning to share in her Lord's Passion, [Lukardis of Oberweinar] prayed that [Christ's] experience of pain might always be present to her own experience. [The Lord said to her in response:] 'Place thy hands against My hands, and thy feet against My feet, and thy breast against My breast, and in such wise shall be so much helped by thee that My pain will be less.' And when the servant of God had done this she felt interiorly the most bitter pain of the wounds both in her hands and in her feet and in her breast... (pp.14–15)

A traditional healer in the !Kung tribe of the Kalahari Desert, Kinachau describes his dancing, in which a longing to unite with his god is actualized (Katz 1982): 'I felt num [the kundalini energy] in my stomach. I felt it rising. I felt it shiver and shiver... You breathe hard and fast, your heart is pounding. You run around because the "num" is shaking and agitating you violently' (p.84). 'Num grabs you and throws you up in the air' (p.89).

A witness to Kinachau's experience, Richard Katz (1982), describes what he saw:

> Kinachau sits up... His look is glazed, and his body trembles spasmodically. He returns to dancing and, after three full turns around the circle, goes over to one of the peripheral "talking" fires and begins to heal. As he pulls the sickness from each person, Kinachau's whole body

shakes roughly and his legs tremble violently, the tendons sticking out.
His jerking hands quiver rapidly over each person's chest... He shrieks
out the characteristic deep howling sounds which express the pain
involved in pulling out sickness. (p.65)

Often, the bodily experience for the mystic includes much physical pain. The
medieval saints left vivid accounts of their pain. Hildegard of Bingen writes
of her aching 'in the marrow of her bones and the veins of her flesh' (Petroff
1986, p.139). Hadewich similarly suffered: '...all my separate limbs
threatened to break...all my separate veins were in travail' (Petroff 1986,
p.194). St Elizabeth of Schonau (Petroff 1986) attempted to describe her
experience of her body: 'after this vision, I remained exhausted with illness'
(p.161); 'I remained in that state of violent bodily agitation' (p.162); 'with
great physical suffering I came into ecstasy' (p.167). !Kung healers speak of
the pain. Richard Katz (1982) describes it this way: 'Healers speak again and
again of the searing pain...in the pit of the stomach. One healer said: "Num
got into my stomach. It was hot and painful...like fire. I was surprised and I
cried"'. (p.45)

Underhill (1911) explains that psycho-physical disturbances are often
the result of mystical experiences: 'The nervous and vascular systems rebel
against a way of life, they don't adjust' (p.60). St Theresa said that the power
of her movement was lost and her breathing and circulation were diminished.
For some, it is impossible to speak or to open their eyes (Underhill 1911).
Another medieval saint, Blessed Angela of Foligno, writes: 'I didn't
remember to eat. And I wished that it were not necessary to eat' (Petroff
1986, p.259). In his autobiography, Gopi Krishna (1971) writes:

Aversion from food is a common feature when the rising of the kundalini
is sudden (p.195). I had not to eat for pleasure or the mechanical
satisfaction of hunger, but to regulate the intake of food with such
precision as not to cause the least strain on my oversensitive and
over-stimulated nervous system. (p.86)

The Buddhist nun, Seng-Kuo, from Ceylon, 'would go into Samadhi for
whole nights on end, her spirit remaining continuously in Buddha-lands. At
such time her body was like a withered tree, and people of shallow
comprehension suspected that she was dead' (Conze et al. 1990, p.292).
James Hillman writes in his commentary on Gopi Krishna's initiation: 'Again
and again we shall come to passages in the text which emphasize the

enormous physical cost of the experience. It is important to realize…that transformation…is exhausting' (Krishna 1971, p.97).

There are times, in the mystic's journey, when physical death becomes a real possibility. Epstein (1988) explains in her insightful book about the great text of Jewish mysticism, the *Kabbalah*: 'For this was the moment when the soul so longed to escape the body that it could inadvertently result in the disciple's death' (p.97). Krishna (1971) writes: 'I felt instinctively that a life and death struggle was going on inside me in which I, the owner of the body, was entirely powerless to take part, forced to lie quietly and watch as a spectator the weird drama unfold in my own flesh' (p.152). A !Kung healer has this to say about death: 'As we enter kia, we fear death. We fear we may die and not come back' (Katz 1982, p.45).

It is interesting to note what the Buddhists say about the challenge of death. Suzuki (1962) writes: 'Eternity, for Zen, is not a posthumous state of affairs. To live in eternity is to tap the infinity of the moment… No one is prepared to take that last step until he has first exhausted all his other resources, and finally stands emptied of all contrivances for meeting life. Only then will the need for reality drive him to the final abandoning of his self. The practice and discipline of Zen is to bring one to this point… The great Death is also the Great Awakening' (p.xvi).

At this time in the Western world, in response to our deepening need for authentic spiritual experience, all we can do is to return to our physical selves. Individuals practicing Authentic Movement can have experiences in their bodies that are not unlike those just described by mystics. What follows are examples of movers' attempts to write about direct experiences of the numinous in the practice of Authentic Movement. These experiences all occurred for individuals after many years of personal therapy followed by several years of Authentic Movement practice.

A man named Allan periodically encounters a specific energy field that moves from inside his body up and out. He says:

> I feel the pushing up from my torso and diaphragm. It's as if a strong life force is pushing up from within me and my body has to follow… Once out, a large golden ball emerges from my body – I carry it around the room in both hands, arms outstretched…I am very large…

For a period of a year I repeatedly witnessed Elena, who was watching her own hands being cut off. After unsuccessfully searching for an explanation within her personal history and personality, she finally accepted this experience, surrendering to its fullness, its lack of emotionality, its specific kinesthetic demands. We subsequently learned that in the earliest form of Jewish mysticism, called Throne Mysticism, the mystic began his descent to the Merkabah, 'the visionary journey of the soul to heaven [by having to stand upright] without hands and feet' (Scholem 1961, p.52).

Michelle wrote this in her journal after moving in the studio:

> I was being pulled to a standing position. I felt as though every cell in my body was being mobilized into an upward motion. My face was lifted up toward the sky light; my arms began to move in an upward fully extended gesture which I held for a very long time…perfectly still, perfectly light. Then my body began to shake and tremble as I released or was released from the experience. I felt as though I was being moved by something more than the 'little' me or ego 'me.'

Another woman, Lauren, wrote in her journal after moving:

> I lie still and become more still. In fact, I am so still the word doesn't work anymore, because I come to an experience where there is much activity, but only on a deep kinesthetic level. I am empty, with no density inside, and no density around me, surrounded by nothing, yet incredibly awake and sort of becoming like sound with no form.

Satprem (1984) writes about this: '…beyond a certain level of consciousness, it is no longer ideas that one sees and tries to translate – one hears… When the consciousness of the seeker is clear, he can hear the sound distinctively; and it is a seeing sound…' (p.224).

Jody describes the experience of light after pulling her limbs slowly in toward her torso: 'I see and feel an explosion from the base of my spine – a white ball diffusing into white light. It is gentle and slow. A "boom," but quiet, in slow motion. It fills my entire back and literally jars me, giving me a jolt'.

Mystical texts are replete with reference to light. Hildegard of Bingen writes: '…that a fiery light of the greatest brilliance coming from the opened heavens, poured into all my brain and kindled in my heart and my breast a flame' (Petroff 1986, p.151).

The following example is of an experience of image within a transcendent state – which is different from fantasy or active imagination. A vision occurs within a mystical state and, therefore, is made of light, or what has been described as electrical energy. In a transcendent state, as Underhill (1911) explains, the self embodies the image or vision.

Anna wrote this vision in her journal after lying unusually still for a long period of time, feeling very tired and weighted:

> Feminine white hands caress the stones in a circle. I come down from the sky onto the pole in the middle. I spin. Roots grow from my feet. Branches reach from my arms from my mouth. My third eye grows a branch which is holding a rabbit who sits on top of the full green tree.

For a period of six months, Julie spoke simply and shyly, after moving, about a kinesthetic experience, the sensation of falling into nowhere. She wrote in her journal:

> This is not an easy task, this surrender to such a life threatening situation, but it brings a release...when I just endlessly fall THROUGH DARK AND EMPTY NOTHING... If I surrender and fall more deeply into the material, I must let go of meaning, of attachment to any semblance of things, which once anchored my life, even my physical being.

MYSTICAL EXPERIENCE AND THE EMOTIONS

As the body transforms, so does the self. The experience of the self, internally, in relationship to others and to the natural world, is altered. The personalities of some mystics are much more visible in their writing about this than others. For example, the lives of medieval Christian visionaries are more available, more explicitly portrayed in biography and autobiography, than the lives of Jewish mystics, who seemed to experience more 'personal reticence' (Scholem 1961, p.16). In this context it is also interesting to note that there is strikingly little recorded biographical material concerning Jewish women who were mystics. Scholem (1961) tells us that Kabbalism is historically and metaphysically masculine. It was made for and by men.

The phenomenon of resistance and its relationship to surrender regarding mystical experience is repeatedly discussed in many traditions. Underhill (1911) tells us that the mystic 'goes because he [or she] must...without hope or reward' surrendering '...self and all things' – into 'the annihilation of selfhood' (p.83). Eliade (1964) describes 'the resistance to "divine election" as mankind's ambivalent attitude toward the sacred' (p.109). He tells us that the 'shaman struggles for a long time with unknown forces before he finally cries: "Now the way is open"' (p.294). It is unusual for the human psyche to do just this without struggle, conflict, terror, despair and a feeling of helplessness. Richard Katz (1982) describes resistance to kia among the !Kung:

The aspiring healers try to regulate their condition. When they feel kia coming on, they involuntarily draw back from and at times actively resist this transition to an altered state. Others help them to overcome this resistance and to strike a dynamic balance between the oncoming intensity of kia and their fear of it... The num must be hot enough to evoke kia but not so hot that it provokes debilitating fear...the correct amount is critical. (p.47)

Scholem (1961) describes the Jewish men who were mystics: 'They glory in objective description and are deeply averse to letting their own personalities intrude into the picture... It is though they were hampered by a sense of shame' (p.16). Petroff (1986) writes of the Christian medieval visionaries: 'Descriptions of physical pain and weakness associated with ecstatic states, accompanied by statements of shame or embarrassment are frequent...' (p.41).

Petroff (1986) discusses Hildegard of Bingen's writing as:

typical of most women visionaries in its mingling of self-confidence and humility. [...] For in the marrow of her bones and in the veins of her flesh she was aching, having her mind and judgement bound, so that no security dwelt in her and she judged herself culpable in all things. [...] She has been protected from pride and vainglory by these feelings of fear and grief. (p.139)

Underhill (1911) describes the fear as not only of the inner experiences themselves but of deceiving themselves and others in their struggle to believe that what is happening to them is real. This is not at all an unrealistic fear. Epstein (1988) mentions that 'the Jewish sages have always therefore warned that it is impossible for the average person to have a real prophetic dream without a considerable admixture of worthless information' (p.143). Petroff (1979) also discusses the great difficulty for the Christian mystics to 'distinguish between one's own mind and the true information' (p.51). She explains how the initiate can't yet see her own new forming self and instead sees herself as less significant than others see her. Guyon, a Christian mystic, writes of his feelings of doubt: 'I could not perceive of any good thing I had done in my whole life' (Underhill 1911, p.38).

Petroff (1986) describes the great effort made by the Beguine visionaries 'to be in the world but not of it' (p.207). This conflict caused tremendous pain for mystics in many traditions. Underhill (1911) describes St Theresa's awesome struggle with this split: 'At times she persuaded herself that she could enjoy both [worlds] which ended mostly in complete enjoyment of neither' (p.214).

Underhill (1911) writes of other excruciating emotional conflicts which mystics suffer. She discusses their feelings of deprivation and inadequacy. Visitors are often experienced as torture. They see a tiny detail of imperfection in themselves and inflate it. They have a 'wild desire to see god, to die. They can't touch earth and they can't get to heaven' (Underhill 1911, p.386).

Eliade (1964) discusses the ascetic practice for shamans as an annihilation of secular personality. He writes of the silence and depression that often follow ecstatic states. Hillman discusses this in his commentary on Gopi Krishna's experiences:

> The alternation of his states of consciousness throughout the years, especially the loss of heavenly joy time and again, is also described by the alchemists. They said the stone must be coagulated and dissolved again and again. The more it alternated between these opposites the more valuable it became. This lesson is hard to learn, for after every peak experience one wants to 'hold it', and after each valley experience one feels guilty, lost, and humiliated. (Krishna 1971, p.237)

The impact of such dramatic change in the body and the emotions challenges the mental health of an individual. Eliade (1958) discusses this: '"Possessed" by the Gods or spirits, the novice is in danger of completely losing his psychomental balance' (p.68).

The Kabbalists were not unaware of the danger of insanity, especially when the mystic was compelled to confront the demonic beings (Epstein 1988). Participatory visions, for the medieval Christian mystics, were the most dangerous in terms of their sanity. Sometimes, 'the visionary so fully identifies with the archetypal experience of grief that she is incapable of observing her vision or reflecting on what she has seen until the vision is over' (Petroff 1979, p.60). When the conscious mind fuses with the image, psychosis is possible.

Because of the great stress on the body and psyche, some initiates become psychotic, some die. A crucial factor in this regard is the clarity of ego consciousness and the strength of the boundary between such consciousness and the experience of the numinous. There is, of course, little written about those who, for whatever reason, do not find themselves able to survive this complex journey. We most often read about those who manage to return to tell the story. Those initiates somehow learn a way to balance surrender and will, form and formlessness, body and spirit. In such a process they manage to stay in touch with the daily life just enough. It is said of St Catherine: 'When she was needed, she always came to herself' (Underhill 1911, p.248).

In the practice of Authentic Movement, when individuals are experiencing various aspects of a mystical journey, the emotional effect is evident. So much of what has just been discussed is familiar in the speaking and the writing of movers and witnesses: shyness, shame, fear, insecurity, a sense of deprivation, confusion, fear of psychosis, fear of death, as well as bliss, rapture, ecstasy.

Many struggle with physical symptoms that do not fit tidily into Western medical phenomena and fall haphazardly into what is broadly referred to as New Age diseases. Many doubt the experiences of the numinous, working hard to find explanation within personality theory. Others resist the intensity of the energy for excellent reasons. Feeling a great inability to describe these experiences, they suffer from frustration, fear of being misunderstood and fear of being judged as inflated, and, finally, deflate the experiences in order to remain safe.

In the practice of Authentic Movement we are learning how to distinguish mystical experiences from unresolved personal history, how to safely help regulate their intensity, how to receive and integrate such material into developing consciousness. In doing so we are learning how to witness the organic evolution of these energies into new form.

MYSTICAL EXPERIENCE AND DEVELOPMENTAL THEORY

Mystical experience, like the unfolding of personality, can occur developmentally. In many mystical traditions there are stages through which the initiate evolves. These stages provide an understanding, an order, a way of containing the whole. However, many experiences of the superconscious do not occur within a tidy developmental framework. These isolated occurrences can be related to any of the specific stages, can occur from the same energy source, can be exactly like those experiences that happen sequentially, but simply are not recognizably experienced within a developmental spectrum.

Halifax (1982) describes the stages in the shamanic tradition, from death to rebirth to return:

The deepest structures within the psyche are found in the themes of descent to the Realm of Death, confrontations with demonic forces, dismemberment, trial by fire, communion with the world of spirits and creatures, assimilation of the elemental forces, ascension via the World Tree and/or the Cosmic Bird, realization of a solar identity, and return to the Middle World, the world of human affairs. (p.7)

Underhill (1911) lists the five stages that the Christian mystic experiences: awakening, purgation, illumination, mystic death and union. As mentioned earlier, in Throne Mysticism the early Jewish mystics passed through 'heavenly halls or palaces' in a journey called 'descent to the Merkabah.' There are seven gates of entry, which finally lead to the 'perception of His appearance on the throne' (Scholem 1961, p.44). It can be different for many Zen Buddhists because the appearance of symbols do not necessarily contribute to their journey. Yet there is a path clearly described by the ancient Zen masters which aspirants follow.

Within these basic and developmental stages of transformative experience there is meaning and complexity in each stage that, again, is similar among the different traditions. What follows is a brief discussion of three of these stages: descent, union and return.

Descent

A distinguished Buddhist priest and philosopher, Yoshinori (1983), writes: 'In the mystical traditions of all times and places, conversion is said to begin with self-purification, with a catharsis of soul' (p.16). Eliade (1958) writes of the descent that the shamanic initiate is required to make in which he or she inevitably 'encounters' monsters (p.62).

Petroff (1979) explains that the first step for Christian visionaries is almost always a direct encounter with evil. Theresa of Avila writes of her experience: 'I saw in his hand a long spear of gold and at the iron's point there seemed to be a little fire. He appeared to me to be thrusting it at times into my heart and to pierce my very entrails...' (Underhill 1911, p.292).

In each tradition these early stages, with or without visions depicting such experience, describe the initiate's experience of loss of his or her physical body through fire, torture, being devoured or dismembered. Death of the self as one has known it inevitably precedes rebirth.

Union

The arrival in the Upper Realm often includes a meeting with God. Enoch writes of his encounter in the Old Testament: 'And there I saw One, who had a head of days, and His head was white like wool' (Epstein 1988, p.50). Union with God is experienced in a myriad of ways. Scholem (1961) explains that in the ecstatic state, the mystic is his own Messiah. For many Kabbalists, union includes letters and words (Scholem 1961): '...every spoken word consists of sacred letters, and the combination, separation, and reunion of letters reveal profound mysteries...and unravel...the secret of the relation of all languages to the holy tongue... In this supreme state, man and Torah become one' (p.135). The great Christian mystic, Eckhart, writes about union:

> In my breaking-through...I transcend all creatures and am neither God nor creature: I am that I was and I shall remain now and forever. Then I receive an impulse which carries me above all angels. In this impulse I conceive such passing riches that I am not content with God as being God, as being all his godly works, for in this breaking-through I find that God and I are both the same... (Merton 1968, p.114)

A renowned Buddhist scholar, Blofeld (1972), describes it this way: 'Reality will flash upon us, the whole universe of phenomena will be seen as it really is...' (p.31). The great and recent spiritual leader in India, Sri Aurobindo, writes: 'Thou art He... Such is the Truth that the ancient Mysteries taught and the later religions forgot' (Satprem 1984, p.170). In the *Taittiriya Upanishad* it is found: 'The Spirit who is here in man and the spirit who is there in the sun, lo, it is One Spirit and there is no other' (Satprem 1984, p.171). Regardless of the framework within which this union occurs, in each tradition it is undeniably positive, more than worth the great suffering that precedes it. The initiate becomes whole, one with the universe.

In the practice of Authentic Movement the unitive stage is reflected on three different levels. With a very practiced mover, union can occur between the moving self and the internal witness. One no longer sees oneself lifting one's arm, it simply lifts. This can look like pre-egoic experience, to use Ken Wilber's framework, but, in fact, it is trans-egoic (Wilber 1980). Experience in the unconscious state can look like experience in the superconscious state. The difference is that in the unconscious state the presence of ego is not yet established and, in the superconscious state, the fully formed ego has been transcended.

Second, union can occur between the witness and the mover when both are simultaneously without self-consciousness and without the experienced density of personality. They are each completely clear and separate beings, and yet united. This can look like merging but, instead, it is union. Gopi Krishna (1971) writes of this when speaking of man's relationship to his god, though it is interesting to wonder about its application here: 'The seer and the seen – reduced to an inexpressible sizeless void which no mind can conceive…or any language describe' (p.208).

In Zen this unity is discussed in relationship to the subject and the object becoming one. A contemporary Buddhist scholar, Maseo Abe (1983), discusses this phenomenon. Perhaps mover and witness could be substituted for subject and object: 'So long as the field of self-consciousness, i.e., the field of separation between subject and object, is not broken-through, and so long as a transference from that standpoint does not occur, a real self-presentation of reality cannot come about' (Abe 1983, p.9).

Third a mover can experience union with his god. Any, or all, of these experiences can look like work in the unconscious, rather than superconscious, but the difference is that ego-consciousness has been expanded toward the numinous. These experiences can only occur safely after healthy ego structures are developed.

Return

After the exhausting and impeccably demanding journey of the initiate, after the torment and the terror, the light and the ecstasy, the bone-aching and the emptiness, inevitably, the one who has travelled returns home again. Campbell (1956) explains the task of return:

> The hero may have to be brought back from his supernatural adventure by assistance from without. That is to say, the world may have to come and get him… After such utter bliss, why would the human psyche choose to leave it and return to the embodied state of humanity? A choice is necessarily made, sometimes consciously, sometimes unconsciously. (p.207)

Perhaps the return has become even more difficult in the Western world because there is rarely a container or community which believes in, honors and correctly receives the initiate. Campbell (1956) continues:

> How render back into light-world language the speech-defying pronouncements of the dark?… How communicate to people who insist on the exclusive evidence of their senses the message of the all-generating void? … The first problem of the returning hero is to accept as real, after an experience of the soul-satisfying vision of fulfillment, the passing joys and sorrow, banalities and noisy obscenities of life. Why re-enter such a world? Why attempt to make plausible, or even interesting, to men and women consumed with passion, the experience of transcendental bliss? (p.218)

The process of return just described essentially has two aspects: the internal experience of the one who has been transformed – the impeccable struggle toward clarity, balance, and integration of the new energy now active within the person – and the equally impeccable task of bringing that embodied energy into clear and correct relationship with the collective. Coming back is not enough. Coming back brings an unwritten, unstated, often unwanted responsibility in relationship to the community.

What follows is an example of work in an Authentic Movement experience, which illustrates an aspect of the phenomenon of return. Hilary writes:

> I witnessed for hours without moving until I felt I would explode. I had to walk out of doors, up the hill to a clearing. Once there I felt I was witnessed by God. I was completely contained by everything around me. When I returned to the studio I looked at my witness and knew that I had been seen. I sat down and felt the presence of God come inside through my womb. It felt like a divine child.

She then began to move inconspicuously with other movers, dancing, crying, laughing, engaging completely in the fullness of the movement that was occurring among them. This experience was reminiscent to me, as a witness, of the tenth of the series of the ox-herding pictures. Bancroft (1979) discusses these pictures, which depict the development of Zen life: 'In the tenth and last picture, he returns to the world, a free man, doing whatever he does with the whole of himself because there is nothing to gain' (p.96).

In the practice of Authentic Movement some movers encounter mystical experiences which either happen outside of a developmental framework or do not appear to be sequentially related. Others have mystical experiences which seem to evolve developmentally. We are now witnessing several movers who have spontaneously begun a descent in which there seems to be an inherent order. Their experiences reflect work at various places on the spiral toward wholeness. What follows is material from the journal of one mover, Rebecca, in which she describes different stages in the development of her mystical journey:

> I come to the killing fields. The sea of endless white where I come to die away the features of my reality. I tremble; I do not come willingly. I know the stakes are high. It is really a matter of one death or another...I trick myself in murderous ways. I let the ripe time rot in inertia or procrastination... This is another letting go. Hanging on to illusion is a

different and I believe more terrible death than letting go; but this letting go is a descent into unknown pain, perhaps memory. I can only guess how painful by the measure of my own resistance to this action.

I begin by sitting, feeling too much, feeling sick and aching. Rest. Empty. By Maria I am comforted. I want the drum... I go to Audrey's drum and sit for a long time: I lay my head on the drum; I scratch the drum. I listen. Carefully. Many sounds in the collective. I must go back to the burning fire. I go. I sit. I extend my spine. I fall into the direct heat. I burn and burn. There is a shift from red to white. I am white in the fire. Pure hot in the burning. Time is called.

She ends the week-end with this entry in her journal:

Search hard to find the gift, until
Your fingertips are shred to bone and
your eyes are water-hollowed stone.

Suffer, until breath itself no longer
visits freely, but hardly fills the
spongy billows, sucked in narrowly
in service of pain's hard thrust.

Beat, the empty, bloodless chambers
of your heart. Burn, until faith
and surrender are the last dim
embers on earth.

A year later, after repeated experience of death, she wrote the following poem in her journal about new life:

Moving to this new place, now so white
with stillness and emptiness
alive in every molecule. Inside
I am the beating wings of
one hundred birds with
winter
coming on.

I begin to suspect that I am in an initiation process that has little to do with psychology... getting these contents into the psychological realm is, in fact, dangerous to me. When I clear away the dross of my psychology, not deny it, but let it run its own inevitable course, then there is this particular circle in which I am being and becoming conscious. I'm in an ancient and external place. Nature teaches me. I dwell with such immense energy that is ordered in mystery. It is all so vibrant, tender, and fierce.

The practice of Authentic Movement

It is important at this point to look more closely at the form of Authentic Movement itself and some of the other aspects of it that are similar to mystical practice. The constant external container in Authentic Movement is the relationship between the mover and the witness (Adler 1987). We begin with dyads which allow movers and witnesses an intimate and safe container out of which trust and clarity can develop. The evolving relationship between the two is reflected in the writing of Santiveva, an eighth century poet and mystic, when he describes the 'practice of contemplative identification with other beings. This he calls either meditation on the "sameness of self and others" or the "transference of self and others"... Whoever wishes to quickly rescue himself and another, should practice the supreme mystery: the exchanging of Self and other' (Gimmello 1983, p.69). The Mahayana Gampo-pa writes:

> Spiritual friends are like a guide when we travel in unknown territory, an escort when we pass through dangerous regions and a ferry-man when we cross a great river... When we go there without an escort, there is the danger of losing our body, life, or property; but when we have a strong escort we reach the desired place without loss. (Gimmello 1983, p.81)

The mover, in the presence of her witness, works with her eyes closed. The Bal Shem Tov told his disciples '...when you wish to yoke yourself to the higher world, it is best to worship with your eyes closed' (Epstein 1988, p.118). St John of the Cross said: 'If a man wishes to be sure of the road he treads on, he must close his eyes and walk in the dark' (Ross 1960, p.243). In Authentic Movement practice eyes are closed for similar reasons, to enhance connection with one's inner life. Usually, inner life includes, even if it is unconscious, an awareness of the numinous.

With eyes closed, the mover's task is to wait and to listen, to trust in the possibility of 'being moved', instead of moving, as Mary Whitehouse (1963) so beautifully explained. Listening means concentrating. Concentration is the central force of all mystical practices. Satprem (1984) tells us that 'any concentration releases a subtle heat' (p.281) and that in concentrating the expanding consciousness 'may silently and quietly focus on the desired object and become this object' (p.116).

There is constant talk in the studio about seeing. The mover strives to see herself more and more clearly via her internal witness. The witness struggles with the developing capacity to see herself as she learns how to see her mover. And seeing her mover means owning her own projections, judgements and interpretations so that she can bring a clear presence to her mover. Clear presence means seeing what is actually there. Satprem (1984) says: 'If we are powerless, it is because we do not see. Seeing, seeing wholly, necessarily means having power' (p.270); 'In inner silence, consciousness sees' (p.116).

Castaneda insists that we 'learn to see' (Larsen, 1976 p.183) and Satprem (1984) reminds us:

> If our mirror is not clean, we can never see the true reality of things and people, because we find everywhere the reflection of our own desires or fears, the echo of our own turmoil... In order to see, it is obvious that we have to stop being in the middle of the picture. Therefore, the seeker will discriminate between the things that tend to blur his vision and those that clarify it; such essentially will be his 'morality'. (p.71)

Suzuki (1980) writes: 'There must be actual seeing on the physical plane, and over and through this seeing there must be another sort of seeing... It is not that something different is seen but that one sees differently' (p.36). Merton (1968) describes Zen in an uncannily similar way in which we are trying to describe moving and witnessing:

> The monk is 'trying to understand' when in fact he ought to try to *look*. The apparently mysterious and cryptic sayings of Zen became much simpler when we see them in the whole context of Buddhist 'mindfulness' or awareness, which in its most elementary form consists in that 'bare attention', which simply *sees* what is right there and does not add any comment, any interpretation, any judgement, any conclusion. It just *sees*. (pp.52–53)

> The trouble is that as long as you are given to distinguishing, judging, categorizing and classifying – or even contemplating – you are super-imposing something else on the pure mirror. You are filtering the light through a system as if convinced that this will improve the light. (p.7)

In the practice of Authentic Movement the mover's internal witness has developed in relationship to a gradual internalization of her external witness.

Originally, the external witness held consciousness so that she, the mover, could open to the unconscious. Now her internal witness holds consciousness for her as she finds more space to open to other sources of energy.

In the Rig Veda there is a striking statement about the internal witness: 'Two birds beautiful of wing, friends and comrades, cling to a common tree, and one eats the sweet fruit, the other regards him and eats not' (Satprem 1984, p.44). Sri Aurobindo describes it this way: 'All developed mental men...at certain times and for certain purpose...separate the two parts of the mind, the active part, which is a factory of thoughts and the quiet, masterful part which is at once a Witness and a Will' (Satprem 1984, p.49).

Perhaps the internal witness progressively evolves into the clear self as unconditional loving presence becomes manifest. As mentioned before, many mystics believe that God is the clear self. In the Tao Te Ching there is an exquisite description of what the expanding and developing internal witness might be:

> The Tao flows everywhere,
> Creating,
> Inspecting, remaining silent and unknown,
> It rejects nothing,
> Possesses nothing,
> Encourages but does not dominate.
> Being quiet,
> Uncritical,
> Nonpossessive,
> It does not sign its name,
> It is hardly recognized by anyone,
> It is too small to see.

After several years of dyad and triad work, the mover enters the witness circle with an increased ability to concentrate, less density from unresolved personality issues and an increasingly clear internal witness. Because of the strengthening of internal witnessing by the movers, the collective of external witnesses gradually shifts from a more personal responsibility of holding consciousness for an individual mover toward the freedom to see from a broader perspective. The circle of witnesses begins to participate in a collective consciousness which can include what Wilber (1980) calls 'super-consciousness.' In this format witnesses often see a collective myth, a ritual, or simply feel in the presence of an energy larger than one individual can hold.

Also within the witness circle, there appears to be a gradual and subtle shift for movers. Often, the movement is less emotional, with less interference from the negative aspects of internalized parents, unresolved trauma and current conflict. Sometimes, a specific gateway into the numinous is experienced within the exact same movement pattern that held the most significant childhood trauma. For example, I witnessed a woman, over a period of two years, explore and finally fully re-live trauma that occurred specifically in a crib in her infancy. After such work had been integrated 'enough,' the exact movement pattern that once had elicited infant trauma suddenly elicited what she called transpersonal experience when she moved within a witness circle.

The circle is an ancient, archetypal form which appears in rituals, celebrations and ceremonies in which the sacred is honored or expressed. The shamans bring their visions back to the circle of their people, where they are enacted and/or danced by the community. The Hasids dance their dances of joy and praise in circles. The !Kung surround their dancers, who invite the num energy to rise for healing purposes, with a circle of people who sing in support of the process. Satprem (1984) agrees with the bodhisattvas that '...no individual transformation is possible without some degree of collective transformation' (p.348).

Ritual often spontaneously occurs in Authentic Movement circles, within an individual's work and within the collective. Spontaneous ritual occurs frequently for Alice. As her witness, I experience myself in the presence of high order and ancient form. She describes it this way:

> I have often found myself embodying, enacting very particular, specific movement gestures, specifically directed by some unknown certainty within me. Often I don't understand why I feel compelled, beckoned to do what I do. Many times when I have completed the movement sequences I return to my place in the circle, open my eyes, and realize I have been in another place/realm, another zone of awareness.

In any ritual impeccability becomes a critical element. Any movement of an individual or a group becomes increasingly specific, precise, as the inherent order reveals itself. Precision is an essential element in transformative experience. Hillman (Krishna 1971) writes: 'The psyche has an affinity for precision; witness the details in children's stories, primitive rituals and primitive languages, and the exactitude with which we go about anything that is important' (p.97). Impeccability within the occurrence of any mystical experience appears to be essential for the survival of the individual, for the survival of the collective, for the completion of the process.

Eliade (1958) writes of 'man's profound need for initiation, for regeneration, for participation in the life of the spirit' (p.134). In our longing to rediscover the mysteries, to participate in ritual, it is extremely important not to impose acts that do not organically evolve out of the experience itself. Because of the gift and the burden of ego consciousness, we can be informed and even nourished by rituals from other cultures, but we must patiently continue to listen for our own expression embodied of collective consciousness. How will we begin again to find the place, light the fire, say the words or dance the dance? As Satprem (1984) says: '...all we want is our own little river flowing into the Infinite' (p.2).

Conclusion

After the above discussion of some of the similarities between mystical practice and the practice of Authentic Movement, it is necessary before closing to briefly discuss some of the differences. The major difference is that unlike mystical practice, Authentic Movement is a practice which has not evolved out of or in relationship to a religious belief system. Instead, it evolved originally out of the art of dance. Mary Whitehouse, Joan Chodorow, myself and many individuals who participate in the development of this form came to it originally as dancers. People come to the form to learn how to listen to their bodies and, in the process, some are guided from within toward experiences beyond ego consciousness.

In the practice of Authentic Movement there is no church, synagogue, dojo or temple representing a holy place where participants meet. There is no priest, rabbi or lama. There is no god whom individuals endeavor to find. There is no teacher who guides the individuals in relationship to religious texts or belief systems. Without a master, without a bible, often without any former direct experience of a god, the mover projects her clear self onto the witness until she is ready to own it. As this ownership is integrated, the individual moves toward wholeness until, at times, she becomes one with what Underhill (1911) calls her 'indwelling Deity.'

Unlike the mystic whose experiences have, in the past, tended to evolve out of specific religious symbols, teachings and collectives, in Authentic Movement practice we are evolving into a collective in which the conscious individual is full member. In doing so we find our only external guide to be the form itself, which is free of any symbols, doctrines or promises.

The discipline of Authentic Movement offers a safe container in which individual and collective experience can become transformed, perhaps because of the evolution of the clear self. Again, Satprem (1984) offers guidance:

> We do not seek to 'pass' on to a better existence but to transform this one. (p.243)

> Everything seems to be happening up above, but what is happening here? … We need a truth that involves also the body and the earth. (p.238)

> First, we must work in our individual body, without seeking any escape, since this body is the very place where consciousness connects with Matter; and secondly, we must strive to discover the principle of consciousness that will have the power to transform Matter. (p.185)

> We are here imprisoned in Matter… There are not a hundred ways of getting out of it, in fact there are only two; one is to fall asleep…and the other is to die. Sri Aurobindo's experience provides a third possibility, which allows us to get out without actually getting out, and which reverses the course of man's spiritual evolution, since the goal is no longer only above or outside, but right inside. (pp.261–262)

> We need a way to be opened that is still blocked, not a religion to be founded. (p.289)

To transform, we must descend into the body: 'The more we descend, the higher the consciousness we need, the stronger the light' (Satprem 1984, p.260). Sri Aurobindo, the Mother and Satprem write voluminously about this process of light descending into matter, thereby transforming it, resulting in 'enstasy,' which is ecstasy in the body (Satprem 1984, p.198). They speak of 'luminous vibrations' (Satprem 1984, p.205). 'The day we learn to apply this Vibration…to our own matter, we will have the practical secret' (Satprem 1984, p.284). Satprem (1984) reminds us of what we all must know but somehow forget: 'One discovers only oneself, there is nothing else to discover' (p.216).

References

Adler, J. (1987) 'Who is the witness? A description of Authentic Movement'. *Contact Quarterly*, Winter, 20–29.

Abe, M. (1983) *Nishitani's Challenge to Western Philosophy and Theology*. Paper presented at the Annual Meeting of the American Academy of Religion, Dallas, Texas, 19–22 December.

Bancroft, A. (1979) *Zen: Direct Pointing to Reality*. London: Thames & Hudson.

Blofeld, J. (1972) 'Introduction'. In H. Hai *The Zen Teaching of Hui Hai on Sudden Illumination* (John Blofeld, trans.). New York: Samuel Weiser.

Blyth, R.H. (1960) *Zen and Zen Classics. Volume 1*. Tokyo, Japan: The Hokuseido Press.

Buber, M. (1958) *Hasidism and Modern Man*. Atlantic Highlands, NJ: Humanities Press International.

Campbell, J. (1956) *The Hero with a Thousand Faces*. Cleveland, OH: World Publishing.

Conze, E., Horner, I.B., Snellgrove, D. and Waley, A. (1990) *Buddhist Texts Through the Ages*. Boston: Shambhala Publications.

Eliade, M. (1958) *Rites and Symbols of Initiation*. New York: Harper & Row.

Eliade, M. (1964) *Shamanism: Archaic Techniques of Ecstasy*. Princeton, NJ: Princeton University Press.

Epstein, P. (1988) *Kabbalah: The Way of the Jewish Mystic*. Boston: Shambhala.

Fry, C. (1977) *Selected Plays*. Oxford and New York: Oxford University Press.

Gimmello, R.M. (1983) 'Mysticism in its contexts'. In S. Katz (ed) *Mysticism and Religious Traditions*, pp.61–88. Oxford: Oxford University Press.

Grof, S. (1985) *Beyond the Brain: Birth, Death, and Transcendence in Psychotherapy*. Albany: State University of New York Press.

Hai, H. (1972) *The Zen Teaching of Hui Hai on Sudden Illumination*. (John Blofeld, trans.). New York: Samuel Weiser.

Halifax, J. (1982) *Shaman: The Wounded Healer*. New York: Crossroad.

James, W. (1982) *The Varieties of Religious Experience*. New York: Penguin Books.

Katz, R. (1982) *Boiling Energy: Community Healing Among the Kalahari Kung*. Cambridge, MA: Harvard University Press.

Katz, S. (1983) 'The conservative character of mystical experience'. In S. Katz (ed) *Mysticism and Religious Traditions*, pp.3–60. Oxford: Oxford University Press.

Krishna, G. (1971) *Kundalini: The Evolutionary Energy in Man (with Psychological Commentary by James Hillman)*. Boulder: Shambhala.

Larsen, S. (1976) *The Shaman's Doorway: Opening the Mythic Imagination to Contemporary Consciousness*. New York: Harper & Row.

Merton, T. (1968) *Zen and the Birds of Appetite*. New York: A New Directions Book.

Meyerhoff, B. (1974) *Peyote Hunt*. Ithaca, NY: Cornell University Press.

Moyne, J. and Barks, C. (1984) *Open Secret: Versions of Rumi*. Putney, VT: Threshold Books.

Neihardt, J.G. (1979) *Black Elk Speaks*. Lincoln, NE: University of Nebraska Press.

Nishitani, K. (1982) *Religion and Nothingness*. Berkeley, CA: University of California Press.

Otto, R. (1923) *The Idea of the Holy*. Oxford: Oxford University Press.

Petroff, E. (1979) *Consolation of the Blessed*. New York: Alta Gaia Society.

Petroff, E. (1986) *Medieval Women's Visionary Literature*. New York: Oxford University Press.

Ross, N.W. (1960) *The World of Zen: An East-West Anthology*. New York: Vintage Books.

Satprem (1982) *Mind of the Cells.* New York: Institute for Evolutionary Research.

Satprem (1984) *Sri Aurobindo: The Adventure of Consciousness.* New York: Institute for Evolutionary Research.

Scholem, G. (1961) *Major Trends in Jewish Mysticism.* New York: Schocken Books.

Suzuki, D.T. (1949) *An Introduction to Zen Buddhism.* New York: The Philosophical Library.

Suzuki, D.T. (1962) *The Essentials of Zen Buddhism.* New York: Dutton.

Suzuki, D.T. (1980) *The Awakening of Zen.* Boulder: Prajna Press.

Underhill, E. (1911) *Mysticism: A Study in the Nature and Development of Man's Spiritual Consciousness.* London: Methuen & Co.

Unno, T. (1984) *Emptiness and Reality in Mahayana Buddhism.* Paper presented at the Symposium in Honor of Keiji Nishitani, April 25–28.

Yoshinori, T. (1983) *The Heart of Buddhism.* New York: Crossroad.

Whitehouse, M.S. (1963) 'Physical movement and personality'. *Contact Quarterly,* Winter 1987, 16–19.

Wilber, K. (1980) *The Atman Project: A Transpersonal View of Human Development.* Wheaton, IL: The Theosophical Publishing House.

CHAPTER 14

The Collective Body[1]

Janet Adler

Things are one; things are many.
The intellect cannot grasp these two simultaneously, but experience can,
if it will.

(Blyth 1960, p.58)

Embodiment of the collective: Belonging

I forget. I am a Western woman and I forget. I am a Western woman and I forget that a source of my longing is related to my great desire to belong. I am a Western woman and have learned that embodied personal consciousness is my goal. The physicist, Peter Russell (1992), beautifully articulates my concern about this goal when he asks:

> Is each of us simply an isolated consciousness, bound by space and time to the body we inhabit? One among five billion other self-conscious individuals who have been given a brief window of experience onto this world? [...] Can we be sure that our individual self is not part of some eternal consciousness temporarily peeking out through the senses of this body into the physical world around? [...] Could my sense of separateness be just an illusion? (pp.144–145)

Illusion or not, separate is how we feel. We forget that the human psyche cannot endure without belonging. Within the last century, change away from

1   Revised paper, previously published in the *American Journal of Dance Therapy Vol.18*, no.2, 1996 and presented as a keynote speech at the First International Dance/Movement Therapy Conference 'Language of movement,' Nervenklinik Spandau, Berlin, Germany, 1994.

tribal living has accelerated dramatically. For countless centuries preceding this change, we belonged before we asked 'who am I?' We were born belonging, not only to a tribalbody but we belonged to the earthbody. We were held by a sacred vessel. As the Western world has developed, we have increasingly been urged first toward the question: 'Who am I?', forgetting about the essential relationship between the individual and the interconnectedness among all beings, encouraged to leave the sacred circle.

I am grateful for the insistence of the question 'who am I?' for the privilege of personal consciousness. I am grateful for the opportunity to heal original wounds and thus change my experience of myself and my experience of others. Individual development is a remarkable aspect of freedom. Because of this freedom, I have learned to look at many parts of myself, to see how these parts create myself, to see the impact of these parts on my body and, finally, to see that I am my body. This sorting through the parts, a very Western way of understanding, has offered a particular kind of learning, resulting in a particular kind of self-knowledge. This knowledge can feel life-saving. And yet, at the same time, it becomes life-threatening if we dare to assume it is enough. Individuals consistently reach for this deserved and blessed freedom and the unraveling of our world becomes more and more visible. It is not enough when the development of the self excludes an integrated relationship to the whole.

In Daniel Quinn's (1992) novel, *Ishmael*, a gorilla, who is the teacher, says:

> You [humans] know how to split atoms, how to send explorers to the moon, how to splice genes, but you don't know how people ought to live (p.89) ...I have amazing news for you. Man is not alone on this planet. He is part of a community, upon which he depends absolutely. (p.101)

The problem: too many of us don't feel part of anything, really, except the system we create in our schedule books.

In the best of all possible Western worlds our sons and daughters are becoming conscious as they leave home and move into the larger experience of the collective world. These days they hear about global problems, are asked to help save their world. But these young adults are just barely learning about the presence of their internalized mother and father! And, of course, they feel they must understand these aspects of themselves so their own children, now in the wings, don't suffer as they have.

But they are told that the world's children – people, animals, forests – are suffering and on the brink of annihilation. This possibility of consciousness of the end of the planet is peculiarly new for the human psyche. Television, literature, even the corporate world, talk about environmental and global questions with a new sense of urgency. Now, instead of just discovering work and a mate, instead of just creating a home and babies, our children must somehow remember that they are part of a larger whole and that the whole is suffering in a particular way.

This is an idea, not a knowing. Most have not grown up as members of a circle – their parents are not members of a circle. Their experience of the extended family, perhaps the nuclear family, is splintered, segmented, not held by or felt to be in relationship with a visible, constant collective. Their recent heritage has taught them the supreme importance of their individual future, getting ahead, gaining power, moving up the ladder.

Over-emphasis on individual development encouraged outside of a sacred circle has contributed significantly to the creation of unbearable rage, isolation and despair. In response, the desire to return to one's unquestioned place in the circle can be awakened. But we can easily romanticize possible membership in the collective without fully understanding the shadow aspects of belonging, why the circle has become absent. Our work in the Western world has been fiercely concerned with freeing the individual from the bonds of religious, political and familial rule. Accepting one's place in the circle could threaten this process of the development of the self. If membership is unconscious, the loss of freedom results. Unconscious commitment to a group ideology, participating in a mass psychology, means loss of freedom for all people involved.

Individualism, independence, even ego development, can threaten conscious membership in a collective when such processes are not in correct relationship to the whole. However, individuation, which is described by Jung (1961) as 'coming to selfhood' or 'self-realization' (p.365), can enable us to richly and responsibly enter our place in the collective. Now our unprecedented task, perhaps unknown to our ancestors, is to bring the gifts of individuation into conscious membership in the whole, to find a way to be uniquely ourselves inside a sacred, conscious circle.

How we discover this is a great mystery. Willing membership just with our minds cannot create the shift in consciousness for which we long. The shift must be an embodied shift. It is in our bodies where the phenomenon of life energy, a physical reality, is directly experienced. One by one, knowing (and knowing implies consciousness), knowing in our bodies that we belong, creates a collective body in which life energy is shared. I imagine the collective body as the energetic consciousness of the earthbody, which includes all living beings. It is the body-felt connectedness among people, profoundly related to the source of our humanity.

Becoming conscious of our part in the whole through direct experience of membership allows exploration of the relationship between the personal body and the collective body. When our individual bodies have been wounded because of our suffering, we often are opened toward embodied personal consciousness. Our earthbody is wounded. Can we, because of personal consciousness, become opened toward consciousness of the collective body? Can we create a sacred, conscious circle that evolves organically from the knowing body of each member?

Embodiment of the collective: Spirit

If we are longing for direct experience of this unitive state with the whole, we are longing, by definition, for access to our souls. One cannot have a mystical experience or access to soul without getting a glimpse of the inter-connectedness of all things. Mystics from the beginning of time have known this, but in the history of Western civilization mystics have been at the fringe of society, their absence supporting our forgetting. We have forgotten how mystical experience comes about, that it occurs in our bodies because we are a microcosm of the whole.

Can we remember that our bodies are more similar than different? Can we remember that the basic structures of our planet are repeated in the basic structures of our bodies? Mandelbrot, a contemporary scientist, discovered the phenomenon of scaling or fractal geometry (Shore 1993). John Briggs (1992), a contemporary teacher and writer, tells us that fractals are a new pattern, which could provide a powerful incentive for turning our attention away from the activity of the 'parts' of nature toward the activity of the whole. This geometry describes the astounding similarity of form in the patterns of nature. For example, blood vessels, tree roots and river beds have the same basic structure. We, as human beings, have the same basic structure! Embodying collective consciousness means extending such knowledge in our minds toward finding a way to directly experience this membership. I believe we are starving for access to such experience because we cannot endure the pain, the isolation, the despair of the separateness, from our own spirit and from each other. I believe these two are inseparable.

Embodying spirit frees me to remember that I am you and you are me, an ancient practice of many mystical traditions. If you are me, you know how afraid I am, how hopeful, how doubting, how strong, how vulnerable I am.

You know that I'm doing the very best I can and how deeply I need to be seen, embraced. If I am you, I know of your fear, your hope, your doubt, your strength and vulnerability. I know you are doing the very best you can and that you desire to be loved as you are. Remembering that 'I am because we are' can encourage a freedom from fear and doubt. Such freedom enables hope and strength.

Authentic Movement and the collective body

The practice of Authentic Movement provides one way for us to learn about this freedom. In this form we can begin to trace the evolution of the development of collective consciousness through the experience of each body, as unconscious material in mover or witness becomes conscious in the presence of others. Thankfully, there are endless ways in the world for individuals to become conscious of membership. I need to begin to mark some within my practice as my need to know, not think about, the web of interconnectedness is urgent.

The ground of the discipline of Authentic Movement is the relationship between the moving self and the witnessing self. The heart of the practice is about the longing, as well as the fear, to see ourselves clearly. We repeatedly discover that such an experience of clarity is deeply and inextricably related to the gift of being seen clearly by another and, just as importantly, related to the gift of seeing another clearly (Adler 1987).

The mover, who is the expert on his own experience (Weir 1969), works with eyes closed in the presence of the witness, who sits still to the side of the movement space. The mover listens inwardly for the occurrence of impulse toward movement. This movement, visible or invisible to the witness, shapes the mover's body as it becomes a vessel through which unconscious material awakens into consciousness. As he internalizes his witness's desire to accept him, to accept his suffering as well as his beauty, embodiment of the density of his personal history empties, enabling him at times to feel seen by the witness and, more importantly, to see himself clearly. Sometimes...it is grace...the mover embodies a clear presence.

The witness practices the art of seeing. Seeing clearly is not about knowing what the mover needs or must do. The witness does not 'look at' the mover but, instead, as she internalizes the mover, she attends to her own experiences of judgement, interpretation and projection in response to the mover as catalyst. As she acknowledges ownership of her experiences, the density of her personal history empties, enabling the witness at times to feel that she can see the mover clearly and, more importantly, that she can see herself clearly. Sometimes…it is grace…the witness embodies a clear presence.

A central aspect of the theoretical structure of the form is that each person, without hurting oneself or another, is free to choose to do what he or she must do, constantly balancing surrender and will in the process. In the midst of such concentration on owning one's own experience as mover or witness it matters that others are attempting the same practice, thus trusting some inherent order in the collective. Trying to be a good group member, putting the imagined needs of the group before individual needs, is not what is intended. When each individual does what he or she must do, regardless of content, we notice that the group as a whole 'seems' to be in synchrony.

This synchrony could be related to the presence of each individual's internal witness, which develops in relationship to the clarity and compassion of the external witness. The internal witness becomes awareness itself, silent and clear. It can evolve out of a developing and discerning ego which accepts, rejects, debates, protects, exposes, tracks, guides our experience of reality. It is the process of the development of the internal witness that creates the possibility of consciously choosing membership in a collective.

Wishing to better understand this organic interconnectedness between individuals and the group, my intention has shifted in the last several years in my teaching practice from focus on the intimacy of interpersonal work within the structure described above to focus on the whole. With the dyadic work between the mover and the witness as ground, movers now always move within a circle of witnesses. Within this newer format, whether moving or witnessing, people are invited to remember that they are not participating alone. Like most individual bodies, the collective body is in the process of becoming conscious.

The only way I know how to become conscious of my relationship to the collective body as a whole system is into and through my own body. My body is my teacher. Joan Halifax (1993) quotes the Zen monk Dogen: 'You should know that the entire earth is not our temporary appearance, but our genuine human body' (p.202). I can think about my body as a collective: millions of one cell units; thousands of two separate cells in relationship; a multitude of clusters of cells creating organs, bones, muscles; many clusters in many configurations which make my whole self; and, finally, the energy inside and around me, which could be called spirit.

How does the human body, as a collective in itself, mirror the collective body? In the collective body we can see the intrapersonal work of each person, like each cell doing its job. We can see combinations of two people in relationship, the interpersonal connection, like two cells working together. Now, like a cluster of cells creating an organ, such as the heart, we can see clusters of people, some small like the family and others including more people, like a village. Just as many clusters of cells create a whole person, many villages create counties, states, nations, the whole world. And like the spirit within and around the individual person, there is energy in the universe within and around the earth.

Stories: The collective body becoming conscious

There are stories from my practice of Authentic Movement about movers and witnesses which mark, for me, the evolution of the conscious development of the collective body. I have selected, among a plethora of potent stories, a few to discuss here. It is important to remember that stories are not what actually happened. Stories are about what the storyteller perceived as happening. As I tell you these stories about people's experience I am including in the first two stories the feelings they experienced while moving, which they shared with us later when they were speaking about their movement. Participants in my workshops are professional adults – therapists, artists, nurses, lawyers and social workers. I am grateful to each participant for making possible my questions, my learning.

One person / One cell

I begin with one person in the whole world, whom I have named Marie. This woman closes her eyes and enters the movement space, focused totally on her own work. As usual, she has a small blanket with her. She lies down on the floor and barely moves for twenty to sixty minutes at a time. She feels like a baby. She feels completely alone. Now she remembers: her mother was seriously ill and taken away for many years to a hospital. She and her siblings were cared for by their grandmother, a sixty-five-year-old arthritic woman. She hears her grandmother's voice saying what a good baby she was, never crying. Now, again, she remembers nothing. She simply is still and alone. Like one cell in one body, Marie is one human being on the earth. Her isolated experience occurs in the Authentic Movement studio, in the midst of nineteen other possibly isolated experiences, individuals bringing unconscious material into consciousness through embodiment.

Two people / Two cells

After a year's work in which lying still was her primary experience as a mover, another mover, whom I shall name Andrea, accidentally encounters Marie. Andrea is crawling around with her eyes closed, as if she is searching. She finds many different movers doing different things but she keeps searching. She does not know for what she is searching. Now she touches Marie, who seems to be barely breathing she is so still. Andrea stops. She strokes the side of Marie's face with the back of her hand and begins to weep. As she cries over this body, she slowly remembers her last days with her dying little child, four years ago. She experiences a depth of pain which had been forgotten, too terrible to remember, re-enter, re-live.

Now Marie starts to move in new ways, opening toward remembering, re-entering, re-living her last memories of touch from her mother, perhaps before she left or during brief visits. Her mother stroked her face with the back of her hand exactly the way someone is now touching her.

This is a synchronistic, unrehearsed encounter between two adult women, both graced by an opportunity to bring unconscious material into consciousness through embodiment, this time because of each other. For both women, energy which has been physically locked within the cells is now being expressed, released and thus available for new growth in the future. This mutual exchange, this direct experience, is not unlike the meeting of two cells in a body, being where they must be when they must be there, doing what they must do.

A village / A cluster of cells

Another year passes. Ten witnesses are in a circle around ten movers. Today Marie, as a mover, walks slowly around the room, encountering people and then moving on. Now she is lying down on this side of the circle, moving slightly. Bert is pacing outside the witness circle. Now he enters the circle, crawling, and begins to make angry noises. As his movements intensify and his sounds become roars, he crawls across the circle and out the other side into a corner of the room. He is thrashing from side to side, hitting the walls, roaring loudly. Now Marie gets up, leaves the room, comes back with her blanket, wraps herself in it, curls up on the floor and quietly begins to cry. Jake goes to the corner where Bert is roaring and sits quietly nearby.

Andrea, who is also a mover, stands at the edge of the circle, feet widely planted, and conducts, as if an orchestra leader. Bert thrashes more and more audibly in the corner. A witness, whose gaze is riveted on Bert, begins to cry silently as her hands go to her neck. Dianna, a mover, is lying on her back, tapping her hands lightly on the floor as she sings nursery rhymes. Joanna, another mover, crawls very slowly toward Marie, whose crying intensifies as she rhythmically throws her torso over her knees.

Suddenly, Bert bolts from his corner and heads toward Marie on his hands and knees. Joanna, hearing his approach, races him there, crawling. Arriving first because she was closer, she scoops Marie into her arms. Now Marie, safe in the arms of a woman, screams and sobs, her body fiercely contracting and releasing. Bert continues to make sounds and tries to touch Marie with his face. Lila, another mover, wraps her arms and legs around Joanna and Marie, creating a barrier between them and Bert. Ingrid, also a mover, tries to directly engage Bert in battle. He tolerates this interruption only briefly and goes back to Marie, but with reduced ferocity. Now Lila tentatively strokes his hair and, as he quiets, he gently touches Marie, who is no longer crying but is still safely held by Joanna.

After the movement time, movers and witnesses speak of their experience, not only bringing consciousness to what had been unconscious within their idiosyncratic personal history but finding their part in the whole as the story unfolds. Bert talks of his rage and his memory of the terrible physical presence of the man who repeatedly abused him when he was a young boy. Marie tells how Bert's angry noises awakened her feeling, encouraging her to express her own pain.

Jake is now realizing that when he sat near Bert in the corner he was re-entering his childhood experiences, his need to stay near his deaf brother, as if to protect him from his parents' confused and erratic responses. As Andrea heard the raging she found herself conducting, re-entering, re-living her efforts to control her father's rage at her when she could not save her dying child. Dianna tells us that nursery rhymes were a familiar cadence — her mother trying to soothe her when her father lost his temper. The witness with her hands on her neck tells us how she experienced Bert as a caged lion and how her experience of him being trapped awakened her claustrophobic terror of being caught in the unconscious web of her family.

Joanna speaks of her experience as an abandoned baby in a hospital and how she felt when she heard a baby cry in an unsafe room. She had to protect the baby. Marie tells us that when Joanna scooped her into her arms it was then that she could fully and safely surrender to her pain, her rage at the neglect of being left alone and unattended for long periods of time when she was a baby. Bert responds by speaking of his great need to get to the unprotected child in himself, somehow connecting his innocence with the power of his abuser. One witness said: 'I saw a caged lion whose cub had escaped. He was only trying to get to his cub. He wasn't going to hurt it.' Lila, the woman who wrapped her long limbs around Joanna and Marie, suddenly speaks. Just now she is remembering how often she tried to mediate between her father and her mother, quietly, hoping no one would notice. Ingrid hesitantly speaks of her anger toward her husband and how it was ignited as she heard Bert roaring. She tells us of her relief as she embodied her anger.

This unrehearsed, synchronous unfolding of events creates a village story. Movers and witnesses participate within the complexity of their individual personalities, doing what they each must do. It is the story of a collection of people bringing unconscious material into consciousness, through embodiment, because of each other. It is not unlike a cluster of cells, like the heart, in which each cell is doing what it must do, resulting in a pumping heart.

The whole earth / The whole body

In the next story we leave the details of personal history and see qualities of the human psyche which exist regardless of personality. If we follow the above mentioned metaphor, we move from a village story or cluster of cells to a phenomenon shared by most of humanity on earth, thus to the whole body. Almost everybody, at some point in development, fears their own death. At this time, it is interesting to note, many also fear the death of our earth.

Members arrive at a workshop full of the pain of challenging experiences which occurred in the previous weeks. Jake speaks of a persistent intestinal disease. Joanna speaks of being in another city, far away, with her mother, who is suffering from a double mastectomy. Another woman tells us of her two major abdominal operations in six weeks. Ingrid reports on her recent hip replacement. Lila describes moving again to a new house, the third move in six months. And Dianna mentions the fact that she continues to lose weight but the doctors do not know what is wrong. Judd has returned to the group after major surgery and radiation therapy, which have visibly affected his appearance. He is wearing an oversized jacket, a hat and a large shawl. He does not speak. Exhaustion, immobility and lack of protection seem to be shared experiences by most group members.

In our first session of moving and witnessing eight movers sleep, two snore! The second day, six people arrive late because they were lost! Marie is one of these participants. When she comes into the studio she decides to be a witness and draws as she sees, a not uncommon mode for certain witnesses. Movers come back from the movement time and speak of their pain. Marie asks to show her drawing but there is no time left.

In the afternoon I suggest that we return to the dyadic work for two reasons: to practice witness skills in an effort to strengthen the witness circle, thus reinforcing the strength of the container, and to give movers the intimacy of one-to-one work, thus reinforcing trust and safety in relationship to their material. But everyone wants to be a mover. No one wants to be a witness. The resistance to witnessing is palpable, people saying they are too tired or that they need to be witnessed and thus wouldn't be good witnesses. I choose to attempt to keep strong boundaries in the structure of our time together and so we work carefully with witnessing skills for the next few sessions. Each time we all come back together to discuss our process, Marie asks to show her drawing. Because of the amount and intensity of material in the group, there is no time.

On the third day of the retreat it is time for a long circle in which people can move or witness whenever they wish. Judd is the first to enter the empty circle. In the course of the last two days he has gradually shed his outer garments. Now we can see him more clearly as he slowly sways back and forth until he loses his balance, begins to fall, catches himself and then begins to sway again. The witness circle feels strong as others choose to move, each coming closer to themselves in the presence of each other. The energy continues to be mostly low, quiet and pained.

At the end of the long circle movers and witnesses speak of their experiences. Jake is angry because I rang the bell too early. Andrea is angry because Dianna spoke too long. Others speak about their exhaustion and pain. Theresa suddenly asks: 'What is going on here?' Judd's fist comes slamming down into the center of the circle as he insists: 'We must name it!' Lila says: 'Fear of physical illness and death.' Ingrid says: 'It is as if we are in bardo, the gap, the place between life and death.' Marie shouts: 'I'm going to show my picture now!' and holds up a charcoal drawing of the bardo state, a drawing of people wandering around in black capes, not knowing. Relief among the group is visible. The collective embodiment of the fear of death makes it available for consciousness. Naming it, 'holding' it together, somehow makes it more bearable. Collective consciousness again made it possible for each to understand better his or her particular role, including Bert – for whom the theme concerning fear of death had no particular meaning at this time.

Judd now speaks of his fear of his own death, describing how he feels it in his stomach. This brings a universal fear back down and into one body, grounding the collective in an essential way. After all, the collective is a manifestation of a collection of individual bodies, individual lives. In this case the personal life of each man and woman grappling with the fear of his or her own death in the presence of each other is the collective body becoming conscious.

Now, the last day, the witness circle is unusually strong. Movers are running, shouting, leaping, piling on top of one another. I see eight people in a people pile, the first morning I saw – and heard – eight people sleeping! We need our tribe desperately. We need to feel membership, especially in relationship to the mysteries, the unknown, the ways in which spirit moves.

The universe / Spirit

The last story is about spirit, the energy inside and around the body. On our earth, most all people know at some point in their lives a fear of death. But in the universe at large, which could be called the energy inside and around the earth, death is inseparable from birth, time and space merge, material disperses and reforms, particle and wave become indistinguishable. In the universe a high order is manifest indefinitely. This order or clarity in the universe, whether perceived or not, could be understood as the witness circle, the clear presence, containing the earthbody.

The story I am about to tell is a projection of my experience as a witness, which is another way to participate in the collective body becoming conscious. As we share our experiences of witnessing the whole or being movers within the whole, we understand a little more about belonging. When witnessing this particular long circle, which occurred in Italy where twenty-five women from different European countries joined me to study and practice the form of Authentic Movement, I experienced a fullness of response to each individual as well as to a collective story.

I have named this story 'The Call.' Each time a voice called out, a particular archetypal aspect of the human psyche was acknowledged, accepted. In this story I saw how new energy repeatedly, cyclically accrues from life, how it is gathered, contained, dispersed back into the collective through one body, then another, then another. I saw an embodiment of my experience of our present state on this planet.

We all began as witnesses, experiencing the empty center. Slowly, one by one, some witnesses chose to move and others held the container by continuing to witness until they chose to move and movers chose to witness. And so the story begins:

I see a senior woman standing on the edge of the circle, facing out, her arms folded in front of her: a gatekeeper on the edge of the earth. At her feet, I see a woman wrapped in a blanket: a baby, new. I see innocence.

A woman walks to the center of the circle, her arms slowly lifting, calling.

I see a woman pounding, yelling, pulling her hair: destruction, despair, hatred, pain. I see suffering.

A woman suddenly stands, reaching her arms straight out to her side, calling.

I see three movers on the other side of the circle laughing, playing, tumbling: joy, beauty, love. I see freedom.

A woman begins turning, calling, a long steady call.

I see a woman standing, holding her hands in front of her as if she holds a thick tube reaching from the floor to the ceiling. She moves very little but tension visibly builds in her body, her focus strong and steady: energy accruing in one body. She releases the tension, pounding her heel into the floor: a body as vessel shattering, birthing new energy, which is sent into the earth through her heel. I see transformation.

A woman lies flat on the floor, calling into the earth.

Women clap and sing in rhythm with the pounding heel, and come to their feet, one by one, stomping and chanting: new energy is dispersed, flowing into many bodies.

I see one woman, crouched at the feet of the dancers, hiding her face: the one not ready.

A woman suddenly moves backward to the wall, screaming: fear of the unknown manifest as the new energy escalates.

Another woman, acknowledging fear, meets the screaming woman until the terror evaporates: fear of the unknown shared and thus contained. These two women – who is leading, who is following? – slowly re-enter the circle. Now a third woman walks with them. They walk so slowly.

The second woman continues, out the other side of the circle, arriving at the open window, calling out into the hills: a call to the gods for help.

A woman calls out from the other open window on the other side of the room: in response, in support, calling the gods for help.

I see a woman lying near the edge of the circle, silent, unmoving: the one who does not know what to do.

A woman sits on the floor with her legs open, breathing harder and harder: labor before a birth.

A woman wraps her legs from behind around the birthing woman. She pushes her pelvis forward, into the back of the birthing woman. Now she reaches up, out of her efforts and calls, a call for new life.

A woman is weaving shapes in the air with intense focus, directly in front of the woman who sits with her legs open: the cosmic mid-wife.

I see a woman moving around the entire outside of the circle, stepping into long deep strides, droning: the cosmic shaman, containing it all.

Again and again, I see a woman sitting on the floor with her legs open, breathing harder and harder: labor before a birth. Will new life occur? This birth is not about an individual who will save our earth. This is the birth of the collective body.

Now I see a woman sitting in a corner, raging: anger, frustration, violence, hopelessness.

A woman crawls toward her, waiting, listening at her feet. I see compassion.

The clock tells me to lift the bell and let it ring. It is time to rest. It is not time for the birth. How is readiness determined? For now, like children, we are in the process of remembering something we once knew long ago and, simultaneously, we are glimpsing our potential for discovering something completely new, something we have never before experienced. In the meantime, we are loving the best we can.

References

Adler J. (1987) 'Who is the witness?' *Contact Quarterly*, Winter, 20–29.

Blyth, H.R. (1960) *Zen and Zen Classics. Volume 1.* Tokyo, Japan: The Hokuseido Press.

Briggs, J. (1992) *Fractals, the Patterns of Chaos: A New Aesthetic of Art, Science and Nature.* New York: Simon & Schuster.

Halifax, J. (1993) *The Fruitful Darkness: Reconnecting with the Body of the Earth.* San Francisco: HarperSanFrancisco.

Jung, C.G. (1961) *Memories, Dreams, Reflections.* New York: Random House.

Quinn, D. (1992) *Ishmael.* New York: Bantam.

Russell, P. (1992) *The White Hole in Time: Our Future Evolution and the Meaning of Now.* San Francisco: HarperSanFrancisco.

Shore, S. (1993) 'The fractal geometry of experience'. *Annandale 133*, 1, 12–19.

Weir, J. (1969) Personal communication.

Joan Chodorow

Joan Chodorow's Papers

It is thirty-five years now since I began to study with Mary Starks Whitehouse. I was in my mid-twenties and in the midst of the transition from teaching dance to becoming a dance therapist. I was engaged with the inner-directed world of Jungian analysis that had long been central to Mary's life and work. Inevitably, my experiences with Mary became deeply interwoven with analysis and with my developing practice as a dance therapist. In addition to the profound experience of movement as active imagination I studied each of Mary's papers as they became available. When I met Janet Adler ten years later, I felt a similar sense of kinship and was deeply impressed with her and inspired by her work and her writings. Janet made essential links between dance therapy and psychotherapy that no one had made before, providing a lens that let me see the richness and strength of Mary's contribution in even greater depth and differentiation. It is a great honor now to follow the contributions of Mary and Janet as I add my own to the historical works of this volume.

The following essays show the development of many of my ideas over a period of seventeen years, from 1974 to 1991. As I reflect on my writing style, it ranges from some early efforts that feel formal and stiff to the more spontaneous quality of the interview. I offer them now essentially unchanged, with all their imperfections, and trust that the questions they explore remain vital and alive today.

The interview conducted by Nisha Zenoff in 1986 leads all the way back to the love I felt at the age of seven for the moving imagination, first on a trapeze and then in ballet. In 'Philosophy and Methods of Individual Work in Dance Therapy' (1974) I discuss outer-directed and inner-directed ways of working and try to show how both are essential aspects of dance therapy practice. 'Dance Therapy and the Transcendent Function' (1977) was my first attempt to go more deeply into the connection between Jung's active imagination and the practice of dance therapy. 'Dance/Movement and Body Experience in Analysis' (1982/1995) is my first contribution to the Jungian literature, an interweaving of many resources. 'To Move and be Moved' (1984) presents for the first time my ideas about the origins of expressive movement in the psyche. I discussed the personal unconscious, the cultural unconscious, the primordial unconscious, and the Self, and tried to differentiate the movement themes that emerge. 'The Body as Symbol' (1986) introduces five symbolic events that seem to reflect certain stages of developing consciousness during the first year and a half of life. All of this material was further developed in my book *Dance Therapy and Depth Psychology: The Moving Imagination,* published in 1991 by Routledge. In 'Active Imagination' (1991) I tried to show how all the creative arts psychotherapies can trace their roots to Jung's early contribution. My long and continuing passion for this material led me recently to edit and introduce a volume entitled *Jung on Active Imagination,* published in 1997 by Princeton University Press.

My analytic practice, teaching and writing continue as a dynamic triad. I am writing a book now about active imagination as a comprehensive method of psychotherapy, based on my understanding of the intrinsic forms of the imagination. I shall work also as editor with Louis Stewart on his opus *Affect and Archetype: Foundations of the Psyche.* For me, the great gift of authentic movement is to work symbolically with the raw material of the unconscious. As the primal stuff of impulse and image emerge as symbolic physical action, we enter the realm of the imagination in both its wounding and healing aspects. We don't have to understand the natural healing function of the imagination in order to benefit from it. But the questions are essential as we move toward a deeper understanding of why we work the way we do.

Joan Chodorow
January 1998

CHAPTER 15

An Interview with Joan Chodorow[1]

Nancy R. Zenoff

Joan Chodorow is a dance/movement therapist and Jungian analyst practicing in Fairfax, California, a small, peaceful town across the Golden Gate Bridge from San Francisco. She is a graduate of the C.G. Jung Institute of Los Angeles and a member of the Jung Institute of San Francisco. She has been actively involved in dance/movement therapy for the past 24 years.

She studied with Trudi Schoop and Mary Whitehouse in the early 1960s, then received her MA degree in psychology and dance therapy from Goddard College. She was one of the first dance therapists in California and one of the first to be licensed as a marriage, family and child counselor. In 1972 she co-ordinated the first California regional American Dance Therapy Association (ADTA) Conference, was elected Vice-President of the American Dance Therapy Association in 1972 and served as its President from 1974 to 1976. She can be seen in the ADTA film *Dance therapy: the power of movement.*

Joan has made a unique contribution in dance/movement therapy by putting the wordless into words. Since 1971 she has written numerous articles and publications on the philosophy and practice of dance therapy. Two of her early writings – *What is dance therapy, really?* and *Philosophy and methods of individual work in dance therapy* – were among the first efforts to build a theory of movement therapy, particularly of individual work. When they appeared, these articles were among the few written teaching materials available. From that beginning she has continued to share in written form the record of her evolving thought, as represented by her articles *Dance and body experience in analysis* (1982; 1995), *To move and be moved* (1984), *The body as symbol: dance/movement in analysis* (1986).

1   Interview previously published in *American Journal of Dance Therapy*, Vol. 9, 1986.

Today, in addition to her private practice, she continues to write, teach and supervise students and therapists. For many years she has been teaching an intensive summer course in Switzerland.

Joan's enthusiasm, dedication and love of her work are clearly evident as she speaks. As she talks, one senses a subtle non-quite-expressed movement; it seems she could as well dance as speak what she has to say. It is a movement that provides an open space for a person to be and to move with her – in that person's own way.

Through the years of involvement, Joan retains a freshness, liveliness and curiosity about movement of the human body and about the moving body's relationship to the psyche. There is always newness to be discovered, to be met with a sense of wonder and joy.

Joan welcomes me to her home with a warm smile and twinkling blue eyes. We meet for the interview in her studio at one end of her home where she sees clients. On a wall near us at one end of an otherwise open expanse of bare hardwood floor are shelves filled to overflowing with sand-tray figures, ready to enter the waiting sand tray. Outside, on a wood-railed balcony, are art supplies for use when talk, sandplay or movement wants to turn into another form of expression.

In this atmosphere of warmth, welcome and choice Joan and I seat ourselves on soft comfortable chairs and begin to talk.

I: 'Joan, how did the world of dance and movement therapy begin for you?'

JC: 'It began with the world of dance. Like so many of us, dance was the center of my childhood and teen years. As a young adult, I danced; I was a dancer and dance teacher. But what led me to dance therapy was working with pre-school age children. Up to that point, my idea of teaching was to train young dancers. Then my world turned around completely when I was given a group of three-year-olds to work with. I couldn't teach them any kind of ballet technique. The only way I could learn about how to be with them was to watch them. What I saw was that everything they did was a mirroring of the world in movement: when they saw something, they watched it and imitated it. In that way the children learned about the world through their bodies. It was a revelation for me.

When I started working with those very young children I realized that there was a whole other way of using movement.
And that was, to learn about the world and to learn about
each other. My imagination opened through these little
three-year-olds. Whatever they were interested in was what we
did in class. For example, that particular group of children was
very interested in bugs. We happened to be in an East L.A.
studio that had a lot of bugs in it, so we would look at the
bugs and watch the way they walked and try to walk like bugs
did. And we also remembered and enacted fairy tales, scenes
from nature, family relationships – all the things the children
were interested in. We would think of what an older brother
or sister is like and how would they move.'

I: 'How did you make the transition from watching the bugs and
thinking about the brothers and sisters to where you knew
you were doing dance therapy?'

JC: 'It's just that those years of work with very young children,
and their parents and teachers, gave me an understanding of
development that's been essential to every aspect of my work
as a dance therapist, verbal psychotherapist and Jungian
analyst. Children develop a sense of who they are through
symbolic play. As adults, we do the same thing but call it
creative imagination. Any in-depth approach to psychotherapy
helps us develop a sense of who we are through the
imagination. In a sense, active or creative imagination is play –
play with images.

All of us have ways of giving form to the imagination, and for
some of us it has to be through the body. Some of us imagine
best through our bodies. I discovered this when I was about
seven – and my father built me a trapeze. It was an ecstatic
kind of experience to swing back and forth on that wonderful
trapeze under an old cottonwood tree. I would literally wait
through the day at school to get home and spend the rest of
the afternoon on the trapeze, hanging from my arms, legs,
knees – often upside down. When I was moving, I could
imagine myself as anything in the world. My imagination
opened up when my body was moving; I knew that that was

my way into a very special world. I would now call it, perhaps, by different names.'

I: 'By what names?'

JC: 'Relationship of conscious and unconscious or relationship of
         psyche and soma – that sort of thing. It basically was going
         into the world of the imagination while at the same time
         remaining grounded in the world of the body – that is, the
         world the way it is. For me, it happened most fully through
         movement, through the body. I started ballet lessons around
         the same time. My first teacher, also when I was around seven
         or eight – her name was Jane Denham, a beautiful young
         dancer – she taught strong technique but, toward the end of
         each class, she also made time for improvisation. The children
         formed a magic circle and, one at a time, we'd go into the
         circle and become anything in the world or we could enter
         any imaginary landscape or we could be ourselves and interact
         with any imaginal being. Those moments were what made the
         dance so wonderful. Did you have something like that?'

I: 'I had the ocean.'

JC: 'I think the trapeze was a way simply to be with myself. Then
         dance became a way not only to be myself but also to
         communicate with others through the imagination. Once I
         began dancing, I knew that that was what I wanted to do. I
         became very focused and committed, as young dancers are.
         You just devote your whole life to that.'

I: 'Were you a professional dancer?'

JC: 'Yes, I was a professional dancer in my late teens and early
         twenties. My main ballet teacher was Carmelita Marocci.
         Carmelita has a kind of passion about the purpose of dance.
         She taught ballet technique but it was all in the service of
         expressing powerful images – to touch the heights or depths
         of human experience. But when I began to get jobs dancing,
         the jobs that were available around Hollywood in those years
         called for a very different approach to dance. I took the jobs
         that were available in nightclubs, summer stock, musical
         comedy. I did those for a couple of years. Some of it was good

work but most of it was depressing. It was far from the imaginative, emotional experiences that had made me want to dance in the first place.

So I went into teaching, at first just as a way to work in between performing, but when I began working with children and teaching ballet to children and incorporating the magic circle – that is, improvisation as part of the ballet classes – I knew that I wanted to teach more than to perform. Shortly after the transition from professional dance to teaching, I began working with the nursery school children, and that was when the whole world opened up. I began to understand that the same thing we think of as the child developing fully into who she or he is is absolutely intertwined with the creative process. For some children, movement is the best way. Dance is an enrichment for everyone. But some of us, by nature, are ourselves most vividly when we are moving, expressing ourselves through the body.

That was the transition. In 1962 a social worker invited me to come up onto a psychiatric unit and work with the autistic children. I remember the first day I went up there. As I said, I had no psychological training. I had a strong background in dance and I could work with children. I had learned from the pre-school children to follow what they were interested in rather than impose my ideas. But it was a powerful experience, those early weeks of working on the children's psychiatric unit.

This was old County Hospital in Los Angeles. As I remember, you went onto an elevator and went up to the sixth floor. Staff were dressed in white uniforms and patients were dressed more the way that I was dressed. Many of us have had these experiences in institutions. I remember carrying the phonograph, the records, the scarves and the drum up the elevator, and no one quite knowing what classification I was, whether staff or patient, because you had to wear the proper uniforms, which I didn't.

The first time I went up there it was exciting and also difficult because I had never seen psychotic children who were hallucinating. Some of the children were also blind. Some were deaf. Many were just mumbling to themselves. You could not tell whether their eyes were rolled back because of an inner vision or whether their eyes were rolled back because they couldn't see. It was an old building and the staff were doing their best. I remember a room with peeling yellow paint and radiators. Some of the kids were climbing on radiators. Others were walking on their toes or creeping on the floor – very much in their own worlds.

And somehow I had the sense that if I could just put on wonderful music, it would change everything. As I remember, I put on a Russian Hopak. There were a couple of staff and a couple of children who liked the music. We somehow got into a loose circle, with the children moving in and out of it. Some of the kids were shrieking and boisterous. The circle was not imposed, we just started running around. We were stamping and doing different kinds of clapping and other things and the more active children joined in. And then there was a little boy who thought it would be more interesting to get down to his knees and bark like a dog. I'd been working with nursery school children enough to know that that was the thing to do. So I got down on my knees and joined him in the barking and some of the other children began to bark. But then a little girl wandered off – one of the children on her toes with her eyes rolled back. So I took off the folk dance music and put on a Debussy piece with a cloud-like sound to invite her back in. I passed out some scarves. I think many of us must be familiar with what happened next: the scarves disappeared into the clothes and mouths and other body openings as they do with many of those kids. Yet somehow the energy and music and movement kept us connected. Later, when I put on a Mexican hat dance, some more of the attendants came and joined in. We ended up having as wonderful a time as we could. And when it was over, some of the children cheered and others wandered off and mumbled to themselves. The tired-looking attendants clapped and smiled. The chief psychiatrist had been watching from behind the one-way glass and what was reported to me was that he said: "The children have never gotten such good exercise. Hire her."'

I: 'The first dance therapist in that hospital!'

JC: 'So what people got was a sense of the spirit and the good exercise. I guess I became a dance therapist that day.

That happened in 1962. My daughter was three years old. I was going through a divorce and had started Jungian analysis, or was about to start. I can't exactly recall the sequence but all these things converged. And in that same year I began to study with Trudi Schoop and Mary Whitehouse.'

I: 'You studied with them both at the same time?'

JC: 'Right. I'd had my first experience with Trudi in 1956 when I was teaching ballet at Dance Center on Western Boulevard in Los Angeles. Trudi was a world-famous dancer who had settled in Los Angeles. I had heard all about her, I knew that she did wonderful pantomime and I wanted to study with her. But I was nineteen years old then and not yet ready to learn what she had to teach. At that time, I was still contained in the style of ballet. I was dancing professionally and had begun to do some teaching. When I took Trudi's class that first time, she had us do all kinds of things. After an energetic warm-up, she led us through progressions across the floor, one after the other. We improvised around a variety of sensory images, played with imaginary balls of different sizes and weights, did lopsided walks as we struggled to carry an imaginary suitcase.'

I: 'You just looked as if you wanted to get up and dance it. Please do.'

JC: 'I loved it, I was excited, but also increasingly uneasy. As a ballet dancer, I was used to being in control of my body. Trudi's class demanded more freedom than I could handle at the time. As the momentum built, we were imagining and expressing the widest range of dramatic experiences. At one point I lost touch with the motivating image. People seemed to be giving themselves over to the compelling, rhythmic music and letting it carry them across the room. All I know is that I did the same thing, just hurled myself into the space. I must have gone unconscious because I couldn't remember what I'd done. I just found myself landing on both feet, hard, on the other side of the room. I was out of breath. My heart was pounding. I had this awful feeling that somehow the ultimate shadow had emerged and I hadn't seen it but everyone else had. It was more than I could deal with at the time. I felt embarrassed and awkward and didn't want anyone to know how awkward I felt, so I just kept going in the same direction, up the steps and into the dressing room. I pulled some street clothes on over my leotards and left. It took five years of growing up before I felt ready to come back to study with Trudi Schoop.'

I: 'So, in 1962 you came back to work with Trudi.'

JC: 'Yes. By then I was studying with Trudi, studying with Mary. I was in my first analysis with Kate Marcus, who was one of the founders of the Jung Institute in Los Angeles. I was learning about what life is like as a single mother. Lori was three then. I had a storefront ballet studio in East L.A. called the Community Dance Studio. I'd begun a collaboration with Ethel Young, who was the director of Heights Cooperative Nursery School, which was across the street from my studio. Our most intense collaboration was through the mid-sixties, but we still keep in touch. Ethel and I developed a way of using the arts as the core curriculum in early childhood education. Some of that material was used later on in the development of Project Headstart. All of the arts – dance, painting, clay, self-decoration – these were seen as many languages through which the children could express and interpret their experiences, grow into themselves.

Those were years of tremendous learning for me. There was the analytic work, which was essentially sitting in a chair across from a wise old woman and talking about dreams twice a week for about four years, and there were the studies with Mary, which were connected to the analytical work because it was so introverted – it involved going inside and listening for an impulse and then giving it enough attention to let it emerge as action, as movement. And, at the same time, I was studying with Trudi. There we were more likely to enact the movement and it was the fulfillment of the movement that would erupt the related emotion.'

I: 'When you worked with them, did you consider yourself a "dance therapist"? The American Dance Therapy Association was not even founded yet.'

JC: 'Right. I knew that Trudi was a dance therapist and Mary wasn't sure she wanted to call it dance therapy, but I knew that she was using movement as a therapeutic process. I was very interested in someone named Marian Chace who was doing something at St Elizabeth's Hospital. At that time I'd just written a little booklet about dance in nursery school programs. I wrote to Marian Chace and sent her my booklet and she wrote back some nice things about what I'd written and sent me a packet of all of her publications. So I knew that there was dance therapy.'

I: 'Did Marian's use of dance with patients seem similar to ways you were working?'

JC: 'Many of her ideas were familiar but some were not. There was the recognition – "Oh, yes, of course" – and then there was also new information. The emphasis in her work was more on the group interaction and I was beginning, even with the children, to be equally interested in the individual interaction.'

I: 'Joan, my introduction to you was at the 1971 ADTA Conference in Washington, DC. I remember watching a videotape that you made of your work with individuals. Were you doing groups as well? Did you actually ever work with Marian Chace?'

JC: 'Never met her. Never worked with her. We just had that exchange by letter, sharing things we'd written. There was such excitement in those years. We knew that something important was happening, knew that something was starting all over the country. I remember going to the public library in downtown LA, looking through the psychological abstracts for any reports I could find about dance therapy.'

I: 'What did you find?'

JC: 'I found that somewhere – Minnesota comes to mind, but it might have been some other place – in some mental institution, as they called it in those days, they had done a ballroom dance program for patients. And it said that this was helpful and people felt better after the experience. But even that kind of report was scarce.'

I: 'Would you say some more about your involvement with Mary Whitehouse and her influence on your work?'

JC: 'Mary's work had a whole different quality. At that time, she and Jane Manning shared a studio on Santa Monica Boulevard in West LA. There were groups and she also worked one-to-one. When I began with her in 1962 I still tended toward deliberate, stylized movement. What happened with Mary in the early days is that I'd start to move and she'd say "No." And then I'd stop and she'd encourage me to wait. And I'd wait and then I'd start to move again and she'd say "No!" So I did much more waiting than moving in the early months of our work. Then, gradually, I got the sense that I really could let something happen, that I didn't have to pour so much energy into the image. I didn't have to form it consciously. It had its own form. I learned that I could listen to my body and something would happen, then something else would happen.

It was similar to the way I was working with dreams in my analysis, where you would take an image and give it your attention and, as you give it your attention, it changes. And then you give it more attention and see what develops out of that. By attention I mean getting interested in what's going on and imagining what it might be about. Mary taught me to pay attention to and move from images and bodily-felt sensations. You would wait to see what comes up and follow it, and then you'd find yourself in a different landscape, interacting with whoever or whatever appears.

Both Trudi and Mary in those days, as I remember, started their classes – they both called them classes – with warm-up techniques. Mary had studied with Mary Wigman and Martha Graham. But her warm-ups gave more attention to the details than I'd ever experienced. It was the kind of thing where she'd want you to sense the quality of the movement. She would have you work with a particular transition. For example, if it had to do with opening arms from the top, she'd have you stay with just that moment when the arms begin to separate and open wide. Or she would use what we might now call sensory awareness in the midst of a warm-up, and that was a new experience for me – to give that much attention to little, minute movements that were so simple to do. From there we would go into the inner-directed work where you would find a space in the room, close your eyes and go inside and wait. And try not to move too quickly, not to plan on making it too formed but just to let it happen. The words that I remember most strongly from Mary have to do with "let it happen," and every so often she would also say – she said these things in her writing too – "No praise, no blame; just let it happen."'

I: 'Joan, I'm not only interested in your teachers' impact on your work, I would also like to know how you are different from your teachers. What makes you who you are? Listening to your description of your development, I can picture you as that seven-year-old on the trapeze or as the young dancer working with autistic children in the hospital. And here we are, sitting in your studio. You, Joan Chodorow, dancer, dance therapist, Jungian analyst, teacher, writer – so many worlds. Will you say something more about you?'

JC: 'The question of how we are different from our teachers is so important. One of the things that happens when we are deeply connected to our teachers is that we want to be just like them. I wanted to be just like Carmelita. But she is a very different person than I am, with a very different body. Her way of moving had a compactness that I couldn't even begin to do well. When I was studying with Trudi I wanted more than anything to have that kind of comic genius, but I don't. I remember working with Trudi at Camarillo, where she would go into a back ward of depressed people and she would say: "Oh my God, look what you're doing! How can you be so gloomy?! Why do you have your head in your hands?" And all of a sudden, those alienated, seemingly inert, people came to life and began to laugh – that wonderful, healing laughter of self-recognition. But when I have tried to do the same thing, it hasn't worked. They just ignored me and got their feelings hurt.'

I: 'Your description of your work with Mary and Trudi seems like an example of the tension between the opposites.'

JC: 'My part of that may be a birth order issue. I am an only child and so that kind of synthesis, of sensing myself as one who has to put two worlds together, is a very natural kind of stance. Because you're right, there weren't that many people who went back and forth many times each week to study with both Trudi and Mary. But it was natural for me and it helped me, mainly because of the genius of each of these women. I never felt that either tried to be possessive but they each gave fully of their gifts. I can't say that I've done a synthesis of the two but I know that I wouldn't be who I am today had I not studied with these two women.'

I: 'Joan, who are you today? If I were a student of yours, how would I describe your impact on my work?'

JC: 'Students do tell me every so often. I think there is a general theme that has to do with permission to be themselves, to find their own way of working.

         Maybe this is it: Trudi is herself and that's the model, that's the lesson. It isn't that anyone else should try to be like Trudi, it's that Trudi is like herself. So then the lesson is for me to be myself and for my students to be themselves. We are really speaking about the process of individuation.'

I: 'Would you talk about how you use movement in analysis?'

JC: 'Movement is not essential for everyone but it is essential for
        some. And its helpful for most people. Yet there are people I
        work with who rarely feel the need to leave their chairs. They
        are able to enter the imaginal world without getting up to
        move. I'm comfortable with that because that's their way. I
        think what's more important to me nowadays than whether
        someone moves or not is whether we are able to open to the
        imagination or not. There are many ways of opening to the
        imagination and each person has to find his or her own best
        way.'

I: 'You said that for some it is essential. How do you or they
        know that it is essential? What are your clues?'

JC: 'In my experience people generally know when they want to
        move. They know that in order to go into the world of the
        unconscious they've got to ground it in the movement of their
        own body. Some people are able to just imagine by leaps and
        bounds. You don't know how they get from here to there. For
        myself, I'm not quite connected when I imagine in that way.
        That kind of fantasy feels disembodied. But when I move my
        body through the images, I've truly entered into that world.
        That kind of vision world is as vivid as this day world or the
        dream world. The people who come to work with me want to
        do analysis and most of them want movement to be part of it.
        So we do analysis. That means we talk about dreams, fantasies,
        life experiences, what's going on between us. We sit in chairs
        or we sit on the floor. We do sandplay, use art materials.

        Whenever there is a feeling of wanting to move, every person
        seems to approach it differently. There are some people who'll
        come and talk for fifteen minutes and then move for twenty,
        thirty minutes and then talk a little bit toward the end. Others
        will come in and, before anything is said, they'll close their
        eyes and begin to move. It is like a ritual beginning. They
        simply go into that world and see what comes. After they're
        through, they'll bring it to an end, make a transition, and we
        may or may not talk about the movement that just happened.
        They're just as likely to be quiet for a while and then say:
        "Where's the clay?" and then form an image. Then we might

sit down and talk about dreams. People often remember their dreams or early childhood experiences while they're moving. Or we might talk about how it felt between us while they moved, how they were aware of my watching the movement or what it stirred up in me as I watched the movement.

It's different for every single person. Some people just move from what their own bodies want to do. Other people will see a specific image, sometimes like a guide person who appears in their imagination. The inner guide moves and the mover mirrors or follows or interacts with the imagined figure. For some, it's primarily a rite of entry into the analytic hour, where you get into your body and you separate from the everyday world. Movement and attending to the body experience can simply be a way of opening to the unconscious. And then we'll sit down and talk about dreams or something else. There's no particular form.

Whether we're talking or moving or engaging the symbolic process some other way, there's a kind of awareness that goes on. For me, whatever comes up from the unconscious usually has four aspects: one aspect is how is it happening here between us; another aspect is how is it happening in the person's life right now; the third aspect is what are the earliest memories from childhood similar to that same kind of experience; the fourth aspect brings in universal or mythic images.

Any kind of affective eruption usually has these aspects: it is in some way present in the therapeutic relationship, it's present in the person's life – there may be some early personal history to reconstruct – and this personal experience is related in some way to experiences others have known. This fourth, larger perspective does not take away the pain but it can restore a quality of dignity to the most chaotic or despairing symptom.

In one of his letters, Jung described active imagination as his analytical method of psychotherapy. Active imagination clearly includes dance/movement as well as all of the other art experiences. But it also includes imagining around transference and countertransference issues and possibilities of what the symbolic meanings might be of complexes that erupt in everyday life. In its most basic sense, active imagination is opening to the unconscious and giving free rein to fantasy, while, at the same time, maintaining a conscious viewpoint.'

I: 'In your writings you have talked about the presence of the witness, the analyst. What is that presence?'

JC: 'Its holding a particular kind of tension, because you bring your total being and total attention to the relationship. This is true whether you are sitting in chairs or whether the person is moving. But the experience is often more powerful when the person is moving and you're not distracted by words. Movement goes so directly to the emotional life.

I feel it is important to bring who I am and not try to clear myself or make myself too centered. When I have put a high value on being centered or receptive, I have found that I tend to split from the parts of me that are not like that. To the degree that I foster any particular attitude, its opposite tends to get constellated in the unconscious. So I have learned to just let myself be how I am and contain it.

What we are talking about now has to do with deliberately opening to the unconscious yet not identifying with it. In other words, opening to the imagination doesn't mean merging with the images and off you go. Opening to the imagination means being yourself with all your strengths and weaknesses and noticing what you are imagining.

A book that was published by Chiron is entitled *The body in analysis*. It is a collection of papers that were given at a conference. I have a paper in it entitled *The body as symbol*. In it I try to describe something of the experience of watching movement. It has so many facets. I describe what it is to watch a little piece of movement and how many perspectives come into that. So much happens in the moment of watching movement that if you try to write it all down, it goes on for pages.

There are so many different levels of witnessing. You notice
what the body is doing. You are curious, interested in what the
body is doing. You are noticing that. But you are also noticing
the emotional tone and if there is an infantile quality to it,
something of a parental, caretaking, nurturing feeling may
come up. Or if there is a family history in the mover of being
neglected or being mistreated in some way, those kinds of
indifferent or rejecting countertransference responses can also
erupt.

Then there is the whole realm of what does this person's
movement stir up in me from a larger cultural perspective?
How has this attitude or movement sequence appeared in art,
how has it appeared in literature or mythology? What
paintings come to mind, what poetry or music comes to mind
as I watch the person move? In what way does this express a
universal human experience? So it ranges from questions
about what is this body doing to imagining all kinds of
possibilities about the person's life history, particularly the
early history that tends to come up so often in movement. It is
all there while you are watching but most of it is like the
dream world – you can't retrieve all of it. Some of it stays but
you don't remember everything. In a sense it has a ritual
quality. It is as if we enter sacred space.'

I: 'Is the sacred space that you are talking about related to what
         you have referred to in your writing as "participation
         mystique"?'

JC: 'The "participation mystique" is a phrase that Jung used to
         describe what we might call merging. It is when we are able to
         drop our boundaries in the presence of another. Sacred space
         is kind of like the inside of the magic circle. It is like the
         therapeutic container. Dora Kalff described a "free and
         sheltered space."

         There is a tension we have to hold as we witness movement.
         On the one hand we deliberately open ourselves to the
         possibility of merging: participation mystique. It is like what
         Mary spoke of when she described a quality of movement

with the word "inevitable." The witness is so connected to what the mover is doing that you feel you know what is going to happen next.

But then, on the other side of it, there needs to be differentiation, a conscious analytic or therapeutic viewpoint. So it is like a continuum that ranges from an alert, conscious differentiated aspect on one side, to a merging, imaginative aspect on the other. The mover also develops the capacity to bear the tension of such inner opposites.

It seems to me that we can learn a lot about the structure and nature of the psyche by watching people move, and that is a very great contribution that we have to make. We can learn about the psyche through any aspect of therapeutic process but particularly through the relationship of the mover and the witness. We can learn so much about our own emotional and imaginative processes as we watch. And the mover is able to do the same thing.'

I: 'Would you give an example?'

JC: 'The material that I am working on next has to do with Jung's view of the psyche as a comprehensive structure that takes into account not only a personal unconscious but a cultural layer as well, which mediates between the personal and the primordial unconscious. This helps us understand where the movement is coming from. Although it is probably true that every complex has personal, cultural and primordial aspects, you can see the difference between a completely raw, untransformed emotion and our more differentiated developed forms of expression and communication.'

I: 'How involved are you in teaching now?'

JC: 'This year, for the first time, I will be teaching candidates at the Jung Institute in San Francisco about the use of movement as a form of active imagination. It is a new course entitled *The body in analysis*. I've also been teaching regularly in the public seminars program. And I continue to teach an annual summer course that started in 1975. Lou Stewart and I have been teaching it together for the last four years. This year it will be in Zürich. Next year we will have it back here in the Bay area. What this leads to is our collaboration. We learn so much from each other.

Lou is an analyst, one of the founding members of the San Francisco Institute. He has been updating Jung's model of the psyche from two essential perspectives. One has to do with stages of development and the other has to do with the role of specific primal affects and their transformation into psychological functions and attitudes. His model helps us to see emotion as the bridge between body and psyche.'

I: 'Joan, when you talk about Lou, your collaborator and husband, your eyes sparkle!'

JC: 'Yes, we were married just about a year ago.'

I: 'Earlier you talked about divorce and being a single mother, and I am delighted for you that you can now talk about your collaboration with Lou and have it be not only professional. What was your involvement with the founding of the American Dance Therapy Association in 1966? Were you one of the original members?'

JC: 'No, I was not one of the original members. I did receive the original invitation but was in the midst of moving from Los Angeles to Santa Barbara and the letter got lost. So I did not join that formal group of charter members. But I joined as soon as I got settled. So I think it was in 1966 or 1967.

The first experience I had of an American Dance Therapy Association's conference was 1971. I had been working at the Santa Barbara Psychiatric Medical Group since 1968 and I brought some videotapes of my work there to the meeting in Washington, DC. The tapes showed that movement could be a primary, in-depth form of psychotherapy for individuals as well as groups. There were both individuals and groups on that tape. Alma Hawkins was at the conference. She presented the work she was doing, which involved opening to the imagination through movement. We flew back to Los Angeles together and talked about our work and about the conference. We also started planning – Barbara Govine, Alma Hawkins, and I had agreed to do the next year's conference in Santa Monica.

We organized two conferences that year – a California regional meeting and the American Dance Therapy Association national conference. The smaller regional meeting was held in February 1972 in Santa Barbara. From that we got a beginning sense of dance therapy in California. The American Dance Therapy Association board sent Sharon Chaiklin, who was then the president, to attend. At that point we were all so excited. We wanted dance therapy to become a recognized profession. We hoped a day would come when you could say "dance therapist" and people wouldn't say "Dance what?!"'

I: 'And when were you president?'

JC: 'I was elected Vice-President in 1972 and did that for two years. Then I was President from 1974 to 1976. It was an enormous commitment, a lot of work. The process of establishing a brand new profession in the world has been incredible. Even now, pioneer work goes on every time we do lobbying in the legislative halls and write letters. But in those early years all of it was for the very first time.'

I: 'Joan, you always seem to have a focus and direction in your work. What is your focus now?'

JC: 'Analytic practice is clearly my main work. I became an analyst in 1983. It was a six-year, post-graduate training program. My educational background is so atypical. After completing post-graduate training as an analyst, I am now going to get my PhD, which is kind of backwards. I am going into an external degree program with Union Graduate School. I think it will allow me to write a book that I have been writing in my mind for several years.'

I: 'What will the book be?'

JC: 'It will be on this work, on the use of movement to give form to the imagination. It will develop a theoretical base of emotions as bridge between body and psyche, drawing strongly on the work that Lou has been doing. It will talk about active imagination in the Jungian tradition, about dance therapy and about this work.' (Editor's note: the book *Dance Therapy and Depth Psychology: The Moving Imagination* was published in 1991 by Routledge.)

CHAPTER 16

Philosophy and Methods of Individual Work[1]

Joan Chodorow

The foundation of individual work in dance therapy is a one-to-one relationship growing in an ambiance of trust. Such a base is common to many therapeutic experiences and is in no way unique to dance therapy. It is critical, however, as little growth can happen without it.

In the beginning all we have is two people, therapist and patient, who meet in a predictable place at regular time intervals. The patient may bring to these meetings a history of relationships where he had to falsify his feelings in order to be accepted. The tragedy, of course, is that even if he succeeded in winning approval, he could not receive it. The approval was not for himself but for his façade and, therefore, he was always left with nothing. It is from interactions with his therapist and others that the patient will begin to feel safe enough to learn, perhaps for the first time, to show himself as he really is.

The importance of the relationship between therapist and patient cannot be overemphasized as it is the difference between teaching dance and doing dance therapy. There is no question that a good teacher is therapeutic (the word means 'To serve, take care of'), as is a good mother, a good friend or beautiful surroundings. However, the teacher tends to focus on the material or techniques to be taught, whereas the therapist gives his major attention to the patient. Mary Whitehouse (1970) described the change in herself as follows:

> It was an important day when I recognized that I did not teach Dance, I taught People... It indicated a possibility that my primary interest might

---

1   Paper previously published in *Dance Therapy: Focus on Dance VII*, AAHPERD, 1974.

have to do with process, not results, that it might not be art I was after but another kind of human development. (p.273)

Individual vs group sessions

A patient might start with individual dance therapy sessions because he feels too threatened or too exposed in a group, or because he is so withdrawn or so aggressive that he is literally unable to function in a group, or because certain material has come up in psychotherapy that needs to be explored or specifically worked with in movement.

On the other hand, another patient might choose to start with group dance therapy because he feels apprehensive about the intensity of individual work, or because for him a group means safety and anonymity, or because group work is available to him and he cannot afford the cost of individual work, or because he has worked in individual psychotherapy and his therapist feels that he can now best benefit from a group experience. Beyond these, there are many other possibilities in numerous combinations.

The first approach: Structuring

Within the individual dance therapy session I generally find myself using one of two approaches, although at times I may use both within the same session. In the first approach I assess the patient's movement repertoire and set definite goals regarding the patient's potential range of response. For example, if I see that the patient is restricted to weak movement, shallow breathing and an overall quality that might be described as monotone, I will use any technique available to help that person go beyond his present boundaries. I might use structured movement or breathing exercises that concentrate on contrasting uses of time, space and energy qualities, or we might together recapitulate the entire sequence of normal development in movement, from infancy to adulthood, emphasizing and repeating whatever he did not get enough of. We might work with fantasy and imagery ('be a striking fork of lightning,' 'be a powerful giant monster') or work with dance-drama and pantomime to help the patient express some of his own feelings, especially those that may have 'shut down.' This patient may need especially to express such feelings as attacking anger, bursting joy or quivering anticipation.

Ethnic forms that emphasize specific body parts can be particularly helpful to bring alive 'dead' parts of the body. One patient worked for months on the strongly grounded heelwork of Spanish dance techniques and I recently spent four or five full sessions teaching a woman the undulating pelvic-centered movements of the belly dance. The interpersonal aspect of this involves my validation of the patient's new and often threatening experience. The woman's pelvis was locked because as a child she was given the message that sensual and sexual feelings were bad and never to be felt, much less enjoyed. I taught her how to move sensually, both seriously and for the fun of it. In every way – through words and touch and movement and voice and feelings – I was able to convey to her a different message from the one she had learned as a child. She was able to receive it and, eventually, to delight in her own good sensations and feelings.

The more structure I use, the more the interactions between myself and the patient take on the qualities of a caring parent-child relationship. This can be critically important for the patient whose parents never took the trouble to teach him anything. A very disturbed patient once told me (as I corrected her at the ballet barre) 'If my mother had made me do things this way, I wouldn't be sick now.' Such highly structured sessions might include studies of basic rhythms, ballet and contemporary dance technique or ethnic dance forms.

With this structured approach, much of my energy goes into planning and motivating, as I am usually trying to evoke a specific response. This approach deals with increasing the patient's conscious awareness of himself and others, his range of movement possibilities and his corresponding feeling experiences. Most of such movement is planned but, often, the planned movement is designed to contact deep feelings. At that point it becomes unplanned and spontaneous.

The second approach: Authentic response

This spontaneous break from planned into unplanned movement leads us to the second approach. Here the external structure is barely perceptible and my motivating leadership role will change to one of participant or observer.

This second approach is harder to describe because it involves listening to and dealing with the less known parts of our psyche – the preconscious and that which Jung (1961) described as the unconscious. This kind of work takes people into a deep self-sensing awareness that is clearly a state of consciousness markedly different from experiencing oneself and relating to others in everyday situations. The movement response is unplanned, authentic and deeply satisfying.

To illustrate this, I am thinking of a young woman, an outpatient, who came into the studio one day feeling hyperactive and uncomfortable. We went into stretching and yawning as a warm-up and then I asked her simply to take any position and 'listen' and allow herself to move whichever way she needed to move. We used no music as I wanted her to rely only on inner cues. She started moving many different ways, with no apparent sense to it, nor did she allow a rhythmic momentum to build. Something would start and then she'd cut it off and then something else would start. Gradually, though, her movement began to integrate spontaneously with her breathing and her attention focused in on the moment-to-moment process of what she was doing. Her air shapes, which at first were sporadic and unformed, became defined and, by the end, she was moving slowly and purposefully, creating a space for herself. At the very end, she was sitting on the floor, legs folded, spine easily stretched upwards as she made smaller and smaller circles with the top of her head, using the base of her spine as a fulcrum. These last movements were very subtle and very centered. She was breathing easily and looked marvelously peaceful and grounded. When she opened her eyes she had a string of insights that included a realization that the hyperactivity was her mask for a very real need to assert herself positively in her interactions with others – to metaphorically claim her own space.

Another patient recently experienced this type of work for the first time. It was toward the end of our fifth session together. I asked if she could contrast two aspects of herself, outgoing and withdrawn. In the past she had felt that she could not, but this day she agreed. In choosing music for her withdrawn self, she described 'slow and depressed and dreary' and we used the final theme of the score from the film *Charley*. She started lying on the ground, waiting, just listening to the music. When she started to move, it looked as if everything she did was a tremendous effort, as if each limb and her head and trunk weighed hundreds of pounds. She was deeply involved in the experience, which lasted about three minutes, and the feeling was of overwhelming sadness and resignation. It was very, very real. As the music stopped, she started to sob very softly and I held her and rocked her for a long time. This woman had been in therapy for years but had not allowed herself to cry before.

Closing one's eyes facilitates entry into such inner worlds. When we are asleep we dream spontaneously, but we can also learn to dip into that same stuff of which dreams are made and allow its emergence in movement. The unconscious manifests itself in many ways, including dreams, primary process type urges and psychosomatic symptoms, but it also, if allowed, manifests itself continually and at all times in the way we move. There is a stream of movement impulses available to each person all the time. The impulse to move in this manner comes when one can let go of all conscious control and identify with oneself as perceived through sensations and images. An impulse might lead to movement that takes only a few moments to unfold but a sequence of impulses, or self-directed authentic movement, can go on for a very long time.

Sometimes, authentic movement is preceded by random activity and fragmented gestures. This seemingly aimless movement may go on for some time before one begins to notice a clarification and increasing sense of definition and purpose. From here, a development toward some form of resolution or release can occur, usually resulting in new experiences and insights. I have seen the process described above completed in minutes or it may be spread over weeks or months. The release may be cathartic in nature, discharging and subsequently assimilating old, previously dissociated feelings. Or it may be a quietly gentle experience of centering, of discovering a condition of harmony between inner feelings and outer expression. Whether it is intense or gentle, I believe that authentic movement ultimately leads towards integration of the personality.

The two approaches

The first of the two approaches described depends on the therapist to provide the goals and the structure. Specific forms are introduced to help the patient make connection to his unexpressed feelings and to help him internalize a sense of order. When I am working with patients who are psychotic, I use this approach exclusively. I suspect that even inside a psychotic person there is some kernel of innate order but it is a difficult task to help him sort out and get in touch with it when he may feel surrounded and overwhelmed by inner chaos.

The second approach depends more on the presence of a stronger internal structure. In fact, it draws almost entirely from the patient himself, trusting in his innate integrity to lead the way. It is usually especially exciting and satisfying to a patient who has functioned efficiently in the outside world but feels his life and relationships to be empty, mechanical and meaningless. Somehow, this internally generated action can put people in touch with the vastness of their full potential.

I have separated my way of working into two such distinct approaches for purposes of clarification. In reality, there is often a constant interchange, an ebb and flow back and forth between the two. When working within the boundaries of the first approach, I keep constant feelers out for the patient's readiness to flow into a spontaneous expansion of whatever movement quality we are working on. And, conversely, when working with authentic response, I am watching carefully to see if the natural movement impulse is being allowed fulfillment or whether it is cut off by the patient's lack of flexibility in movement behavior. When this inhibition occurs, we will often switch back to an external structure in order to work on extending the patient's range of movement possibilities.

Conclusion

I have discussed individual work in dance therapy and put the highest priority on a patient-therapist relationship that is built on trust. It is this focusing on the interpersonal relationship rather than the movement technique itself that is one of the most important differences between doing dance therapy and teaching dance. It requires the deliberate creation of a safe environment in which the patient can have the opportunity to discover the authenticity within himself and it involves non-verbally 'giving permission' for the patient to dare to be himself. There are special conditions that indicate a need for individual sessions as there are other conditions that indicate a need for group work. The dance therapist accommodates to these special conditions and needs by working individually with the patient whenever the therapeutic relationship is best enhanced through this approach. Finally, we have explored two approaches to movement: an approach which is most appropriate in working with psychotic patients and patients who can benefit from getting more in touch with the external world and an approach which flows in the opposite direction as the patient learns to touch the source of his inner reality. Whether these approaches are used interchangeably or whether it is more therapeutic to stay exclusively with one or the other depends on the moment-to-moment needs of the individual. In a larger sense, both approaches are essential as an individual's health and comfort depends greatly on achieving a balance between his inner and outer worlds.

References
Jung, C.G. (1961) *Memories, Dreams, Reflections.* New York: Random House.

Whitehouse, M.S. (1970) 'Reflections on a metamorphosis'. In R. Head, R.E. Rothenberg and D. Wesley (eds) *A Well of Living Waters: Festschrift for Hilda Kirsch*. Los Angeles: C.G. Jung Institute.

CHAPTER 17

Dance Therapy and the Transcendent Function[1]

Joan Chodorow

Introduction

The psychology of Carl G. Jung offers many concepts of interest and importance to the field of dance therapy. And many dance therapy concepts, especially those which emphasize the body experience as a bridge between consciousness and the unconscious, offer enrichment to Jungian psychology. This paper will attempt to relate aspects of dance/movement therapy to Jung's concept of the transcendent function and his associated method of active imagination.

Jung's view of emotional dysfunction is that it is most often a problem of psychological one-sidedness, usually initiated by an over-evaluation of the conscious ego viewpoint. As natural compensation to such one-sided viewpoint, an equally strong counterposition automatically forms in the unconscious. The most likely result is an inner condition of tension, conflict and discord.

The concept of the transcendent function arose out of Jung's attempt to understand more deeply how one may come to terms with the unconscious. He found that there is an innate, dynamic process which serves to unite opposite positions within the psyche. It draws polarized energies into a common channel, resulting in a new symbolic position which contains both perspectives. 'Either/or' choices become 'both/and,' but on a new and

---

1   Paper presented at the first Regional Congress of the International Association for Social Psychiatry, Santa Barbara, California, 1977, and the First International Conference of the American Dance Therapy Association, Toronto, Canada, 1977. Previously published in *American Journal of Dance Therapy*, Spring/Summer 1978.

unforeseeable level. Thus the transcendent function facilitates a transition from one attitude to another. Jung (1916) described it as '...a movement out of the suspension between two opposites, a living birth that leads to a new level of being, a new situation' (p.90).

Movement approaches to consciousness and the unconscious

We see that two opposite positions within the psyche – conscious and unconscious – must first be differentiated, then integrated. In order to differentiate and explore the worlds of consciousness and the unconscious, we shall approach them from the perspective of movement and the body experience.

Time and space

The relationship between consciousness and the unconscious is basically one of mutual compensation and complementarity. Each of these complementary worlds functions under an entirely different set of laws. Our approach to comparing them will be to see how time and space are known in the conscious world and how they are known in the world of the unconscious. Consider for a moment the profound differences between the way one experiences time and space when wide awake and when dreaming. The entire question has particular importance to the field of dance therapy because time and space are the dance therapist's most familiar tools.

In dreams, as in the cosmos, time and space are without boundaries, without limit. In the world of the unconscious, time is simultaneous – past, present and future merge into one. Space is infinite. The shape and substance of objects, people, even one's own body, can change from moment to moment. Distances too are flexible and often in a constant state of metamorphosis. This deep, vast world of the unconscious serves as the source of our very being, the well-spring of all human art, culture and religion. It is also the world of the psychotic, who lives directly under its influence.

Our everyday consciousness, on the other hand, is definite and directed. It is this reliable, focused, conscious process that has made civilization and scientific development possible. In this externally focused world, time and space have clearly defined limits. Time is linear and generally moves in a single direction. Relative to the laws of the unconscious, space is stable and finite. One major task of consciousness appears to involve accurate perception of time/space limitations and the capacity to function within them.

However, the crucial issue for consciousness must include bringing unconscious material to light and integrating it into the total personality. Jung called this the process of individuation – the process of becoming whole.

Therapeutic approaches

When movement is used in psychotherapeutic intervention, it activates both conscious and unconscious processes. By its very nature, movement as a therapeutic tool will explore, strengthen and integrate multiple aspects of the human psyche. However, in order to determine specific interventions, the dance therapist needs a sense of direction. This includes knowing whether the immediate goal is to move toward the unconscious or toward a more conscious, concrete reality.

For the purpose of greater clarity and understanding, we'll look at these two contrasting approaches available to the dance therapist. However, it's important to keep in mind that 'In reality, there is often a constant interchange, an ebb and flow back and forth between the two' (Chodorow 1974, p.24). The first approach emphasizes conscious, everyday reality, especially regarding time and space limitations, and it works to strengthen ego boundaries. The psychotic person usually derives great benefit from such work. Here the dance therapist attempts to evoke specific movement responses which will help the person cope more effectively with the external world. For example, use of structured rhythms, working within clearly organized spatial patterns, intentional use of weight, etc, will help the person develop a more realistic body image and strengthen his or her conscious viewpoint.

The second approach concentrates on using movement as a means of opening to the unconscious and will most likely involve some dissolution of ego boundaries. Here the movement may be based on more internally generated rhythms, spatial patterns may be more diffuse and the person's eyes may be closed or have an inward focus. Awareness of and attending to selective aspects of inner reality becomes a central focus. As the brain receives an ongoing but diminished flow of sensory input, it may begin to create its own internal experience through increasingly vivid imagery and, at times, body image distortion (Wilbarger 1976). Such navigation through the non-rational world of the unconscious can facilitate profoundly important insights and new levels of integration for people who have already developed a strong ego position.

Labananalysis

Although different words are used, many dancers, as well as dance therapists, have developed ways to differentiate, explore and integrate what we here call conscious and unconscious. There is one especially comprehensive theoretical structure called Labananalysis, which enables us to study the movement process in its full depth and immensity. This framework was created by Rudolf Laban (1971) and has been continually developed by Irmgard Bartenieff (1980), Marion North (1972), Warren Lamb (1965, 1978) and their associates.

We shall touch on the Effort/Shape aspect of this theory and then turn to some of Trudi Schoop's clinical work, which deals with integration of consciousness and the unconscious. Effort/Shape is a system of movement observation and analysis which offers a powerful tool for the study of unconscious and conscious processes. Effort gives us a way of looking at a person's intentional attitudes toward *Time* (fluctuating between leisurely and urgent), *Space* (fluctuating between indirect and direct), *Weight* (fluctuating between lightness and firmness) and the ongoing *Flow* of muscular tension (fluctuating between greater and lesser control). Depending on the way we combine these elements, the movement experience may strengthen our connection to the objective external world or it may relate us to our more subjective inner world.

The Full Effort actions, which combine a single element each of Time, Space, Weight and Flow, are examples of intense actions usually related to an external activity. Similarly, the Basic Efforts, which combine a single element each of Time, Space and Weight, are directed toward the outer world.

Effort combinations which cause us to turn so deeply inward that we become almost lost in subtle moods and shades of long-forgotten feelings are the Internalized Drives and the Inner Attitudes (also called Incomplete Efforts). Internalized Drives combine an element of Flow with two other elements. They are, therefore, Timeless, Spaceless or Weightless states, powerfully reminiscent of many dream experiences. The Inner Attitudes have an even more elusive and transitory quality. They are combinations of only two elements and evoke a wide and dramatic range of internal experiences.

Effort/Shape is one component of Labananalysis which also includes Space Harmony and the Movement Fundamentals developed by Irmgard Bartenieff (1980). As Effort/Shape depicts the quality of movement, Space Harmony deals with the body's relationship to Space and Fundamentals deals with the body's relationship to itself. Just as Jung has given us a psychology which encompasses the vastness of our potential, Laban's work offers us a movement-based model for human wholeness. Each presents a framework through which we may study the same ultimate reality.

Schoop's work with the 'Ur'

Trudi Schoop (1978) contrasts our ordinary relationship to time, space, energy (and our usually limited sense perceptions) with an experience she calls the 'Ur.' 'Ur' is a German word which translates roughly into such English words as 'primal' or 'archetypal.' To help people clarify their ordinary reality, she asks them to dramatically represent what it feels like sometimes to have too little time, space or energy. The resulting improvisations show in a stylized way how people cope with the demands of everyday life. To get into the 'Ur' experience, she asks people to imagine how they would move if there were no limits. How would you move if time were without end? If this moment could go on forever, how would you experience your body? How would you move if there were no limits to this space we are in? If there were no walls, no buildings, no obstructions of any sort – if there were only open space in all directions, to the horizons and the horizons beyond – how would you move? How would you feel? These movement experiences tend to be very powerful, often reflecting a genuine transcendence of the two worlds. People increase their awareness of how they've been relating to the external world while discovering their resources for inner renewal. By working with physical representations of such opposite positions in the psyche, Trudi Schoop creates a greater acknowledgement of both and a functional balance between them.

From the dawn of history, dance/movement has been used to effect such intrapsychic changes, as well as to effect changes in the larger environment. In a 1930 seminar on Zarathustra, Jung (1934) stated:

> You can dance, not only to produce the union with yourself, or to manifest yourself, but in order to produce rain, or the fertility of women, or of the fields, or to defeat your enemy. The idea of an effect, of something produced, is always connected with the idea of dancing. (p.46)

Active imagination

The aim of the transcendent function is to realize the original potential wholeness of the psyche. Jung (1917) described it as '...a natural process, a manifestation of the energy that springs from the tension of opposites, and it consists in a series of fantasy-occurrences which appear spontaneously in dreams and visions' (p.79). In later years he incorporated this dynamic process into his developing concept of an archetype of unity which he called 'the Self' (Hannah 1953).

To facilitate the transcendent function, he discovered a meditative procedure which he called 'active imagination.' Its value is two-fold. First, it helps us to support those internal processes which activate the transcendent function. And, second, it is designed to liberate the patient through his or her own efforts, rather than through dependence on the therapist. This means that the procedure is meant to be done by the patient alone, away from the analyst. The analyst may supervise the patient at the beginning but the emphasis is on how one may learn to deal autonomously with the ongoing stream of unconscious material that continues unceasingly throughout life.

Since this paper is about dance therapy and the transcendent function, we shall concentrate primarily on the first value of active imagination. Our exploration is of the relationship between an inner-directed movement process and the transcendent function. Although most of the work discussed assumes a therapeutic setting, much of it can also be done independently.

The major danger of active imagination involves being overwhelmed by the unconscious. Therefore, it will be utilized most fully by relatively stable individuals who possess a sufficiently strong ego viewpoint that conscious and unconscious may encounter each other as equals. For less stable individuals, the dance therapist might choose to carefully structure a variety of separate movement experiences to explore different aspects of each component. Independent involvement with the total procedure should be attempted only by individuals capable of withstanding a powerful confrontation with the unconscious.

Several of Jung's associates have continually developed the method, organizing his ideas more fully and adding the resource of their own experiences. Marie-Louise von Franz (Dallett and Lucas 1977) has outlined four specific components or steps of active imagination: (1) opening to the unconscious, (2) giving it form, (3) reaction by ego, (4) living it. We shall use this four-part framework to explore active imagination and the unique power and integration movement and the body experience bring to the process.

First component: Opening to the unconscious

The first step in active imagination is familiar to many psychological approaches and forms of meditation. It involves a suspension of our rational, critical faculties in order to produce the fertile void which allows emergence of unconscious contents. The dance therapist offers potent resources to this initial step.

Rather than approaching the task from a one-sided mental attempt to get the mind to empty itself, the dance therapist offers the body experience. Use of relaxation techniques, special attention to breath, development of sensory/kinesthetic awareness, awareness of body parts and how they relate to each other – all are important keys in opening doors to the unconscious.

The unconscious manifests itself through an ongoing stream of body sensation and mental imagery. Its relatively formless products may include inner throbbings, pulsings, tinglings, pressures, surges, waves of differentiated and undifferentiated energies, inner voices, sounds, words, fantasies, feelings, moods, memories and impulses. At the point where we begin to give these raw materials a form, we move toward the second component of active imagination.

Second component: Giving it form

Mary Whitehouse (1987) describes movement as originating in a specific inner impulse which has the quality of sensation. Just as active imagination in fantasy involves following the visual image, active imagination in movement involves '...following the inner sensation, allowing the impulse to take the form of physical action...' (Whitehouse 1987, p.17). A woman describes her experience of active imagination in movement:

> Seated on the floor with my legs crossed, I attended to the rhythm of my breathing. Gradually, this took me into a circular rocking movement, at first very small and safe. With increasingly strong impulses, I began to rock further away from my secure center. New surges of energy pushed me far over to one edge, then another and another. I was barely suspended on the edges now and felt afraid of falling. I let the movement subside and was flooded with feelings and memories.

This type of experience always carries an element of surprise. It has a quality of immediacy and heightened perception. It usually involves total attentiveness to the movement process itself, with or without associated imagery. It may be low key or highly charged with emotion.

Another sort of internally-generated movement appears to originate from image rather than sensation. Instead of following the inner sensation, fantasy-based movement appears to follow and reflect the ongoing stream of visual imagery. It sometimes lacks the spontaneous quality of sensation-based movement yet it, too, may be of crucial importance with respect to the transcendent function.

Perhaps artists are most familiar with the second component of active imagination as it involves the most overt aspect of the creative process. The emphasis is to securely anchor the unconscious material by externalizing it in a definite form. Jung (1916) suggests that different people will need to do this in different ways. Those who see images or hear voices inside themselves must find a way of giving tangible form to their experience – usually by writing it down. Others may want to use their hands to give a more direct form to the unconscious through various art materials or through automatic writing. Of movement, he says:

> Those who are able to express the unconscious by means of bodily movements are rather rare. The disadvantage that movements cannot easily be fixed in the mind must be met by making careful drawings of the movements afterwards, so that they shall not be lost to the memory. (p.84)

Drawing can be a marvelous way to document the movement experience. In addition to sketching realistic figures or other indications of the actual movements, it is of immense value to express the essence of the movement experience in a more abstract form. This may be through drawings, clay or virtually any other media.

Another possibility is that upon completion of the internally-generated movement experience, the person flashes back over the process to remember the most vivid parts of it. In a wide variety of ways it may then be transformed into a repeatable choreographic statement.

Writing is also available. It can involve anything from objective notation of the actual movements and qualities to use of poetic metaphor.

It is through the therapeutic relationship that we find still another means of securing the movement experience. Unlike inner visions of many other internal processes, dance/movement can be clearly seen by another person(s). Thus the movement process is simultaneously an inner experience and an external communication. As the dance therapist is likely to have highly developed movement observation skills, accurate feedback is available to the client. This sort of shared interaction often brings up powerful issues of transference and countertransference which must be explored as part of the total therapy process.

Finally, to make use of current technology, there is the video-tape recorder, a tool which gives instant playback of any movement sequence we choose to record.

The reason for such emphasis on documentation is that even the most powerful inner experience must be carefully fixed into consciousness or it tends to slip away. In this second component of active imagination we must reactivate our directed consciousness and put it in the service of the unconsciousness. Thus the unconscious flow remains the core but consciousness, without exerting undue influence, must become involved with the task of giving it form. Jung (1916) describes the product as one '…which is influenced by both conscious and unconscious, embodying the striving of the unconscious for the light and the striving of the conscious for substance' (p.83).

Upon creation of such a product we too often imagine that the process is complete. Although feelings of closure may be appropriate for an artist, the therapeutic task remains unfinished. In active imagination, as in therapy, much remains to be done with the product that emerges.

Creative formulation versus understanding

Before going on to the third step or component of active imagination, we shall pause and reflect on two tendencies that arise in response to a product which reflects inner experience: the way of aesthetic formulation and the way of scientific understanding. If the first tendency predominates, a person may lose the goal of the transcendent function and instead get fascinated with artistic questions and the creation of beauty. If there is a predominance of the second tendency, there is the danger of such analysis and interpretation that the power of the symbol is lost. Each tendency seems to be the regulating principle of the other and a balance of both are needed to facilitate the transcendent function.

Either extreme aestheticization or intellectualization may serve to rechannel an overpowering emotional response. However, Jung (1916) warns that '…they should be used only when there is a vital threat, and not for the purpose of avoiding a necessary task' (p.88). He emphasizes the importance of emotional factors and suggests that affect be a full participant in the transcendent function.

Third component: Reaction by ego

During the first and second parts of active imagination the unconscious has to maintain a position of leadership. Upon entering the third stage it is the ego viewpoint which takes the most active position. The ego must react fully in order to come to terms with the unconscious material.

It is here, perhaps more than at any other stage, that we must clearly differentiate between the dynamics of active and passive imagination. An example of passive imagination would be lying still with eyes closed, watching the pictures in one's head, without personal involvement. In such passive imagination one might fantasize an image such as a fish, then flit to an image of a bird, which might then be replaced by a firefly. These would all be viewed with interest as if watching a film or television show. However, the essential commitment to come to terms with the image is lacking.

In active imagination, by contrast, one actively intervenes at some point – usually by entering into the fantasy one's self. We must give the inner figures credibility equal to ourselves. We must interact with and respond to them with the serious intention of learning from and about each other. Movement, by its very nature, is active. By dancing a figure from the unconscious, one is more likely to be totally involved with the process and more able to seriously own and acknowledge that aspect of one's being.

In one sense, inner or written dialogues may be the most simple way of getting a reaction by the ego because in that way there is a conversation with figures from the unconscious just like a dialogue between human beings. However, the ego viewpoint can also have a strong and effective reaction to a drawing, piece of writing or other product from the unconscious. Faced with such a product, Jung (1916) suggests a Faustian question: 'How am I affected by this sign?' (p.89).

During a movement experience or immediately following it, a seemingly endless variety of such questions might be explored:

- How is this familiar to me?

- What is the earliest memory I have of moving in this particular pattern?

- In what ways is this new to me?

- How come I've never experienced this quality of movement before?

- Which of the new movement qualities might be especially useful in my life right now?

- How would I feel if my mother/father/spouse/child were watching me?
- How would I have been received if I had moved with this quality when I was a child?
- Do I have movement patterns that continually reappear?
- What do I feel while I'm doing them?
- What happens when I stay with the same movement?
- How does that affect me?
- Can I own and accept such an incredibly wide range of feelings?
- What kind of movement am I doing as I experience a particularly vivid image or strong emotion?
- How do they connect?

The Odyssey contains a classic story of a confrontation between conscious and unconscious in Menelaus' description of how Proteus, the sea god, was elusive when Menelaus wanted to engage him in a discussion. Menelaus finally grabbed him. Proteus responded by turning himself into a lion. Menelaus was startled but he continued to hold onto the god tightly while Proteus took on all kinds of forms. He became a dragon, snake, running water, tree and many other creatures and things. Finally, since Menelaus never let go, Proteus became exhausted and resumed his own shape. He and Menelaus then proceeded to start a discussion with the aim of coming to terms with their differences.

The capacity to continuously and consciously attend to the body experience, while impulses from the unconscious are allowed to emerge as physical actions, may be analogous to the story of how Menelaus held on to Proteus. It is through conscious awareness of our movements that their meaning will ultimately be revealed to us.

Jung (1935) describes the ego as a complex datum which is constituted primarily of a general awareness of the body. With sufficient attention to the body experience, it is possible to simultaneously express the unconscious through movement while maintaining an equally strong ego position through ongoing awareness of the body's reality.

Although the impulse to move may spring from a source in the unconscious, the body, which allows the impulse to manifest itself, remains firmly rooted in the fact of its own existence. The actual act of moving creates proprioceptive and kinesthetic feedback which serves to confront the unconscious with the body ego's reality. As the unconscious impulse and the body ego encounter each other's different realities, an intense and fully mutual education is likely to occur.

Since the body has the capacity to simultaneously manifest both conscious and unconscious, it may be our most potent tool toward the transcendent function. In the Zarathustra seminars Jung (1934) stated:

> ...the essence of differentiation, the idea of the Self, could not exist for one moment if there were not a body to create and maintain that distinctness. We may suppose that if the body vanishes and disintegrates, the Self in a way disintegrates, for it loses its confines. (p.236)

And, in *The Symbolic Quest*, Whitmont (1973) suggests that it is through the body experience that the archetype of the Self is first actualized.

Fourth component: Living it

In his autobiography, Jung (1961) writes that it is '...a grave mistake to think that it is enough to gain some understanding of the images and that knowledge can here make a halt. Insight into them must be converted into an ethical obligation' (pp.192–193). His emphasis is on the importance of realizing in actual life what one learned from the unconscious.

This brings up a question of the difference between the ethical commitment he describes and sheer will power. The answer has to do with whether or not there is a genuinely new inner situation. Sheer will power is supported by the ego alone and is likely to be sabotaged whenever the counterposition in the unconscious attempts (in the healthiest way it knows) to call attention to itself. On the other hand, an ethical commitment to put a new inner situation to use will most likely be supported by the archetype of unity, the Self (Dallett and Lucas 1977). Such a commitment may involve some work to overcome old habits but one is unlikely to experience the struggle so often associated with will-power.

Dance therapy offers a head start on this final component of active imagination because, through movement, we can make actual, physical use of any new level achieved. Here we can directly encourage movement qualities and patterns that will both reflect and support recent inner changes.

In the therapeutic relationship this level might involve largely verbal interactions and/or it might involve rather structured movement work. Other possibilities would include free movement improvisation and psychodramatic forms to explore a wide range of options for putting the new insights to use. Still another possibility is that much of the work of this final component has already occurred while working with the other components. Perhaps the most exciting thing about using movement this way is its simultaneous nature – it offers us the essence of a holistic experience.

Clinical application

Teresa had been involved in individual movement psychotherapy for nine months, attending weekly sessions. This day she came into the studio and began to move immediately with a rhythmic side-to-side swaying that gradually folded forward toward the ground into a sort of half-hanging, still swaying slowly from side to side. She gradually sank onto the floor and lay quietly with a quality of absolute stillness. She remained with the silence and stillness, beautifully centered and concentrated. Then she slowly began to move with an increasingly free, loose, spontaneous quality. As it built in momentum, she was drawn onto her feet. Although her movements did not look dangerous, she became so unrestrained that I found myself moving around the room to serve as a protective 'buffer' between herself and cabinet edges or other obstructions.

After experiencing this loose, free quality for a long time, she was drawn again toward the ground. She began to move slowly and sensuously on the floor, folding and unfolding her whole body. This led into a gentle smile of pure pleasure which flowed into soft laughter from time to time. However, after a while, the sensuous quality was replaced by a laughter which convulsed and rocked her entire body. This second type of laughter went on and on, with a feeling she later described as hysterical. After a while, I intervened and asked her to take whatever time she needed to come back. Up to this point she had allowed internally-generated impulses to move her for nearly forty-five minutes.

As she gradually returned to everyday consciousness, her entire attitude changed. She became tense, negative and strongly judgmental toward the parts of herself that had just emerged. Her first words were in a shocked and shaken voice: 'Wow, I really got pretty far out there!' We then talked together about the contrast between her emerging freedom of choice, spontaneity, sensuality and the relative rigidity of her lifelong beliefs and lifestyle. Although she was increasingly able to acknowledge the tension between her two viewpoints, she continued to identify with the most familiar part of herself and maintained an attitude of self-condemnation.

I suggested that we role-play these two aspects of her personality and she agreed. First, we moved together, sharing a harsh, judgmental quality. It was a stylized version of herself as a controlled, respectable matron. Then I asked her to continue the same quality while I began to move similarly to the ways she had moved before. As my momentum began to build, I allowed myself to become genuinely less controlled and she had to find a way of dealing with me. At first, she seemed to ignore me. However, she soon started to move around the edges of the studio, gently protecting me from bumping into obstructions, just as I had done for her earlier. This transition felt amazing. When I moved into some of the pleasurable sensuality she had shown before, she was able to watch me, conveying a tentative sense of validation and acceptance. Soon she joined me and we improvised together. Here we achieved a new kind of integration in our movements, which now included both freedom and control. It was one of the most exciting and intense sessions we had ever had. We ended after a brief, mutual, verbal sharing.

Teresa continued to consolidate the new integration from this session and made profound changes in her life. Although we touched on each of the active imagination components, the process was markedly different due to our interactions.

Because of the trust we had built through our work together, she was able to release her usual inhibitions and move fully from the unconscious. As this happened, I took over part of her ego function that has to do with orientation and tried to protect her. This offered her a new and more nurturing model for how a conscious viewpoint (in this case, mine) might relate to the emergence of unconscious material.

We also used our relationship to keep her experience from slipping away. Although she remembered much of it through her own body experience, my presence served to anchor it even more securely. I watched her move, discussed it with her later, and then incorporated the essence of what I saw into my own movements. As she watched me move the same qualities she had rejected in herself, she came to relate to them in a new way. When she finally joined me, unlike her earlier experience by herself, she was fully conscious. Together, we embraced large amounts of space with the wonderful momentum she showed before, but our freedom now grew from a firm ground.

The question of freedom and control stems from different personal experiences. It also carries the power of a collective human dilemma. Although our work was clearly focused on Teresa's therapy process, I too experienced change. I believe we both emerged with a greater degree of consciousness and integration.

Conclusion

Active imagination has been called 'a dialogue with the gods' (Dallett and Lucas 1977). The same definition can apply to the dance/movement experience. From the dawn of human history, dance has been a sacred language, a way of realizing our connection to the cosmos. Wherever we humans have withdrawn from a direct experience of our relationship to the universe, there too has the power of dance diminished.

In our present time there is increasing energy and attention turned toward transpersonal values. In a sense, human survival now depends on developing a conscious relationship to the vast, collective inner reality we all share. We must learn to come to terms with opposite positions, whether they be within the individual, between two or more persons, or between nations.

To develop most fully the potential of that sacred dialogue which serves to unite the opposites, dance/movement must reclaim its original power. It may then take its place as our most powerful tool in facilitating the transcendent function.

Bibliography

Adler, J. (1972) 'Integrity of body and psyche: Some notes on work in process'. In B.F. Govine and J. Chodorow (eds) *What is dance therapy really? Proceedings of the Seventh Annual Dance Therapy Conference,* pp.42–53. Columbia, MD: American Dance Therapy Association.

Bartenieff, I. (1980) *Body Movement: Coping with the Environment.* New York: Gordon & Breach.

Chaiklin, S. (1975) 'Dance therapy'. In S. Arieti (ed) *American Handbook of Psychiatry.* 2nd ed., Vol.5, pp.703–720. New York: Basic Books.

Chodorow, J. (1974) 'Philosophy and methods of individual work'. In K. Mason (ed) *Dance Therapy: Focus on Dance VII.* Washington, DC: American Association for Health, Physical Education and Recreation.

Dallett, J. and Lucas, H. (1977) Active Imagination Seminar. C.G. Jung Institute of Los Angeles.

Dell, C. (1970) *A Primer for Movement Description.* New York: Dance Notation Bureau.

Dosamantes Alperson, E. (1974) 'Carrying experiences forward through authentic body movement'. *Psychotherapy: Theory, Research and Practice, 11,* 3.

Edinger, E.F. (1974) *Ego and Archetype.* Baltimore, MD: Penguin Books.

Fay, C.G. (1977) *Movement and Fantasy: A Dance Therapy Model Based on the Psychology of Carl G. Jung.* Master's thesis. Goddard College, Vermont.

Frantz, G. (1972) 'An approach to the center: An interview with Mary Whitehouse'. *Psychological Perspectives 3*, 37–46.

von Franz, M.L. (1975) *C.G. Jung: His Myth in Our Time.* New York: Putnam and Sons.

Fry, R. (1974) *Teaching Active Imagination Meditation.* Doctoral dissertation. Lawrence University, Goleta, California.

Hannah, B. (1953) 'Some remarks on active imagination'. *Spring,* 38–58.

Hawkins, A. (1971) 'Work with patients'. In D. Cook (ed) *Dance Therapy, Roots and Extensions, Proceedings of the Sixth Annual Dance Therapy Conference,* pp.67–69. Columbia, MD: American Dance Therapy Association.

Hawkins, A. (n.d.) Theoretical concepts. Unpublished notes.

Hawkins, A. (n.d.) Experiencing process, laboratory. Unpublished notes.

Hillman, J. (1974) 'Archetypal theory: C.G. Jung'. In A. Burton (ed) *Operational Theories of Personality,* pp.65–98. New York: Brunner-Mazel.

Jacobson, E. (1967) *Etiology of Emotion.* Springfield, IL: Charles C. Thomas.

Jung, C.G. (1916) 'The transcendent function'. In *The Collected Works of C.G. Jung* (2nd ed., 1969/1978) (vol. 8). Princeton: Princeton University Press.

Jung, C.G. (1917) 'Psychology of the unconscious'. In *The Collected Works of C.G. Jung* (1953) (vol.7). Princeton: Princeton University Press.

Jung, C.G. (1921) 'Definitions'. In *The Collected Works of C.G. Jung* (1971) (vol.6). Princeton: Princeton University Press.

Jung, C.G. (1931) 'The aims of psychotherapy'. In *The Collected Works of C.G. Jung* (1975) (vol.16). Princeton: Princeton University Press.

Jung, C.G. (1934) *Nietzsche's Zarathustra: Notes of the Seminar Given in 1934–1939* (1988) (Vol. I). (Edited by J.L. Jarrett). Princeton: Princeton University Press.

Jung, C.G. (1935) 'The Tavistock lectures: The symbolic life'. In *The Collected Works of C.G. Jung* (1976) (vol.18). Princeton: Princeton University Press.

Jung, C.G. (1961) *Memories, Dreams, Reflections.* New York: Vintage Books, Random House.

Jung, C.G. (1964) *Man and His Symbols.* New York: Doubleday.

Laban, R. (1971) *The Mastery of Movement.* London: MacDonald & Evans.

Lamb, W. (1965) *Posture and Gesture.* London: Duckworth.

Lamb, W. (1978) 'Universal movement indicators of stress'. *American Journal of Dance Therapy 2,* 1, 27–30.

North, M. (1972) *Personality Assessment Through Movement.* London: MacDonald & Evans.

Schoop, T. (1978) 'Motion and emotion'. Paper and workshop presented at the Southern California Chapter of the American Dance Therapy Association Conference, Los Angeles.

Selver, C. and Brooks, C. (1968) *Report on Work in Sensory Awareness and Total Functioning.* New York: Selver and Brooks.

Singer, J. (1972) *Boundaries of the Soul: The Practice of Jung's Psychology.* New York: Doubleday.

Singer, J. (1976) *Androgyny: Toward a New Theory of Sexuality.* New York: Anchor Press/Doubleday.

Szent-Gyoergyi, A. (1974) 'Drive in living matter to perfect itself'. *Synthesis 1,* 1, 12–24.

Whitehouse, M.S. (1958) 'The Tao of the body'. In D.H. Johnson (1995) (ed) *Bone, Breath and Gesture: Practices of Embodiment,* pp.241–251. Berkeley, CA: North Atlantic Books.

Whitehouse, M.S. (1963) 'Physical movement and personality'. *Contact Quarterly.* Winter 1987, 16–19.

Whitehouse, M.S. (1970) 'Reflections on a metamorphosis.' In R. Head, R.E. Rothenberg and D. Wesley (eds) *A Well of Living Waters: Festschrift for Hilde Kirsch* (1977) pp.272–277. Los Angeles: C.G. Jung Institute.

Whitehouse, M.S. (1977) 'The transference and dance therapy'. *American Journal of Dance Therapy 1,* 1, 3–7.

Whitehouse, M.S. (1979) 'C.G. Jung and dance therapy'. In P. Lewis Bernstein (ed) *Eight Theoretical Approaches in Dance/Movement Therapy,* pp.51–70. Dubuque, IA: Kendall/ Hunt.

Whitmont, E. (1972) 'Body experience and psychological awareness'. *Quadrant, 12,* 5–16.

Whitmont, E. (1973) *The Symbolic Quest: Basic Concepts of Analytical Psychology.* New York: Harper & Row.

Wilbarger, P. (1976). Personal communication.

CHAPTER 18

Dance/Movement and Body Experience in Analysis[1]

Joan Chodorow

Introduction

The role of dance/movement and body experience in Jungian thought and practice remains largely undeveloped. This neglect is despite Jung's own relationship to his body and his love of dancing (Jaffé 1979); his purposeful practice of specific movement exercises to calm and center himself (Jung 1961); his references to body movement as a form of active imagination (Jung 1916, 1929, 1935, 1947, 1976); and his dance/movement interactions with certain patients (Fay 1977; van der Post 1977, 1979).

From his earliest work in the Burghölzli Psychiatric Clinic in Zürich, Jung was fascinated by the mysterious, perseverative gestures made by some of the most regressed patients (Jung 1961). Fay (1977) and van der Post (1979) describe one of his cases. While working with a woman patient who had not been known to speak for many years, he noticed that she continually made certain odd movements with her hands and head. Going on instinct, he shut his eyes and repeated her movements in order to sense what she might be feeling. He then spoke out loud the first words that came to him. The woman responded immediately by saying: 'How did you know?' From that moment, a connection was made. The woman, previously regarded as incurable, was soon able to talk with him about her dreams and was ultimately able to be discharged. After this experience, he frequently relied on the body

---

[1]   Previously published in M. Stein (ed) *Jungian Analysis*. La Salle, IL: Open Court Publishing Co. (1982, 2nd ed. 1995).

experience as a communicative bridge to reach patients who were completely withdrawn (Fay 1977; van der Post 1979).

In discussing ritual, Jung said that the gesture is the most archaic manifestation of culture and spiritual life. In the beginning was the symbolic gesture, not the word (von Franz 1978, 1979). It is obvious that he had an instinctive grasp of movement as the primal means of expression and communication, yet he gave it relatively little attention in the development of analytical psychology. He did, however, take up the nature of the body-mind relationship. Psyche and matter are 'two different aspects of one and the same thing' (Jung 1947, p.215). 'The symbols of the self arise in the depths of the body...' (Jung 1940, p.173). What we call 'psychic' includes both physical and spiritual dimensions (Jung 1929). Jung envisioned the analogy to the color spectrum with two poles, ranging from 'the "psychic infra-red," the biological instinctual psyche' to 'the "psychic ultra-violet," the archetype...' (Jung 1947, p.215). Here he offers a vast foundation upon which others may continue to build.

The Jungian literature

There is increasing interest in the dialectic of expressive movement and the experience of the body in analysis. Kreinheder (1991), Mindell (1985), Schenk (1986), and Sidoli (1993) address the meaning and purpose of somatic symptoms. Schwartz-Salant (1982) takes up the subtle body. Wyman-McGinty (1998) explores the non-verbal nature of somatic memory and the importance of the somatic countertransference. Hubback (1988) and Samuels (1989) look at the experience of the body in early development and in the analytic relationship. Kalff (1971) and Rossi (1986) speak of the role of the body in the development of spiritual life.

Hall (1977) differentiates between enacting and acting out and suggests dance as a form through which dreams may be enacted. Roloff (1993) describes a powerful moment in his work with a child that shows so clearly the child's ability to discover and integrate the meaning of symbolic enactment. Sullwold (1971) presents an impressive account of her work with a child, which includes a description of the two of them becoming immersed in a dance the child taught her. Allan (1988) describes and discusses the therapy of a psychotic child:

> As Luci was best able to relate in the guise of different identities, we decided to...follow her through the fantasy world which she freely

constructed. In other words, rather than denying these fantasies, we, ourselves, participated in their enactment and assumed the roles she assigned to us. We attempted to make tangible some of the inner world sensations and thus validate the reality she was experiencing. (p.158)

Whitmont (1972) traces the historical tradition that produced our separation of body-mind and states that we can no longer operate with this schism: '…our emotions and problems are not merely in our souls, they are also in our bodies…' (p.16). He explores the use of techniques involving body-level awareness and symbolic enactments to deepen and broaden the Jungian analytic process. Bosanquet (1970) suggests that 'touching can, in certain circumstances, promote the analytical process and…prohibition of touching can delay or inhibit this' (p.42). She discusses the role of tactile contact in a case history, in early development, in regression and in the larger society. Greene (1984), Gaumond (n.d.) and McNeely (1987) continue the work of integrating body therapy and depth psychology. Chodorow (1991), Oppikofer (1991), and Wyman-McGinty (1998) focus particularly on dance/movement as active imagination.

The experience of dance can be approached in many ways. Singer (1976) explores psychological androgyny as experienced and expressed through the dances of gods and humans. Blackmer (1989) looks at the rigors of dance training and relates it to the alchemical *opus*. Spencer (1984) works with the image of dance and the dancer in dreams.

Since the early days, psychoanalysis has been known as 'the talking cure.' But underlying the process of verbal dialogue and exchange is the ongoing, continuous dialectic of expressive movement. This deep, non-verbal level is fundamental to the success of psychotherapy.

In his discussion of *Pan/Echo*, Lopez-Pedraza (1977) weaves wonderfully rich images around a therapy based on Echo-like reflections:

The happening of Pan's echo in psychotherapy can constellate a true epiphany of Pan, which is one of the most vivid expressions of the psychotherapeutic relationship. Like cures like…this is where the real symmetry happens, where the dance is, where the psychotherapy of Pan is. It is the expression of two bodies dancing in unison, a psychotherapy of the body. Are we in the psychoid realm of the psyche? Perhaps – but for sure we are in the realm where Pan appears in a psychotherapy within a sort of dance and through body movements, constellating the transference which belongs to him. (pp.84–85)

Perera (1981) describes this experience of empathic mirroring: 'On the deep levels of the transference-countertransference, outer and inner merge and two individuals share one psychic reality in the force field of *participation mystique;* hence it is often hard to discern what affect or image belongs to whom' (p.60).

Hillman (1976) contrasts the medical/diagnostic approach to the body, which emphasizes definition, with the dialectical approach in analysis, which seeks amplification:

> Analysis too pays meticulous attention to the body. It observes and listens to the body as experience. The body is the vessel in which the transformation process takes place. The analyst knows that there are no lasting changes unless the body is affected. Emotion always tears at the body, and the light of consciousness requires the heat of emotion. These affections of the body during an analysis are symptomatic – not in the diagnostic sense – of stages in the dialectic. To take them diagnostically and treat them medically might harm the process. The outbreak of skin rashes, circulation disorders, internal organ complaints, aches and pains, all reflect new areas of body experience, which must often first come about in the guise of ailments until the body can be heard without having to scream for recognition. The analyst also pays the same careful attention to his own body, listening to cues in his own flesh to aid his dialectic. He tries to sense during the hour when he is tired and hungry, sexually excited, slumped in passivity, irritatedly fidgeting, or developing symptoms and illness. His body is a sounding board. This sensitivity is appropriate to the body as experience and fits the analytical work. (pp.145–146)

Woodman (1980) addresses issues of body and psyche throughout a beautifully written psychological study of obesity, anorexia nervosa and the repressed feminine. She suggests dance as a powerful, practical way women may learn to listen to their bodies:

> [It is terrifying for modern women] to give themselves up to their emotions and the music and thus experience their own corresponding depths... That leap into the unconscious, however, is the very link that could connect them to the life force... This is not to recommend that women return to primal dance. Rather it is to suggest that the medium of music and creative dance is one of the surest ways to bring consciousness into the forgotten muscles. The dialogue with one's own body is a form of active imagination. (p.113)

Dance/Movement Therapy

While the use of dance as a healing ritual goes back to the dawn of history, dance therapy is a relatively new profession. The American Dance Therapy Association (1974) defines dance/movement therapy as the 'psycho-therapeutic use of movement as a process that furthers the physical and psychic integration of an individual.' Dance therapy is based upon the assumption that mind and body are in constant reciprocal interaction (Schoop 1974). It is built on psychological and physiological concepts, with an emphasis on the relationship of body and psyche. To use movement in therapy is to work directly with the most basic and primitive aspects of human experience. 'Differences in theoretical conceptualizations may alter the style or technique, but the underlying movement theories are inclusive. Dance therapy offers an alternative method for working within the context of any systematized theory of human behavior' (Chaiklin 1975, p.703).

One approach to dance therapy is based on Jung's psychology. This way of working is known as 'authentic movement,' a term coined by dance therapy pioneer Mary Whitehouse. It is basically dance/movement as a form of active imagination. Janet Adler (1992) describes her understanding of this work:

> ...the discipline of Authentic Movement is defined by the relationship between a person moving and a person witnessing that movement... movers work with eyes closed, slowly bringing their attention inward as their movement becomes highly specific to their own nature and history. Witnesses are invited to focus not only on what the mover is doing, but on their own inner experience in the presence of the mover. As the witness owns projections, judgments and interpretations, the mover is increasingly free to risk, honoring the deepening need to follow movement impulses which are born out of the unconscious. As the body finds form for the expression of what is at first formless material, personal consciousness evolves. (pp.76–77)

Active imagination in movement offers an individual the opportunity to develop a deep, self-sensing awareness – an attitude of inner listening. Out of this receptive state, a movement response may emerge that is unplanned, authentic. Carolyn Grant Fay (1982) writes:

> We work from life situations, body sensations, feelings, and dreams. Sometimes I may have to offer some simple movement to get started, such as rocking, and then we move with what unfolds out of that. Out of

a process of free movement certain patterns of movement may keep appearing and reappearing. These are important cues and need to be explored. (p.9)

Powerful images, feelings and memories may arise out of self-directed movement and out of the relationship that contains it. Because the process involves the use of the body to express the imagination, it tends to take the mover to complexes that can be traced back to the sensory-motor period of infancy and early childhood. The experiences of both mover and witness become intricately interwoven because part of the task of the therapist-witness is to hold the mover (psychologically) and to mirror empathically.

Verbal dialogue and exchange is an important part of the process. There is usually some talking before and after the movement, but less frequently in the midst of it. Self-directed movement ordinarily goes on for twenty to thirty minutes or more. Then there are times when only a few minutes of movement experience produces material for much subsequent reflection and processing. Whether long or short in duration, movement is often followed by a period of natural stillness and continuing inner attentiveness. At this point, verbal exchange may be premature. Art materials are sometimes helpful as a bridge, or poetic metaphor, or simply sitting together quietly. General rules are impractical for this transition because the links connecting movement/body experience, imagery, reflection and verbal processes between two individuals are subtle and complex. Sometimes, the mover has an immediate insight or string of insights about the meaning of the experience. Other times, it may take longer. Sometimes, a transformative experience is deeply felt but cannot be expressed in words.

Rather than attempting to evoke specific behavioral change, this approach to dance therapy relies on the natural development of internally-generated cues. It sees the body as the primary guide to the unconscious. This approach represents an important part of the dance therapy literature and its developing body of knowledge. It is a major focus of studies in some of the graduate-level training programs in dance therapy and an area of specialization for postgraduate studies.

Mary Whitehouse

Mary Whitehouse made a profound contribution to the field of dance therapy and her work offers rich resources to Jungian psychology. From her roots in dance, she was drawn into the experience of personal analysis with

Hilde Kirsch in Los Angeles and into studies at the Jung Institute in Zürich. She became a major pioneer in the field of dance/movement therapy, linking her understanding of movement to the principles of depth psychology.

In the paper entitled *C.G. Jung and dance therapy*, Whitehouse (1979) delineates two major principles – active imagination and polarity – and explores them from the perspective of dance/movement. Polarity is built into the physical body. We are organized via pairs of opposites, physically and psychologically. No human action can be accomplished without the operation of two sets of muscles, one contracting, one extending. As three-dimensional beings, each body axis contains a pair of opposites: up-down, left-right, backward-forward. To sense consciously the simplest body movement is to experience an interrelationship of the opposites.

An example of this may be helpful. The following is meant to be read as if you are listening and responding to the voice of someone you trust. As you read, give some attention to the rhythm of your breathing. Give yourself time simply to notice the taking in and giving out of each breath cycle. Can you find not only inhalation and exhalation but also the two subtle moments of reversal in between? Feel how the inhalation pauses before it reverses itself. And feel that suspended space at the bottom of the breath cycle, where the wonder of renewal continually emerges out of emptiness. You may find that your body has shifted, or wants to shift, towards an alignment that allows air to come in and out more easily. Yawning may occur, or some other transition toward deepening the breath cycle. But give primary attention to awareness. Don't direct, don't inhibit, just let it happen. No praise, no blame. As you continue to attend to your breathing, notice where you feel it. Is it in your throat? Chest? Rib cage? Abdomen? Lower back? Pelvic floor? Do you feel the transformation from coolness to warmth as air enters and leaves you? Notice the tendency to grow, to take up more space with each inhalation. You may feel yourself lengthening (up-down), widening (left-right), deepening or bulging (front-back). There is usually shrinking with exhalation – shortening, narrowing, compressing. With each breath cycle, sense the fullness of your three-dimensionality, the length, width and depth of your body. Sense how breath and body, spirit and matter, have effect upon each other. Then, when you finish reading this paragraph, close your eyes and let your body remember what you've just experienced.

Whitehouse (1958) describes another form of the polarity principle: 'The core of the movement experience is the sensation of moving and being moved' (p.243). To feel 'I am moving' is to be directed by the ego. To experience 'I am moved' is to know the reality of the unconscious. 'Ideally, both are present in the same instant… It is a moment of total awareness, the coming together of what I am doing and what is happening to me' (p.243). Whitehouse (1963) described the origin of movement as:

> a specific inner impulse having the quality of sensation. This impulse leads outward into space so that movement becomes visible as physical action. Following the inner sensation, allowing the impulse to take the form of physical action, is active imagination in movement, just as following the visual image is active imagination in fantasy. It is here that the most dramatic psycho physical connections are made available to consciousness. (p.17)

Whitehouse encouraged people to embody their images from dreams and fantasies and emphasized the importance of staying with the image:

> When the image is truly connected in certain people then the movement is authentic. There is no padding of movement just for the sake of moving. There is an ability to stand the inner tension until the next image moves them. They don't simply dance around. (Frantz 1972, p.41)

Sensation and image

The question of whether internally-generated movement cues are perceived by the mover as having the quality of sensation or image, or both, is most likely related to individual typology. Some people move with depth and authenticity but initially report either no images or only the constantly changing image of their own bodies and/or body parts in motion. It may be that such persons perceive the inner world predominantly through felt body sensations. They may have a powerful emotional response and even a sense of resolution, yet what it is about or where it comes from remains a mystery.

Those whose movements follow and reflect an ongoing stream of inner imagery often move through journeys of mythic proportion. These people usually make intuitive connections between the movement experience and their lives. Following the image alone may lead to some sense of its meaning but without attention to the instinctive body (through felt body sensations), a movement experience lacks emotional spontaneity.

Although one's basic inclination may remain one or the other, active imagination in movement tends to develop a relationship to both sensory and imaginal realms. When felt body sensation emerges as physical action, an image may appear that will give the movement meaning. Or, when an inner image emerges as physical action, the proprioceptive, kinesthetic experience may lead the mover toward connection to his or her instinctive body. The richest movement experiences seem to involve both sensation and image, fluctuating back and forth or occurring simultaneously.

Expression and impression

Dance/movement may fulfill two basic psychological objectives. We have been discussing how it arises out of an internal state – this is movement as a means of 'expression.' Yet it may also be employed to produce emotion, to subdue it or otherwise to have an effect upon internal states – this is movement as a means of 'impression.' Although the latter is a behavioral approach to psychic change, it sometimes has a place in the individuation process. An example is Jung's occasional use of certain Yoga exercises to control an emotional response that might have otherwise been over-whelming (Jung 1961).

Some of us are familiar with the planned and unplanned effects of rhythmic movement. It can take possession of groups. It can incite passions or subdue them. People can be motivated to work, disciplined to march into battle, energized or lulled into passivity: '…rhythm is a classic device for impressing certain ideas or activities on the mind' (Jung 1912, pp.154–155). Like any primal force, movement, particularly rhythmic movement, is powerful and this power must be respected. It merits increasing recognition and study by those who are concerned with depth psychology.

An emphasis on movement as expression or movement as impression may produce two distinct ways of working. Attention to both, however, creates fluctuation and constant interchange. The movement process serves as a bridge between inner and outer worlds, each having an impact on the other. Expression and impression may form an ongoing two-way flow that builds toward new integration.

Case illustration

Anna, a talented professional woman in her early thirties, has been in analysis for nearly three years. Although most of the process is verbal, she also utilizes movement, sandplay and art materials. The following movement sequence will illustrate some of the concepts discussed in this paper.

Recently married, Anna is struggling with the tension between her career and her desire to have a baby. In movement exploration she finds two opposite attitudes. When her right side leads, she finds quick movements that emphasize extension, definition, firmness. When her left side leads, she finds sustained softness – her body gathers inward, her arms gently overlap and envelop a small unseen shape.

After enacting each of these attitudes, she pauses and begins to experience tension between the two. She attempts to find a way of moving that simultaneously embodies both sides but, instead, she is gradually pulled apart into the shape of a twisted, hanging crucifix. As her right arm reaches outward, it is rigid and ineffective. Her left side is awkward as she attempts to encircle a baby with one arm. She begins to cry, yet is able to remain with the symbolic action.

Watching her, the therapist notices that her own body is becoming tense with restricted, shallow breathing. In Anna's pain, she recognizes her own. She now finds herself drawn into the enactment and reflects Anna's body state. Almost as if mirror images of each other, they hang together, twisted by a seemingly unresolvable tension. It is a timeless experience that moves through and beyond personal pain. They remain suspended together, moving only slightly, crying silently until both know that something has shifted. Although the issue is not resolved, there is a feeling of completion and relief. A struggle known by each of them individually, and by many women, has been seen and touched. A synchronistic moment has occurred. When they are ready to talk, the sense of mutuality remains strong. Rather than interpreting, they each tell about their own experience of the movement.

Here simultaneous work on physical and psychological levels has activated the archetype of the wounded healer. As both analyst and patient contact a profound sense of individual and collective woundedness, the depth of their experience constellates the other side of the archetype. As the wound is felt and recognized, it brings some experience of healing.

Like many modern women, Anna expected herself to fulfill all professional and family needs simultaneously. Her ego's attempt to integrate the polarities – soft-firm, gather-extend, slow-quick – all in the same instant was ineffective. In subsequent work she discovered that sequential, fluctuating rhythms can encompass many pairs of opposites. Her family came to include a baby (now growing up); her professional life also developed. As in the movement sequence, the struggle is not resolved but there is some feeling of completion.

Conclusion

It seems that as the Jungian collective turns its attention to the neglected feminine and to the shadow, it cannot avoid attending to the third aspect of this rejected trinity – the body. Jung pointed the way to this in 1928 when he wrote:

> ...if we can reconcile ourselves to the mysterious truth that the spirit is the life of the body seen from within, and the body is the outward manifestation of the life of the spirit – the two being really one – then we can understand why the striving to transcend the present level of consciousness must give the body its due. (pp.93–94)

Bibliography

Adler, J. (1972) 'Integrity of body and psyche: Some notes on work in process'. In B.F. Govine and J. Chodorow (eds) *What is Dance Therapy Really? Proceedings of the Seventh Annual Dance Therapy Conference,* pp.42–53. Columbia, MD: American Dance Therapy Association.

Adler, J. (1992) 'Body and soul'. *American Journal of Dance Therapy 14,* 2, 73–94.

Allan, J. (1988) *Inscapes of the Child's World.* Dallas, TX: Spring.

American Dance Therapy Association (1974) *Proceedings of the Ninth Annual American Dance Therapy Association Conference.* Columbia, MD: American Dance Therapy Association.

Blackmer, J.D. (1989) *Acrobats of the Gods: Dance and Transformation.* Toronto: Inner City Books.

Bosanquet, C. (1970) 'Getting in touch'. *Journal of Analytical Psychology 15,* 1, 42–58.

Chaiklin, S. (1975) 'Dance therapy'. In S. Arieti (ed) *American Handbook of Psychiatry 5,* 2nd ed. New York: Basic Books.

Chodorow, J. (1974) 'Philosophy and methods of individual work'. In K. Mason (ed) *Dance Therapy: Focus on Dance VII,* pp.24–26. Washington, DC: American Association for Health, Physical Education and Recreation.

Chodorow, J. (1978) 'Dance therapy and the transcendent function'. *American Journal of Dance Therapy 2,* 1, 16–23.

Chodorow, J. (1984) 'To move and be moved'. *Quadrant 17,* 2, 39–48.

Chodorow, J. (1991) *Dance Therapy and Depth Psychology: The Moving Imagination.* London and New York: Routledge.

Fay, C.G. (1977) *Movement and Fantasy: A Dance Therapy Model Based on the Psychology of Carl G. Jung.* Master's thesis. Goddard College, Vermont.

Fay, C.G. (1978) 'Five dance therapists whose life and work have been influenced by the psychology of C.G. Jung'. *American Journal of Dance 2,* 2, 17–18.

Fay, C.G. (1982) 'Dance therapy: Who/what/why'. Plenary session of the Conference on Medical Applications of Dance at Baylor College of Medicine, Houston, TX.

Frantz, G. (1972) 'An approach to the center: An interview with Mary Whitehouse'. *Psychological Perspectives 3,* 1, 37–46.

Franz, M.L. von. (1978) *Interpretation of Fairy Tales.* Irving, TX: Spring Publications.

Franz, M.L. von. (1979) Comments made during a panel discussion. Panarion Conference, 21–27 July, Los Angeles.

Gaumond, M. (no date) 'Individuation through body awareness: Eutonia as seen by a Jungian Analyst'. Unpublished manuscript.

Greene, A. (1984) 'Giving the body its due'. *Quadrant 17*, 2, 9–24.

Guggenbuhl-Craig, A. (1971) 'Power in the helping professions'. New York: Spring Publications.

Hall, J. (1977) *Clinical Uses of Dreams: Jungian Interpretations and Enactments.* New York: Grune & Stratton.

Hayes, D. (1959) 'Consideration of the dance from a Jungian viewpoint'. *Journal of Analytical Psychology 4*, 2, 169–181.

Hillman, J. (1962) *Emotion: A Comprehensive Phenomenology of Theories and their Meaning for Therapy.* Evanston, IL: Northwestern University Press.

Hillman, J. (1976) *Suicide and the Soul.* Zürich: Spring Publications.

Hubback, J. (1988) *People Who do Things to Each Other: Essays in Analytical Psychology.* Wilmette, IL: Chiron Publications.

Jaffé, A. (ed) (1979) *C.G. Jung: Word and Image.* Princeton: Princeton University Press.

Jung, C.G. (1912) 'The transformation of libido'. In *The Collected Works of C.G. Jung* (1956/67) (vol. 5). Princeton: Princeton University Press.

Jung, C.G. (1916) 'The transcendent function'. In *The Collected Works of C.G. Jung* (2nd ed., 1969/78) (vol. 8). Princeton: Princeton University Press.

Jung, C.G. (1928) 'The spiritual problems of modern man'. In *The Collected Works of C.G. Jung* (2nd ed., 1970) (vol. 10). Princeton: Princeton University Press.

Jung, C.G. (1929) 'Commentary on "The secret of the golden flower."' In *The Collected Works of C.G. Jung* (1967) (vol. 13). Princeton: Princeton University Press.

Jung, C.G. (1935) 'The Tavistock lectures: On the theory and practice of analytical psychology'. In *The Collected Works of C.G. Jung* (1976) (vol. 18). Princeton: Princeton University Press.

Jung, C.G. (1940) 'The psychology of the child archetype'. In *The Collected Works of C.G. Jung* (1972) (vol. 9, part I). Princeton: Princeton University Press.

Jung, C.G. (1947) 'On the nature of the psyche'. In *The Collected Works of C.G. Jung* (2nd ed., 1969/78) (vol. 8). Princeton: Princeton University Press, .

Jung, C.G. (1961) *Memories, Dreams. Reflections.* New York: Vintage Books, Random House.

Jung, C.G. (1976) *The Visions Seminars. Vol. 2.* New York: Spring Publications.

Kalff, D. (1971) 'Experiences with Far Eastern philosophers'. In J.B. Wheelwright (ed) *The Analytic Process.* New York: Putnam.

Kreinheder, A. (1991) *Body and Soul: The Other Side of Illness.* Toronto: Inner City Press.

Lewis, P. (1992) *Creative Transformation: The Healing Power of the Arts.* Wilmette, IL: Chiron Publications.

Lopez-Pedraza, R. (1977) *Hermes and his Children.* Zürich, Switzerland: Spring Publications.

Mayer, M. (no date) 'A Jungian perspective on breathing and relaxation: In theory and practice.' Privately printed.

McNeely, D.A. (1987) *Touching: Body Therapy and Depth Psychology.* Toronto: Inner City Books.

Mindell, A. (1985) *Working with the Dreaming Body.* Boston and London: Routledge & Kegan Paul.

Oppikofer, R. (1991) 'Vom erleben der emotionen: Emotion und körperarbeit im therapeutischen prozess'. Diplomthesis am C.G. Jung Institute, Zürich, Switzerland.

Perera, S. (1981) *Descent to the Goddess.* Toronto: Inner City Press.

Roloff, L. (1993) 'Living, ignoring, and regressing: Transcendent moments in the lives of a child, a transsexual, and a sexually repressed adult'. In M.A. Mattoon (ed) *The Transcendent Function. Proceedings of the XIIth International Congress of Analytical Psychology.* Einsiedeln, Switzerland: Daimon Verlag.

Rossi, E.L. (1986) *The Psychobiology of Mind-Body Healing.* New York and London: W. W. Norton & Co.

Samuels, A. (1989) *The Plural Psyche.* London and New York: Routledge.

Schenk, R. (1986) *Bare Bones: The Aesthetics of Arthritis. The Body in Analysis.* Wilmette, IL: Chiron Publications.

Schoop, T., with Mitchell, P. (1974) *Won't you Join the Dance?* Palo Alto, CA: National Press Books.

Schwartz-Salant, N. (1982) *Narcissism and Character Transformation.* Toronto: Inner City Books.

Schwartz-Salant, N. and Stein, M. (eds) (1986) *The Body in Analysis.* Wilmette, IL: Chiron Publications.

Sherman, F. (1978) 'Conversation with Mary Whitehouse'. *American Journal of Dance Therapy 2,* 2, 3–4.

Sidoli, M. (1993) 'When meaning gets lost in the body'. In M.A. Mattoon (ed) *The Transcendent Function. Proceedings of the XIIth International Congress of Analytical Psychology.* Einsiedeln, Switzerland: Daimon Verlag.

Singer, J. (1976) *Androgyny.* Garden City, NY: Anchor Press/Doubleday.

Spencer, M.J. (1984) 'Amplification: The dance'. *Journal of Analytical Psychology 29,* 113–123.

Sullwold, E. (1971) 'Eagle eye'. In H. Kirsch (ed) *The Well Tended Tree.* New York: Putnam.

van der Post, L. (1977) *Jung and the Story of our Time.* New York: Random House, Vintage Books.

van der Post, L. (1979) *World Unrest as a Loss of Meaning. C.G. Jung Cassette Library.* Los Angeles: C.G. Jung Institute.

Whitehouse, M.S. (no date) Some thoughts on movement, dance and the integration of the personality. Unpublished notes.

Whitehouse, M.S. (no date) *Creative Expression in Physical Movement is Language without Words.* Unpublished manuscript.

Whitehouse, M.S. (1958) 'The Tao of the body'. In D.H. Johnson (ed) *Bone, Breath and Gesture: Practices of Embodiment.* Berkeley, CA: North Atlantic Books, 1995.

Whitehouse, M.S. (1963) 'Physical movement and personality'. *Contact Quarterly,* Winter, 1987, 16–19.

Whitehouse, M.S. (1968) 'Introduction of videotape: Individual dance and verbal therapy session'. In B. Bird (ed) *Workshop in Dance Therapy: Its Research Potentials,* pp.20–22. New York: Committee on Research in Dance.

Whitehouse, M. (1970) 'Reflections on a metamorphosis.' In R. Head, R.E. Rothenberg and D. Wesley (eds) *A Well of Living Waters: Festschrift for Hilde Kirsch*, pp.272–277. Los Angeles: C.G. Jung Institute, 1977.

Whitehouse, M. (1977) 'The transference and dance therapy.' *American Journal of Dance Therapy*, 1, 1, 3–7.

Whitehouse, M. (1979) 'C.G. Jung and dance therapy'. In P. Lewis Bernstein (ed) *Eight Theoretical Approaches in Dance/Movement Therapy*. Dubuque, Iowa: Kendall/Hunt.

Whitmont, E. (1972) 'Body experience and psychological awareness'. *Quadrant 12*, 5–16.

Woodman, M. (1980) *The Owl was a Baker's Daughter*. Toronto: Inner City Books.

Woodman, M. (1982) *Addiction to Perfection*. Toronto: Inner City Books.

Woodman, M. (1984) 'Psyche/soma awareness'. *Quadrant 17*, 2, 25–37.

Wyman-McGinty, W. (1998) 'The body in analysis: Authentic Movement and witnessing in analytic practice'. *Journal of Analytical Psychology 43*, 2.

CHAPTER 19

To Move and Be Moved[1]

Joan Chodorow

Introduction

In the beginning there was not the word, rather there was the symbolic action – a union of body and psyche. In the beginning dance was the sacred language through which we communed and communicated with the vast unknown. In the earliest times the dancer was both healer and priest.

Then, through the centuries, in the name of progress and civilization, mind and body were split apart. Separate professions developed to attend to the needs of increasingly compartmentalized beings. The instinctive body was seen as a threat because it represented the 'lower,' animal aspects of human nature. As the life of the body was suppressed, so too was the receptive, feminine principle. As clarity, objectivity and differentiation were developed and given highest value, the Moon Goddess, who seeks union, wholeness, completion, was sacrificed. Both the body and the feminine were relegated to the underworld, along with all that is despised and rejected.

C.G. Jung, in his studies of the symbolism of the Holy Trinity, emphasized that it has its counterpart in a lower, chthonic triad. Father, Son and Holy Ghost represent the one-sided values of Western culture – qualities that are masculine, disembodied and 'good.' By contrast, we have devalued qualities related to the feminine, denied the experience of the body and relegated evil to the underworld, where it effects utmost destruction in the darkness of projection and possession.

---

1   One of three papers for a workshop entitled *Body and Psyche* with Anita Green, Marion Woodman, and Joan Chodorow, Discussants. The National Conference of Jungian Analysts, New York City, May 3–6, 1984. Previously published in *Quadrant*, Vol. 17, no. 2, Fall 1984.

As we approach the third millennium, this long-buried underworld trinity increasingly demands conscious recognition. We see it in the development of the women's movement, the resurgence of attention to the life of the body and the life of Mother Earth, and a bare but beginning psychological awareness of the personal, the cultural and the collective shadow.

Human survival may now depend on each individual's capacity to bear the tension of carrying many inner opposites. In *Aion* Jung (1951) suggests that the coming Aquarian Age will require us to relate not only to new aspects of ourselves and each other but to a new God-image – a complex of opposites that includes masculine/feminine, spirit/body, good/evil.

Jungian analysts have a profound contribution to make to this developing new consciousness. It seems essential that as we attend to issues of the emerging feminine, and the shadow, we also attend to the third aspect of this rejected trinity: the living body. Work with the unconscious includes listening to the body as experience (Hillman 1976). We may sense, as the alchemists did, that if spirit has been imprisoned in matter, it is to matter we must go to discover and release the spirit.

Dance/Movement and body experience in analysis

Attention to dance/movement and body experience in analysis is not new. In his 1916 paper on the transcendent function, Jung described body move-ment as one of many ways to express the unconscious. Through the years he continued to refer to a small number of his patients, apparently all women, who used dance and body movement to elaborate or develop a theme: 'Those who are able to express the unconscious by means of bodily movements are rather rare' (Jung 1916, p.84); 'I have come across cases of women who did not draw mandalas but danced them instead' (Jung 1929, p.23); 'One or two women danced their unconscious figures' (Jung 1935, p.173). For some people, men as well as women, dance is the most immediate, powerful way to give form to unconscious contents. For such individuals, dance/movement and body experience may be an essential part of the individuation process.

Body movement as a form of active imagination is similar to sandplay, in the sense that it involves an inner-directed process of symbolic action that usually takes place within the analytic hour. The analyst most often serves as witness and, at the beginning, as in any analytic work, carries a larger responsibility for consciousness. The analysand is simply invited to move and see what happens.

Mary Starks Whitehouse

Mary Starks Whitehouse was a dancer, teacher and pioneer movement therapist. Through her personal analysis with Hilde Kirsch in Los Angeles and her studies at the Jung Institute in Zürich, she began to link her understanding of dance and movement to the principles of depth psychology. Her work has inspired a number of her students to continue its development for use in analysis, dance therapy, choreography, dance performance, dance education, dance ethnology.

Whitehouse was primarily interested in exploring and understanding the inner experience of the mover. She taught her students to move from a specific, inner impulse that has the quality of a bodily felt sensation. She also invited people to embody their images, to dance with and to be danced by the inner other. Whether we are attending to the bodily felt sensation, the inner image or both as our source(s) of movement, this way of working develops in us a more conscious relationship to both sensory and imaginal realms.

Whitehouse was one of the first to communicate clearly what it is to move, and what it is to be moved:

> 'I move' is the clear knowledge that I personally, am moving... The opposite of this is the sudden and astonishing moment when 'I am moved'... It is a moment when the ego gives up control, stops choosing, stops exerting demands, allowing the Self to take over moving the physical body as it will. It is a moment of unpremeditated surrender that cannot be explained, repeated exactly, sought for or tried out. (1979, p.57)

> The core of the movement experience is the sensation of moving and being moved... Ideally, both are present in the same instant... It is a moment of total awareness, the coming together of what I am doing and what is happening to me. (1958, p.243)

In her classes Whitehouse usually started with some warm-up exercises – either leading them or suggesting that people improvise on their own. Then she told people to find a place in the room, close their eyes, attend inwardly and wait for an impulse to move them. She fostered an attitude of yielding – that is, letting oneself be moved by the stream of unconscious impulses and images – while at the same time bringing the experience into conscious awareness.

From this simple yet profound idea there developed a new sensitivity to the origins of movement from different aspects of the psyche. In the following pages we will discuss the personal unconscious, the cultural unconscious, the primordial unconscious and the Self as four different sources out of which movement may arise.

Movement from the personal unconscious

One of the first dance therapists to describe movement from various levels of the unconscious was Janet Adler, who had studied with Whitehouse. She wrote of some movement gestures that seem completely personal, unique to the individual:

> Idiosyncratic movements are most powerfully expressive of the true shadow – the darker, or unknown side – of the personality. They seem to have no meaning to anyone else, and appear unrelated to anyone else's movement patterns. Of its very nature, then, it is difficult to identify an idiosyncratic pattern as such until it is repeated so many times that it becomes clear. Even then I seldom have the slightest idea what it means or where its source lies. These movement patterns or qualities truly reflect the uniqueness and the enormously complicated nature of the individual. (1972, p.48)

As the mover and the witness gradually become aware of an emerging movement repertoire, the idiosyncratic patterns become more familiar. The mover may even find that s/he cannot escape them. No matter what s/he does, a specifically personal gesture or quality is woven through all the ways s/he moves.

Such intensely personal patterns are frequently related to pre-verbal experiences. Pre-verbal memories are vivid when we are able to attend to them – they manifest in both sensory and imaginal realms. But it is difficult to retrieve them because there are no words available to organize and describe the event. By bringing consciousness to the idiosyncratic movement patterns, certain images and affects become available that are typical of stages of development in infancy and early childhood. Many of these gestures seem related to the sleep rituals that ordinarily become conscious when the baby becomes aware of his or her capacity for pretend play.

In a rich interweaving of Jungian thought with recent studies of the affects and their expression, Louis H. Stewart (1981, 1982) has been up-dating Jung's model of the psyche. Writing in collaboration with Charles T.

Stewart, a child psychiatrist, he describes the critical moment in the infant's development when the sleep ritual first becomes conscious:

> Around sixteen to eighteen months of age, the child becomes aware of the semiotic function through the experience of pretense, for example in the miming of an already adaptive behavior pattern like the ritual behavior adopted to ease the transition into sleep (e.g. thumb sucking and fingering the satiny edge of a blanket). The child laughs with joy at this new recognition of Self; and this is pretend play... But let us reflect for a moment on the sleep ritual. This is not a neutral pattern of behavior. It represents one of the landmarks in the child's development. If the transition to sleep and waking is not easily accomplished, the child may be forever prone to sleep disturbances, to excessive fear of the dark, needing a night light, etc. And why is going to sleep difficult? Because it brings together the child's most feared and distressing fantasies, that of being deprived of the presence and comfort of those most dear, and of being left alone in the dark which is peopled by who knows what ghostly phantoms. Thus we consider it no accident that the child discovers pretense in the recognition of the sleep ritual; pretend play begins with the miming of a behavior pattern which has assisted the child in warding off fear of the unknown and soothing the anguish of separation. Subsequent pretend play will be seen to reenact all the emotionally charged experiences of the child's life. (Stewart and Stewart 1981, p.47)

Stewart suggests that bringing the sleep ritual to consciousness is to separate the world parents – it is at this moment we first learn to distinguish between conscious and unconscious. When, as adults, we find ourselves continually returning to a uniquely personal way of rocking, stroking, fingering or holding – a puzzling yet comforting movement pattern – it may be the psyche's way of bringing our attention to this bridge between the two realms of consciousness – that is, helping us attend to the transition between dayworld and dreamworld.

As personal movement patterns emerge, transference issues that reflect the infant parent relationship are likely to become prominent. The feelings, attitudes and complexes of the mover's parents tend at this point to be transferred to the analyst as s/he watches the mover.

Movement from the cultural unconscious

The cultural level of the unconscious has been described by Joseph L. Henderson (1964) as a level that mediates between the primordial unconscious and the cultural forms that provide us with religious, aesthetic, social and philosophic experience.

Janet Adler (1972) seems to be describing movement arising from the cultural unconscious when she speaks of 'culturally symptomatic movements.' In contrast to the idiosyncratic, these movement gestures are more easily understood by both the mover and the witness. For example, a gesture of forcefully pushing one or both hands away from the torso might be culturally read as 'get away' or 'leave me alone' (Adler 1972). A single firm stamp of the foot is usually understood as 'I put my foot down' or 'here I stand.' Gestures that mime different kinds of work and play appear and, sometimes, certain animal-like images are given form. Despair, yearning, frustration, enthusiasm – a whole world of everyday feelings emerges in gestures that can be clearly expressed and understood. These movements may be planned, done with the conscious intent of conveying a specific message, or they may be unplanned, emerging or even erupting spontaneously to the complete surprise of the mover.

Adler (1972) also speaks of how specific body parts can be invested with psychic energy. For example, a body part that carries heightened tension may be noticed but not necessarily understood. Again, a body part that looks and feels dead may draw attention to itself. If the mover can stay focused on the body put as it is, without trying to change it, a meaningful symbolic gesture frequently emerges. As this happens, we are witness to a symbol in the process of transformation as it moves out of the personal unconscious into a form that is culturally understandable.

The cultural unconscious holds a wide range of emotional expression that has a formalized quality. I think here of a recently bereaved woman who had no conscious awareness that Jewish tradition, as well as many others, requires the tearing of a garment or piece of cloth as a formal gesture of grief. She wanted to move, but when she first began to attend inwardly, she became immobilized. The images that came were of self-destruction – hurling herself against the walls, tearing at her own flesh. She then shifted her attention from images to bodily sensations and found that her heart felt as if it was tearing apart. As she stayed with the feelings of her heart being torn, her hands grasped at the sweatshirt she was wearing. Slowly, with a quality that can best be described as 'inevitable,' her hands began to tear through the cloth of her garment.

Movement from the primordial unconscious

And then there are movement themes that have such a different, often non-human, quality that it seems they must come from the depths of the collective unconscious. In *The Structure of the Psyche* Jung (1927) wrote:

> The whole psychic organism corresponds exactly to the body, which, though individually varied, is in all essential features the specifically human body which all men have. In its development and structure, it still preserves elements that connect it with the invertebrates and ultimately with the protozoa. Theoretically it should be possible to 'peel' the collective unconscious, layer by layer, until we came to the psychology of the worm, and even of the amoeba. (p.152)

Movement events that emerge out of such depths have a numinous effect on both mover and witness. The sequences have a seizure or trance-like quality, as if the mover is approaching, or is in, a state of possession.

Sometimes, the quality of movement is chaotic, arrhythmic, disjointed. The mover seems to be struggling to avoid loss of control. Here the gestures are no longer recognizable as repressed personal history. And they are not in a form that is culturally recognizable. These impulses and images can be so alien that they are – or we experience them as if they were – undifferentiated chaos. The mover usually approaches with caution. Most people will simply stop rather than be taken over by such an experience.

At other times, the movement has the quality of a seizure or trance state that does not appear chaotic. The mover seems to be possessed by an animal quality, a nature image or an affect of great intensity. Such movement may emerge for only a second or two or it may sustain itself over a longer time. Here, too, the movement may reflect the mover's struggle to maintain some control. But even though the impulses and images from this level remain other than human, they are more differentiated, or our relationship to them is. We are somehow able to allow such primordial affects to emerge in the form of symbolic physical action.

Stewart's (1982) work on the relationship of affect and archetype is helpful in understanding the movement qualities that emerge. He identifies two major affects of life enhancement: curiosity/interest (*logos*) and play/joy (*eros*). Taken into the primal depths, these affects become seizures of divine curiosity and ecstatic love. When a human being embodies such god-like qualities, an inflation is inevitable. On a movement level, we see a person who is literally 'being danced' by an intensely focused energy that approaches manic excitement or we see one who has become identified with an all-embracing quality of seemingly limitless love, bliss, rapture.

In addition, Stewart and Stewart (1981) describe the four-fold crisis/survival affects and the specific stimulus of each: Distress [loss]; Fear [the unknown]; Anger [restriction]; and Contempt/Shame [rejection]. When touched by these aspects of the primordial unconscious, the mover approaches a state of seizure. Distress descends into the eternal pool of grief and anguish that goes beyond personal loss; fear of the unknown becomes stark terror as the mover dances with and is danced by *Pan*; frustration/anger becomes homicidal rage; contempt/shame calls forth the extremes oi alienation and humiliation. Human beings cannot sustain such intensity for long. Such movement events occur rarely and last only for moments, but they remain unforgettable to both mover and witness.

Movement from the Self

Another group of movement events that come from such depths has an entirely different quality. These patterns are geometric in form, with a strong central axis that seems to balance and counterbalance all the dynamic pairs of opposites possible in a moving body. It is as if the mover is being moved by the ordering and centering process of the psyche. These experiences tend to come as a constellation of the Self at critical stages in the work.

I remember here the movement of a gifted psychotherapy student in her early thirties. She had recently suffered a profound personal loss that made her painfully aware of her tendency to deny the life of her own body. In her previous work with movement she had always yearned toward the sky, barely touching the earth with her feet. Now, in a state of grief, she discovered that her feet were connected to the ground. The rest of her body was able to follow this awareness downward onto the floor. For the next several months, whenever she moved, she remained intimately connected to the ground, rolling, crawling, creeping, crouching and rocking. She became increasingly aware of sensations in her pelvis and movement began to initiate from her pelvic floor. Different images began to accompany this new way of moving.

One image was of blood coming out of her hip joints. She experienced it as a pouring forth of life blood – an image of both woundedness and healing. In the movement she spread it all over herself, outside and in, drinking, swallowing, absorbing. Then, covered with blood, she descended into some caverns. Her pelvis was so alive it led the rest of her body. Light came out of her pelvis, enabling her to see where she was going. At the bottom of the cavern there was a pool of mud. She bathed in the mud and felt grounded, connected, secure. That night she dreamed that her grandmother gave her a sum of money in the form of 'securities.'

At the next session all of her movement centered on pelvic initiation. Finally, she simply sat on the earth, grounded, a primal woman. From this sitting there grew a slow, but increasingly compelling, rhythmic pattern. Her arms, head and torso began to move as a unit, tracing a half-circle through horizontal space, right to the left, counterclockwise. When her body could go no further in the horizontal plane, it shifted to the lateral plane and she completed another half-circle, this one left to right, clockwise, over her own head, like a rising and setting sun. When she could go no further to her right (in the lateral plane), she began the cycle again by returning to the horizontal, counterclockwise sweep. She repeated the cycle over and over with strong rhythmic shifts and a wonderful clarity of spatial intent. Her movement was an integration of two half-circles – one counterclockwise, the other clockwise. She also brought together two planes and four directions, creating a multidimensional, circular cross. It felt like a union of opposites in motion.

Jung (1947) may well have been describing such a movement event when he wrote:

> The chaotic assortment of images that at first confronted me reduced itself in the course of the work to certain well-defined themes and formal elements, which repeated themselves in identical or analogous form with the most varied individuals. I mention, as the most salient characteristics, chaotic multiplicity and order; duality; the opposition of light and dark, upper and lower, right and left; the union of the opposites in a third; the quaternity (square, cross); rotation (circle, sphere); and finally the centering process and a radial arrangement that usually followed some quaternary system... The centering process is, in my experience, the never-to-be-surpassed climax of the whole development, and is characterized as such by the fact that it brings with it the greatest possible therapeutic effect. (p.203)

The mover, the witness and their relationship

It will take a study of greater length than this chapter to illustrate how movement experience weaves into the larger context of Jungian analysis. But it is the therapeutic relationship, with particular attention to issues of transference and countertransference, that is central to the use of dance/movement in analysis.

It is a powerful experience for the analyst to bring his or her full presence to witness the movement of a patient. And it is the quality of the analyst's attentive presence that can create the 'free and sheltered space' that has been so beautifully described by Dora Kalff (1980).

Part of witnessing requires the capacity to open fully to the unconscious, as in any analytic work. Witnessing also provides mirroring for the patient and, often at critical moments, invites a state of *participation mystique*. Yet the witness-analyst must also be separate from the mover and maintain a conscious analytic standpoint for reflection on the meaning of the symbolic action.

For example, in the circular cross movement described above, the witness-analyst was so absorbed in watching the mover that she was drawn into a similar breathing rhythm and similar patterns of muscular tension. As the mover sat firmly connected with the earth, the witness too was conscious of her own pelvic floor. As she watched, she was aware that she felt embedded, even rooted, as both she and the mover sat on the floor.

When the mover began to slowly trace the first half-circle, the witness became alert to the change and noticed that it was in the counterclockwise direction. The witness-analyst remembered a Corn Dance ritual in New Mexico, where for a full day she had watched hundreds of Pueblo Indians move in a gigantic counterclockwise circle. She remembered other experiences when counterclockwise movement had led to a light trance state.[2] As she watched, her earlier state of near merging changed to an attitude of careful attention. She imagined that the counterclockwise circling might go on and on, as it often does. But before her awareness of this possibility was fully formed, the mover paused, rotated her entire torso and completed the circle clockwise. The change was breathtaking. It was a clearly articulated shift from one plane to another and it united two half-circles into a whole, using both the counterclockwise (sacred or demonic time/space) and the clockwise (everyday ego time/space) directions.

---

2   In Christian, Buddhist and certain other traditions, counterclockwise movement is related to the rituals of witchcraft and black magic, but many primal peoples dance in a counterclockwise pattern when they wish to enter the realm of sacred time and space.

As the mover continued to repeat the cycle with increasing clarity and strength, the witness experienced a new sense of order. As she watched the movement, she could feel it again in her own body and, at the same time, she had some understanding of it.

Later, as mover and witness came together, it took some time before there was room for words. They had each experienced the autonomous power of the ordering and centering process of psyche/soma. They both knew that an important passage had been completed.

Conclusion

For me, the core of work with movement in Jungian analysis is the experience of the mover, the experience of the witness-analyst and the relationship between them that serves as container and process. The work is sustained by Jung's vision of individuation:

> When the great swing has taken an individual into the world of symbolic mysteries, nothing comes of it, nothing can come of it, unless it has been associated with the earth, unless it has happened when that individual was in the body... And so individuation can only take place if you first return to the body, to your earth, only then does it become true. (Jung 1934, p.473)

Bibliography

Adler, J. (1972) 'Integrity of body and psyche: Some notes on work in process'. In B.F. Govine and J. Chodorow (eds) *What is Dance Therapy Really? Proceedings of the Seventh Annual Dance Therapy Conference*. Columbia, MD: American Dance Therapy Association.

Henderson, J.L. (1964) 'The archetype of culture'. In S. Karger (ed) *The Archetype, Proceedings of the Second International Congress of Analytical Psychology*. New York or Zürich?

Hillman, J. (1976) *Suicide and the Soul*. Zürich: Spring Publications.

Jung. C.G. (1916) 'The transcendent function'. In *The Collected Works of C.G. Jung* (2nd ed.,1969/78) (vol. 8). Princeton: Princeton University Press.

Jung, C.G. (1927) 'The structure of the psyche'. In *The Collected Works of C.G. Jung* (2nd ed., 1969/78) (vol. 8). Princeton: Princeton University Press.

Jung, C.G. (1929) 'Commentary on "The secret of the golden flower."' In *The Collected Works of C.G. Jung* (1967) (vol. 13). Princeton: Princeton University Press.

Jung, C.G. (1934) *The Visions Seminars. Vol. 2* (1976). New York: Spring Publications.

Jung, C.G. (1935) 'The Tavistock lectures: On the theory and practice of analytical psychology'. In *The Collected Works of C.G. Jung* (1976) (vol. 18). Princeton: Princeton University Press.

Jung, C.G. (1947) 'On the nature of the psyche'. In *The Collected Works of C.G. Jung* (2nd ed., 1969/78) (vol. 8). Princeton: Princeton University Press.

Jung, C.G. (1951) 'Aion: Researches into the phenomenology of the Self'. In *The Collected Works of C.G. Jung* (1968) (vol. 9, part II). Princeton: Princeton University Press.

Kalff, D. (1980) *Sandplay.* Santa Monica, CA: Sigo Press.

Stewart, L.H. (1982) *The Play-Dream Continuum.* Lecture presented at the annual meeting of The Association for the Anthropological Study of Play (TAASP).

Stewart, L.H. and Stewart, C.T. (1981) 'Play, games and affects: A contribution toward a comprehensive theory of play'. In A.T. Cheska (ed) *Play as Context. Proceedings of The Association for the Anthropological Study of Play* (TAASP). Westpoint, NY: Leisure Press.

Whitehouse, M.S. (1958) 'The Tao of the body'. In D.H. Johnson (1995) (ed) *Bone, Breath and Gesture: Practices of Embodiment.* Berkeley, CA: North Atlantic Books.

Whitehouse, M.S. (1979) 'C.G. Jung and dance therapy'. In P. Lewis Bernstein (ed) *Eight Theoretical Approaches in Dance/Movement Therapy.* Dubuque, Iowa: Kendall/Hunt.

CHAPTER 20

The Body as Symbol
Dance/Movement in Analysis[1]

Joan Chodorow

The dance is the mother of the arts. Music and poetry exist in time; painting and architecture in space. But the dance lives at once in time and space. The creator and the thing created...are still one and the same thing.

(Sachs 1937, p.3)

This paper will discuss the use of dance/movement as a form of active imagination in analysis. The history of this work emerges out of two traditions: depth psychology and dance therapy. The roots of both can be traced to earliest human history, when disease was seen as a loss of soul and dance was an intrinsic part of the healing ritual.

The importance of bodily experience in depth psychology has not been fully recognized, despite Jung's interest in and experience of the body and his understanding of its relationship to the creative process. I will take up some of this material; look at the early development of dance movement therapy, with attention to Mary Starks Whitehouse and her contribution to the development of active imagination through movement; and explore the process of using dance/movement in analysis. This will lead to discussion of dance/movement as a bridge to early, preverbal stages of development.

---

1   Previously published in *The Body in Analysis*, The Chiron Clinical Series, 1986.

Depth psychology

Throughout his life, C.G. Jung (1961) seemed to listen to the experience of his own body: 'I hated gymnastics. I could not endure having others tell me how to move' (p.29); 'My heart suddenly began to pound. I had to stand up and draw a deep breath' (p.108); 'I had a curious sensation. It was as if my diaphragm were made of iron and were becoming red-hot – a glowing vault' (p.155). His visions, too, were clearly experienced in his body:

> Suddenly it was as though the ground literally gave way beneath my feet, and I plunged down into dark depths. I could not fend off a feeling of panic. But then, abruptly, at not too great a depth, I landed on my feet in a soft sticky mass. I felt great relief. (p.179)

From his boyhood realization that he had two 'personalities,'[2] Jung was interested in questions about the relationship of body and psyche. His earliest psychological study included observations of unconscious motor phenomena (Jung 1902). His work with some of the severely regressed patients at Bürgholzli led him to question, and eventually discover, the meaning of their peculiar, perseverative, symptomatic actions (Jung 1907). His word association studies involved measurement of physiological changes that occur when a psychological complex is touched. His later speculations about the existence of a psychoid level and his alchemical studies continued to explore the relationship between instinct and archetype, matter and spirit. In an evocative paper entitled *Giving the body its due*, Anita Greene (1984) writes: 'For Jung, matter and spirit, body and psyche, the intangible and the concrete were not split or disconnected but always remained interfused with each other' (p.12).

Adela Wharton, an English physician, told Joseph Henderson that during one of her analytic hours, Jung 'encouraged her to dance her mandala-like designs for him when she could not draw them satisfactorily' (Henderson 1985a, p.9). The room was not large, but a small clear space was sufficient (Henderson 1985b). We know very little about the details of her dance, or

---

2   Personality Number One was grounded in the concrete reality of everyday life, the facts of the world the way it is. Personality Number Two lived in eternal time, the world of the ancestors and spirits, a mythic realm. Jung (1961) wrote: 'The play and counterplay between personalities No. 1 and No. 2, which has run through my whole life, has nothing to do with a "split" or dissociation in the ordinary medical sense. On the contrary, it is played out in every individual' (p.45).

what it stirred in each of them, or how they came together afterwards. But, in his *Commentary on 'The Secret of the Golden Flower,'* Jung (1929) wrote:

> Among my patients I have come across cases of women who did not draw mandalas but danced them instead. In India there is a special name for this: *mandala nrithya*, the mandala dance. The dance figures express the same meanings as the drawings. My patients can say very little about the meaning of the symbols but are fascinated by them and find that they somehow express and have an effect on their subjective psychic state. (p.23)

Jung touched on this theme again in his 1929 seminar on dreams:

> A patient once brought me a drawing of a mandala, telling me that it was a sketch for certain movements along lines in space. She danced it for me, but most of us are too self conscious and not brave enough to do it. It was a conjuration or incantation to the sacred pool or flame in the middle, the final goal, to be approached not directly but by the stations of the cardinal points. (1938, p.304)

As early as 1916, Jung suggested that expressive body movement is one of numerous ways to give form to the unconscious. In a description of active imagination, he wrote that it could be done in any number of ways: 'according to individual taste and talent…dramatic, dialectic, visual, acoustic, or in the form of dancing, painting, drawing, or modelling' (1947, p.202). As with so many aspects of his work, he was far ahead of his time. The idea of using the arts as part of a psychotherapeutic process must have been startling in 1916. The original paper was circulated privately among some of Jung's students and remained unpublished until 1957. Still more time had to pass before the creative art therapies could emerge and be recognized by the mental health community.

Dance/Movement therapy

Dance therapy became a profession in 1966 with the formation of the American Dance Therapy Association. The pioneer dance therapists were all women: dancers, choreographers and teachers of dance, they shared a common passion and deep respect for the therapeutic value of their art. At first, they were without any kind of clinical training and they lacked a theoretical framework. But each of them knew the transformative power of dance from personal experience. Although isolated from each other, they taught in private studios and made their way into psychiatric hospitals and other clinical settings throughout the 1940s and 1950s. Some of them started as volunteers; part-time or full-time jobs were created for them after they established themselves. Dancers, psychotherapists and others came to study and apprentice with the early practitioners, who began to develop theories to support their keen observations. The need to develop a theoretical framework led most of them to psychological and other related studies (Chaiklin and Gantt 1980).

Mary Starks Whitehouse was one of the early movement therapy pioneers. She received her diploma from the Wigman School in Germany and also was a student of Martha Graham. Her personal analysis with Hilde Kirsch in Los Angeles and studies at the Jung Institute in Zürich resulted in the development of an approach which she called 'movement-in-depth' while others termed it 'authentic movement'. In a paper entitled *Reflections on a Metamorphosis* she told the story of this transition:

> It was an important day when I recognized that I did not teach Dance, I taught People… It indicated a possibility that my primary interest might have to do with process, not results, that it might not be art I was after but another kind of human development. (1970, p.273)

Her work has many aspects. She was the first to describe movement from different sources in the psyche:

> 'I move' is the clear knowledge that I personally, am moving… The opposite of this is the sudden and astonishing moment when 'I am moved'… It is a moment when the ego gives up control, stops choosing, stops exerting demands, allowing the Self to take over moving the physical body as it will. It is a moment of unpremeditated surrender that cannot be explained, repeated exactly, sought for or tried out. (1979, p.57)

> The core of the movement experience is the sensation of moving and being moved… Ideally, both are present in the same instant… It is a moment of total awareness, the coming together of what I am doing and what is happening to me. (1958, p.243)

As she developed her approach to movement, she taught her students to become aware of a specific inner impulse that has the quality of a bodily felt sensation:

Following the inner sensation, allowing the impulse to take the form of physical action, is active imagination in movement, just as following the visual image is active imagination in fantasy. It is here that the most dramatic psychophysical connections are made available to consciousness... (1963, p.17)

She was also interested in visual images that come out of the movement experience, as well as images from memories, dreams and fantasies. Whether the images were God-like, human, animal, vegetable or mineral, she encouraged her students to remain in their own bodies and interact with the interior landscapes and personified beings that appeared. There were times when the images themselves seemed to want to be embodied, as if the image could make itself better known by entering the body of the mover. Then her students would experience not only 'dancing with' but they would allow themselves at times to 'be danced by' a compelling inner image.

She developed much of her work through an extremely simple structure. It involves two people: a mover and a witness. Whitehouse was primarily concerned with exploring and understanding the inner experience of the mover. Some of her students, other dance therapists and analysts have been developing the work further toward a deeper understanding of the inner experience of the witness and the relationship between mover and witness. When this work is brought into the analytic *temenos*, many questions arise about how the dance/movement process weaves into the larger context of a Jungian analysis.

Dance/Movement in analysis

The use of dance movement in analysis is similar in many ways to the use of sandplay. Both are a non-verbal, symbolic process that usually takes place within the analytic hour. The analyst serves as participant/witness. It is the quality of the analyst's attentive presence that can create the 'free and sheltered space' that has been so beautifully described by Dora Kalff (1980).

As with other forms of active imagination, the use of dance/movement relies on a sense of inner timing – inner readiness. Sometimes the timing is wrong. For example, when tension or discomfort is building in the verbal work, the idea of moving may be an unconscious form of avoidance. But most people are able to sense when it is time to imagine an inner dialogue, when to move, when to build a sandworld, or use art materials, or write, or bring in a guitar to sing their own song of lamentation or celebration.

The various forms affect each other. For example, when sandplay and movement are both part of the analytic process, analysands may sometimes experience themselves moving as if they were inside one of their own sandworlds, interacting with some of the tiny figures. When this happens, it tends to evoke in the mover an Alice-in-Wonderland quality as she or he meets the imaginal world with intensified interest and curiosity. Whether the mover has grown smaller or the sandworld larger, things are getting 'curiouser and curiouser.' The mover usually meets such a novel situation by becoming even more alert and attentive, learning all she or he can about this strange, yet familiar, landscape and its inhabitants.

Alice may be a particularly useful model of a strong, young feminine ego who is learning how to follow her curiosity (down the rabbit hole or through the looking glass) into an unknown realm – the unconscious. She is wide awake, questioning everyone and everything. The story offers a helpful image for any form of active imagination, that of the ongoing, interwoven relationship between Alice (curiosity) and Wonderland (imagination).

Another similarity between dance/movement and sandplay is that specific themes emerge that seem to follow stages of development in early childhood. More about this later.

Analysts and analysands find individual ways to introduce dance/movement into the analysis. When initiated by the analysand, it may be as spontaneous as the mandala dance described above or there may be much previous discussion and exploration of feelings and fantasies about moving.

When initiated by the analyst, movement may be as spontaneous as a moment of playful, non-verbal interaction or it may be as subtle as the mirroring and synchronous breathing that naturally occurs when we open ourselves to a state of *participation mystique*. An analyst may invite the analysand to enact a specific dream image (Whitmont 1972) or psycho-somatic symptom (Mindell 1982, 1985). Analytic work on a body level may be grounded in a specific approach that includes the use of gentle touch techniques (Greene 1984) or dance and movement may be introduced through a series of workshops and continued in the individual analytic hours that follow (Woodman 1982, 1984).

When the analyst is familiar with and interested in dance/movement as active imagination, his or her analysands are likely to want to move at some point in their work. But there are also analysands who are fully committed to work with the unconscious yet never, or rarely, feel the need to leave their chairs. Some people move every hour, some a few times a year. Some get involved with a particular body level theme and work on it intensely for weeks or months, and then continue on a verbal level.

The movement itself may take no more than ten minutes or it can go on for an hour or more. Sometimes, it is helpful to decide in advance on a time period, perhaps twenty minutes, and have the analyst serve as timekeeper, letting the mover know when to (gradually) bring the movement process to an end.

Physical safety issues need to be discussed. The mover closes his or her eyes in order to listen for the inner sensations and images. But if he or she begins any kind of large swinging, spinning, leaping movements, any kind of momentum that could lead to a collision with windows, furniture or what have you, it is essential that the eyes be open. Even when the quality of movement is smaller and slower, movers have to learn to open their eyes from time to time to keep an orientation to the room. It is difficult to do this without losing the inner-directed focus. But if the work involves a true meeting of conscious and unconscious, maintaining a sense of where one is in a room becomes part of the conscious standpoint. This is easy to say but often extremely difficult to do. When one is moving in this way, the eyes usually 'want' to stay closed. To open the eyes (even a tiny slit) takes a major effort. At times, one's eyes feel as if they are glued shut.

A photograph of a Siberian shaman depicts him in a garment that has ropes hanging from his waist. Heavy metal weights are tied to the end of each rope. The shaman enters an ecstatic state as he begins to dance, whirling around. The ropes with their heavy weights fly out around him – a person could be badly injured if hit by even one of them. The shaman is in a trance but, at the same time, remains conscious and restricts his dancing to an area that is safe. No one gets hurt (Henderson 1985b).

This aspect of the shamanic tradition is similar to the process of active imagination. The essence of both processes requires the capacity to bear the tension of the opposites, to open fully to the unconscious, while, at the same time, maintaining a strong conscious standpoint.

The mover and the witness

Dance/movement usually needs a brief warm-up period. A time to stretch, relax and attend to the depth and rhythm of one's breathing helps to prepare the physical body for inner-directed movement. It may also serve as a *rite d'entrée* into the experience – a time when both mover and witness may become more fully present. After the warm-up, the mover/analysand closes his or her eyes, attends inwardly and waits for an impulse to move, while the witness/analyst finds a corner in the studio where she or he can sit and watch. Movers are encouraged to give themselves over to whatever the body wants to do, to let themselves be moved by the stream of unconscious impulses and images. At the beginning, the witness/analyst carries a larger responsibility for consciousness while the mover/analysand is simply invited to immerse in his or her own fluctuating rhythms of movement and stillness. In time, the mover will begin to internalize the reflective function of the witness and develop the capacity to allow the body to yield to the unconscious stream of impulses and images, while at the same time bringing the experience into conscious awareness.

In movement the unconscious seems to manifest in two recognizable ways: in images and in bodily felt sensations. Some movers experience the unconscious predominantly through a stream of inner visual images. Others may experience it primarily through the body. The initial preference seems related to typology. But the movement process tends to develop an increasingly balanced relationship to both realms. As we learn to listen and respond, our attention usually fluctuates back and forth. Each realm may constellate and enrich the other. A woman describes a movement experience that has the quality of such a dialectic:

My left hand became hard fisted. It was like a phallus. I moved through all levels with this strong, hard, left forearm and fist. Then, the fist opened. It opened so slowly that it was like a reversal from numbness. As my hand relaxed slowly into openness, a large diamond appeared in my palm. It was heavy. I began to move my left arm in slow spirals around myself. I was aware of feeling the sequential, overlapping rotations of shoulder, elbow, wrist, and even fingers. Both arms came to stillness together, joined behind my back. The left hand continued to hold the diamond. Then, the image of the diamond came in front of my eyes. It grew larger, until I could see through it with both eyes. It showed me a vision of everything broken up by its facets. The diamond grew larger, until I was inside it looking out. The light was bright – almost golden. I bathed in it and felt that it was a healing kind of light. Now, my body shape took on the diamond's many facets. I was myself, my own shape, but each part of me had many cut surfaces. It was as if I could 'see' through the myriad facets of all of me. There was a sense of wonder and suspension and peacefulness.

This mover describes a fluctuation and constant interchange between two sources of movement – the world of the body and the world of the imagination.

The experience of the analyst/witness ranges along a continuum that has at its poles two modes of consciousness. They are sometimes described as *Logos*, or directed consciousness, and *Eros*, or fantasy consciousness (Jung 1912; Stewart 1986). They are known by many names. The alchemists spoke of a mysterious marriage between *Sol* and *Luna*.

Let us take a moment and imagine how the same landscape might be affected by sunlight and by moonlight. Sunlight, or a solar attitude, offers us clarity. It enables us to divide what we see into its separate parts. But when it gets too bright, everything becomes harsh, glaring, dry. When the sun is at its peak, we live in a world without shadow. The moon, on the other hand, reflects a mild light. It reveals a moist, shimmering landscape. Everything merges. In the darkness we find an unsuspected unity (Jung 1963).

What does this have to do with witnessing movement? The witness fluctuates between a solar, differentiated, objective, definitive way of seeing, to a lunar, merging, subjective, imaginative way of seeing. The same movement event may be seen and described in many ways:

> As I watch, I see the mover crouch low with her face hidden. Only her arms reach forward, with wide-spread hands pressing flat on the ground. With an increasingly deep cycle of breathing, she slowly drops forward onto her knees and elbows, and finally slides flat onto her stomach, stretched full length on the ground. Her arms draw together in a long narrow shape, slipping between her body and the floor. She rests, breathing deeply.

> As I watch, I let myself imagine and remember what it is like to go deeply inside. I know that this woman was largely ignored during the early years of her life, due to a series of illnesses in her family. As I watch, I feel an ache in my throat and my heart goes out to her. I now see her as if she were a very young infant. I imagine holding her close to my body, we rock back and forth with merging rhythms. As I imagine holding and rocking her, I slowly become aware that I am actually rocking slightly. Later on, I realize that our breathing has become synchronous.

> As she presses her hands into the ground, I experience mounting tension and for a moment, I'm fearful that she'll press harder and harder and suddenly explode. But instead, she slides forward and lies on her stomach. She has now withdrawn so much that there is very little

movement. My mind wanders. I pick at a hangnail. I feel irritated with her, then guilty and irritated with myself. I imagine she is sitting on a volcano. In any case, it feels as if I am: my shoulder muscles are contracted, my jaw is tight, I'm not breathing very much. My mind dimly wonders whether I might be picking up something about her father's cycle of violent outbursts and subsequent remorse. Or is her withdrawal too close to my own way of avoiding anger?

As she kneels low, the shape of her body reminds me of the Moslem prayer ritual. Another image comes: one of the paintings Jung did for his Red Book shows a little figure that bows low, while covering its face. An enormous fire spout is erupting out of the earth in front of the little person. It fills the upper half of the painting with intricately formed red, orange, and yellow flames.

We know from ancient tradition that the Feminine Mysteries are not to be spoken. Yet consciousness demands that we reflect on and, at some point, name our experience. When and how do we speak about the experience of dance/movement? How do we understand the meaning of the symbolic action? Do we interpret it from the perspective of transference and countertransference? When and how do we allow the symbolic process to speak for itself? When and how do we respond to it in its own language?

Dancers know instinctively that there is danger in 'talking away' an experience that is not ready to be put into words. Isadora Duncan was asked to explain the meaning of a particular dance. Her reply was: 'If I could tell you what it meant, there would be no point in dancing it.'

Analysis offers a different perspective, but analysts, too, know the danger of making premature interpretations that would analyze feelings away (Greene 1984; Machtiger 1984; Ulanov 1982).

There are three aspects of dance movement in analysis that we gradually learn to remember: (1) What was the body doing? (2) What was the associated image? (3) What was the associated affect or emotional tone? There are heightened moments when all three are clearly known and remembered by both mover and witness. When we are aware of both physical action and inner image, we are likely to be conscious of the emotion as well. But there are times, just as with dreams, that we remember very little. When the mover is conscious of his or her experience, it can be told. Telling it to the analyst is not unlike telling a dream. But a dream is different from active imagination. Active imagination is closer to consciousness. Also, in dance/movement as active imagination, the analyst is literally present and able to witness the experience as it unfolds. The analyst/witness may be unaware of what the motivating images are until after the movement, when the two participants sit together and talk. Or, the analyst/witness may be so familiar with the mover's previous dream and fantasy images that he or she can sense and imagine the nature of the images while watching. Sometimes, the movement comes from such depths that mover and witness experience a state of *participation mystique*.

When an untransformed primal affect is touched, the mover may 'space out,' or feel dazed, or stuck, or in some other way become numb to it. Or, if the mover goes with it – if she or he merges with the affect/archetypal image – she or he is likely to be taken over by a primal affect, or by resistance to it, or a log-jam of both. At such a moment, the emotional core of the complex is experienced as toxic, even life threatening. At one time it may well have been that.

Sylvia Perera (1981) writes so beautifully as she tells the story of our descent to a realm that has been unimaginable and unspeakable:

> Work on this level in therapy involves the deepest affects and is inevitably connected to preverbal, 'infantile' processes. The therapist must be willing to participate where needed, often working on the body-mind level where there is as yet no image in the others awareness and where instinct and affect and sensory perception begin to coalesce first in a body sensation, which can be intensified to bring forth memory or image. Silence, affirmative mirroring attention, touch, holding, sounding and singing, gesture breathing, nonverbal actions like drawing, sandplay, building with clay or blocks, dancing – all have their time and place. (p.57)

Because much that goes on in the analytic relationship at this level is preverbal, we will turn to some of our earliest experiences as they appear in dance/movement and relate them to certain stages of normal development in infancy.

Sources of movement

An earlier paper (Chodorow 1984) discussed the origins of movement from different aspects of the psyche. Four sources were suggested and illustrated: movement from the personal unconscious, the cultural unconscious, the primordial unconscious and the ego-Self axis. Although every complex has elements that are personal, cultural and primordial, themes that emerge through the body are so immediate that it seems possible and helpful to sense from which level or source it is constellated.

Dance/movement is one of the most direct ways to reach back to our earliest experiences. Movers frequently lie on or move close to the ground. By attending to the world of bodily felt sensations, the mover recreates a situation that is in many ways similar to that of an infant who swims in a sensory-motor world. The presence of the analyst/witness enables re-enactment and re-integration of the earliest preverbal relationship(s). It is here that images of the transference and the countertransference may be most clearly recognized.

This paper will introduce five symbolic events that appear and reappear in the movement process of many individuals. They seem to represent certain stages of developing consciousness through the preverbal, presymbolic developmental period of infancy from birth to approximately sixteen months. The symbolic actions and interactions are: (1) patterns of uroboric self-holding; (2) seeking the face of the witness and, when found, a smile of recognition; (3) the laughter of self-recognition; (4) disappearance and reappearance; and (5) full engagement in the symbolic process via free imaginative use of mime.

Two sources have been essential to my recognition and understanding of these events. Louis H. Stewart (1981, 1984, 1986) has been updating Jung's model of the psyche from the perspective of child development and recent studies of the affects and their expression. Charles T. Stewart (1981), a child psychiatrist, has been developing a theory of play and games as universal processes in ego development. Working individually and in collaboration (Stewart and Stewart 1981a, 1981b), they have gathered a wealth of material from Jung, Neumann, Piaget's observations, Tomkins's study of the affects, and anthropological research into play and games. From these and other sources they have brought together certain phases of ego development described by Neumann, with fully embodied observations of real babies.

Infant and child development is most often studied from the perspective of patriarchal values. For example, Piaget wanted to understand the development of the intellect, so even though his observations demonstrate a development of both imagination and intellect, his theory shows a one-sided emphasis on *logos* functions. Stewart and Stewart (1981a, 1981b) give us a way to understand the development of the imagination. Together, both perspectives form a whole, an ongoing dialectic between the twin streams of life instinct. One stream is *Eros*, as imagination, divine relatedness and the other is *Logos*, as intellect, divine curiosity (Stewart 1986).

In the following pages we will discuss each theme as it appears in dance/movement and explore it from the perspective of infant development. The ego-Self axis is constellated at the threshold of each stage. The experiential core of each passage in the development of consciousness is a startling, even numinous, moment of synthesis and re-orientation.

Uroboric: Patterns of self-holding

Movers tend to explore a very wide range of uroboric self-holding. We see all kinds of patterns: one hand holding the other; thumb-holding; arm(s) wrapping around the torso to hold rib(s), elbow(s), hip(s), knee(s), foot or feet. All of these seem reminiscent of those earliest body experiences when we at first unintentionally find, then lose and find again – and gradually discover what it is to hold ourselves. In infancy the first primal recognition of self may well be that powerful and comforting moment when thumb and mouth find each other:

> We may see that the infant, while sucking its fingers or its toes, incarnates the image of the mythical Uroborus that, according to Neumann, represents the 'wholeness' of that undifferentiated state of self-other consciousness that is characteristic of this developmental state. We can also see in this early behavior the earliest evidence of that aspect of the autonomous process of individuation that Neumann, following Jung, has called *centroversion*. In this light we may understand the infant's behavior in the discovery of sucking its thumb as representing the first synthesis of the psyche following upon the rude disruption of life within the womb, which had more impressively represented a paradisiacal absorption in the purely unconscious processes of life itself. (Stewart 1986, p.191)

When the mover is immersed in self-holding, his or her eyes are closed or have an inward focus. There is usually rocking, swaying or some other kind of rhythmic pulsation. The quality is usually complete self-containment. If the analyst/witness opens himself or herself to a state of *participation mystique*, he or she may join the mover in a timeless state and experience a similar kind of rhythmic self-containment. Shared rhythms of holding, touching, lulling and lullabies are the psychic nourishment of this earliest phase.

If the analyst/witness does not enter into a state of *participation mystique* with the mover, he or she may feel excluded, irritated, uneasy. Alternatively, or even concurrently, he or she may feel shy, embarrassed to watch an experience of such intimate union with self. As with any other analytic work, witnessing requires opening to the unconscious and, at the same time, maintaining a conscious analytic standpoint to reflect on the meaning of the symbolic action and the associated countertransference response.

At times, the experience has a different, perhaps more conscious, quality. There is a sense of wonderment as the mover's hands discover and explore the shape of his or her own body. As the mover's hands shape themselves to the bulges and the hollows, the hard bones and the soft flesh, there is a profound sense of self-recognition – as if meeting oneself for the first time. Both mover and witness often feel as if they are participants in an ancient ritual form. After many years of witnessing women and men spontaneously discovering the shape of their own bodies with their hands, I learned of a myth that demonstrates so clearly such a return to our uroboric origins. The myth of Changing Woman,[3] who presses and molds her own body as she comes of age, is still re-enacted throughout the American Southwest in the form of an initiation ceremony.

First smile: Recognition of other (Approx. second month)

The movement process frequently evokes a special smile that is reminiscent of the infant's earliest recognition of the 'other.' When the movement comes to an end, it is almost always followed by continued inner attentiveness – a period of natural self-containment similar to the uroboric quality. Then, as the mover makes the transition to everyday consciousness, it is as if she or he

---

3   The initiation ceremony is called the *Kinaaldá* by the Navaho. The Apache call it the Sunrise Dance (Quintero 1980). It is an elaborate ritual – a time of rejoicing to mark a girl's onset of menstruation. Her passage to womanhood is announced to the whole community in a dramatic four-night ceremony. Changing Woman had a miraculous birth and grew to maturity in four days. At this time, she had her first menstrual period. The Holy People were living on the earth then and they came to her ceremony and sang songs for her. She originated her own *Kinaaldá*. One of the most important parts of the ceremony was molding her body. Some say that at the first *Kinaaldá*, Changing Woman molded her own body. The pressing or molding was done to honor the Sun and the Moon. Changing Woman was molded into a perfect form. When the first-born human girl became *Kinaaldá*, Changing Woman did the same things for her. She pressed and molded the younger woman's body, thus gifting her with beauty, wisdom, honor and self-respect. The *Kinaaldá* is part of the Blessing Way Ceremony. It is done today as it was done in the beginning (Frisbie 1967; Henderson 1985b; Quintero 1980; Sandner 1979).

is gradually waking up. When the mover's eyes open, she or he usually begins to search the room for the analyst. When the analyst's face is found, there is a mutual sense of reconnection and, most often, the smile(s) of recognition. The mover may have just experienced painful emotions; his or her face may still be wet with tears. But as he or she gradually comes back to the dayworld and scans the room for the analyst's face, there is a meeting and a clear-eyed smile. Even when the quality of the therapeutic relationship is primarily that of two adults, any fully spontaneous smile has at its core the infant's smile when she or he first consciously recognizes the now familiar face of the mother or other primary nurturing adult.

Louis H. Stewart (1984) reflects on the infant's first smile:

> What are the first signs of love in the infant and child? Our Western image of childbirth has been that the mother must suffer and the child come crying into the world. All this has more recently been questioned and there are those who talk about infants entering the world with smiles on their faces and wide awake mothers ready to smile back immediately upon birth. We are far from knowing then what may be the possible potential of the development of love in the child. However, what is observable today is that the mutual smile of recognition between mother and infant does not occur for several weeks after birth. Before that the child smiles under certain conditions of satiety, half awake, half asleep, but in a dazed, glassy-eyed manner. Then there comes a moment, as early as the end of the first month sometimes, when the infant, awake and clear eyed, smiles in what is unmistakably a pleased recognition of the familiar sounds and face of the mother. Soon, within days or weeks, the infant's first joyful laugh occurs. (p.1)

First laugh: Recognition of self (Approx. third month)

From time to time, usually in the midst of movement, the mover laughs. There are many kinds of laughter. This one expresses joy in the sheer exuberance of bodily motion and/or a particular image appears and there is the laughter of self-recognition (Stewart and Stewart 1981b). Piaget (1962) describes such a laugh:

> It will be remembered that Laurent, at 0;2(21), adopted the habit of throwing his head back to look at familiar things from this new position. At 0;2(23 or 24) he seemed to repeat this movement with ever-increasing enjoyment and ever-decreasing interest in the external result: he brought

his head back to the upright position and then threw it back again time after time, laughing loudly. (p.91)

Charles T. Stewart (1981) draws an analogy between the infant's first laugh and a similar moment in the analysis of an adult, reported by D.W. Winnicott. Winnicott's patient was described as a schizoid-depressive man who could carry on a serious conversation but lacked any kind of spontaneity. He rarely, if ever, laughed. In the midst of one of his analytic hours the patient imagined himself doing a backward somersault, similar to the movement made by Laurent when he threw his head back and laughed. Winnicott (1954) writes of his patient:

> On important but rare occasions he becomes withdrawn; during these moments of withdrawal unexpected things happen which he is sometimes able to report... The first of these happenings (the fantasy of which he was only just able to capture and to report) was that in a momentary withdrawn state on the couch, he had curled up and rolled over the back of the couch. This was the first direct evidence in the analysis of a spontaneous self. (p.256)

Joan Blackmer (1982) writes of a dream in which two small, agile tumblers, trained acrobats, turn somersaults. Among her amplifications, she describes their trickster quality:

> They certainly are transformers... The somersault, in itself a moving circle, is a mandala, a symbol of the Self, which causes change through human motion. Psychologically, this represents a change in attitude. (p.8)

The laughter of self-recognition always turns our world around.

Disappearance and reappearance: Object constancy (Approx. ninth month)

There are so many ways that the mover/analysand hides from the witness/analyst – and reappears. The dance/movement structure itself is a game of disappearance and reappearance (as the mover's eyes close and open again). But within the movement, even with eyes closed, the mover may turn away and do some small, intricate gestures that the witness cannot see. If the witness follows his or her curiosity and moves to where the gestures can be seen, the mover may turn away again and the cycle can repeat itself. Often, if the witness stays put, the mover turns around again to where she or he may be seen. Sometimes, peek-a-boo and other hiding games and activities emerge as overt, central, conscious themes in dance/movement enactment.

Separation anxiety develops in the third quarter of the baby's first year. At the same time that the infant begins to struggle with the pain of separating from beloved persons, she or he immerses herself or himself in games of peek-a-boo and intensely investigates problems of disappearance and re-appearance.

> At 0;8(14): Jacqueline is lying on my bed beside me. I cover my head and cry 'coucou'; I emerge and do it again. She bursts into peals of laughter, then pulls the covers away to find me again. Attitude of expectation and lively interest. (Piaget 1952, p.50)

> 0;9(15): Jacqueline wails or cries when she sees the person seated next to her get up or move away a little (giving the impression of leaving). (Piaget 1952, p.249)

> 0;9(20): Jacqueline is lying down and holds her quilt with both hands. She raises it, brings it before her face, looks under it, then ends by raising and lowering it alternately while looking over the top of it: thus she studies the transformations of the image of the room as a function of the screen formed by the quilt. (Piaget 1954, p.193)

As the first smile is the beginning of mother-child differentiation, peek-a-boo and, later, games of hide-and-go-seek continue an ongoing process that leads toward the development of object constancy.

Pretend play: Separation of the world parents (Approx. sixteenth month)

Jung (1963) describes this major passage of consciousness as:

> ...the first morning of the world, the first sunrise after the primal darkness, when that inchoately conscious complex, the ego, the son of the darkness knowingly sundered subject and object, and thus precipitated the world and itself into definite existence... Genesis 1: 1–7 is a projection of this process. (p.108)

A number of passages in the infant's first year create the base upon which a clear separation of dayworld and dreamworld can occur. Neumann (1973a, 1973b) refers to this differentiation of conscious and unconscious as 'separation of the world parents.' In the infant's life this passage comes not through the word but rather through the discovery of non-verbal, symbolic play – that is, the baby discovers that she or he can pretend. It is this first, independent discovery of 'symbolic action' that coincides with the beginning of real curiosity about language:

> Around sixteen to eighteen months of age, the child becomes aware of the semiotic function through the experience of pretense, for example in the miming of an already adaptive behavior pattern like the ritual behavior adopted to ease the transition into sleep (e.g., thumb-sucking and fingering the satiny edge of a blanket). The child laughs with joy at this new recognition of Self; and this is pretend play (Piaget 1962). But let us reflect for a moment on the sleep ritual. This is not a neutral pattern of behavior. It represents one of the landmarks in the child's development. If the transition to sleep and waking is not easily accomplished, the child may be forever prone to sleep disturbances, to excessive fear of the dark, needing a night light, etc. And why is going to sleep difficult? Because it brings together the child's most feared and distressing fantasies, that of being deprived of the presence and comfort of those most dear, and of being left alone in the dark which is peopled by who knows what ghostly phantoms. Thus we consider it no accident that the child discovers pretense in the recognition of the sleep ritual; pretend play begins with the miming of a behavior pattern which has assisted the child in warding off fear of the unknown and soothing the anguish of separation. Subsequent pretend play will be seen to reenact all the emotionally charged experiences of the child's life. (Stewart and Stewart 1981a, p.47)

Similar to the infant's first discovery of pretend play, the dance/movement process in analysis often begins with the miming of a familiar behavior pattern that has served to ward off emotional pain. Also similar to children's play, imaginative mime can lead the mover toward, and eventually through, the emotional trauma that lies at the heart of a complex.

The following descriptions are of three women, each in the early stages of analytic work:

> A woman begins to move by expressing a happy-go-lucky attitude, 'moving on.' Then she pauses and her chest seems to collapse. With a feeling of increasing heaviness, she lowers herself to her knees and becomes overwhelmed by a deeply familiar sense of despair.

> A professional dancer puts on a show that would dazzle Broadway. She then sinks to the ground, becomes very quiet and begins to move slowly. The slow movement is halting and looks increasingly painful. Her body convulses and she seems to be in a trance.

A busy, active executive enacts her overscheduled life. For a moment, she pauses, looks down to the ground and realizes how tired she is. She struggles briefly with her yearning to lie down, and overcomes it by returning to the portrayal of her active life.

Each woman, in her own way, struggles with the tension between an overly bright, adaptive persona and its shadow. As in any analytic process, a pair of opposites will be constellated. Out of the experience of that two-fold tension, a third reconciling symbol will eventually be born: a new inner attitude that contains yet also goes beyond both perspectives.

Carolyn Grant Fay (1977) describes the emergence of such a moving symbol. The mover is a woman who has had many years of analytic work. She does not begin with avoidance of pain, nor does she seek it. She begins by listening deeply:

> I lay for what seemed like a long time, listening inwardly to myself. My throat brought itself to my attention. It hurt and felt constricted and tense, so I let my throat lead me into movement. It led me up to kneeling, then forward, and then slowly across the floor in a sort of crouching position. In my imagination I became aware as I concentrated on the throat that it was red with blood. The heart area was also aching and bloody. Finally my throat brought me up to standing and propelled me farther along. It stopped me suddenly, and I just stood there. At this point, I collapsed onto the floor and lay there motionless. There was no movement...not an image...nothing.
>
> After a while I became aware that the color red from the blood was there at my throat and breast. Little by little it became many shades of red from light pink to deep crimson. A rose began to take shape, rising out of the throat and heart through movements of my arms up, out, and around. The rest of my body down from that area seemed, in the fantasy, to be forming the stem and leaves of the flower. All sorts of superlatives come to me now as I try to express how I felt at that moment: warm, happy, fulfilled, in order, at one with myself. (pp.26–27)

Conclusion

More important than whether we use dance as a form of active imagination is the question of how we can fully engage the imagination. Jung suggests giving free rein to fantasy, according to the individual's taste and talent. Some people have what he called 'motor imagination' (Jung 1938). It is the nature of such an individual to experience life in terms of spontaneous movement activity and to imagine with and about the body. Thus a dialogue is initiated between interest and imagination as twin streams of libido: interest in the body the way it is and fantasies of what the body might be about (Stewart 1986).

As the process of individuation leads us to become who we are, certain analysts and analysands are inevitably led to use dance/movement as part of their analytic work. For those with a motor imagination, dance/movement is simply the most immediate, natural way to give form to the unconscious. Some find dance/movement essential because they feel alienated from the body or because they only know how to direct the body and now sense deeply that they must learn to listen to it. Some turn to dance/movement because it is a direct way to work with certain complexes that were constellated in infancy. It seems that complexes of a preverbal, presymbolic nature are less often touched by the verbal aspects of analysis.

Eliade (1975) wrote: 'Life cannot be repaired, it can only be recreated' (p.30). In analysis, active imagination is that re-creative process; dance/movement is one of its forms.

Bibliography

Adler, J. (1972) 'Integrity of body and psyche: Some notes on work in process'. In B.F. Govine and J. Chodorow (eds) *What is Dance Therapy Really? Proceedings of the Seventh Annual Dance Therapy Conference,* pp.42–53. Columbia, MD: American Dance Therapy Association.

Adler, J. (1987) 'Who is the witness?' *Contact Quarterly,* Winter, 20–29.

Bernstein, P.L. (ed) (1984) *Theoretical Approaches in Dance/Movement Therapy.* Vol.2. (pp.321–342). Dubuque, Iowa: Kendall/Hunt.

Bernstein, P.L. and Singer, D.L. (eds) (1982) *The Choreography of Object Relations.* Keene, New Hampshire: Antioch University.

Blackmer, J.D. (1982) 'The training and experience of a modern dancer: Exploration into the meaning and value of physical consciousness'. Unpublished thesis. Zürich: C.G. Jung Institute.

Chaiklin, S. and Gantt, L. (1980) *Conference on Creative Arts Therapies.* Washington, DC: BlackmanAmerican Psychiatric Association.

Chodorow, J. (1974) 'Philosophy and methods of individual work'. In K. Mason (ed) *Dance Therapy: Focus on Dance VII,* pp.24–26. Washington, DC: American Association for Health, Physical Education and Recreation.

Chodorow, J. (1978) 'Dance therapy and the transcendent function'. *American Journal of Dance Therapy 2,* 1, 16–23.

Chodorow, J. (1984) 'To move and be moved'. *Quadrant 17,* 2, 39–48.

Chodorow, J. (1995) 'Dance/movement and body experience in analysis'. In M. Stein (ed) *Jungian Analysis,* 2nd ed., pp.391–404. La Salle, IL: Open Court.

Eliade, M. (1975) *Myth and Reality.* New York: Harper & Row.

Fay, C.G. (1977) 'Movement and fantasy: A dance therapy model based on the psychology of Carl G. Jung'. Master's thesis, Goddard College, Vermont.

Frisbie, C.J. (1967) *Kinaaldá : A Study of the Navaho Girl's Puberty Ceremony*. Wesleyan University Press.

Greene, A. (1984) 'Giving the body its due'. *Quadrant 17*, 2, 9–24.

Hall, J. (1977) *Clinical Uses of Dreams: Jungian Interpretations and Enactments*. New York: Grune and Stratton.

Henderson, J.L. (1985a) 'The origins of a theory of cultural attitudes'. In *Proceedings of the 1985 California Spring Conference*. San Francisco: C.G. Jung Institute.

Henderson, J.L. (1985b) Personal communication.

Jung, C.G. (1902) 'On the psychology and pathology of so-called occult phenomena'. In *The Collected Works of C.G. Jung* (1975) (vol. 1). Princeton: Princeton University Press.

Jung, C.G. (1907) 'The psychology of dementia praecox'. In *The Collected Works of C.G. Jung* (1972) (vol. 3). Princeton: Princeton University Press.

Jung, C.G. (1912) 'Two kinds of thinking'. In *The Collected Works of C.G. Jung* (1967) (vol. 5). Princeton: Princeton University Press.

Jung, C.G. (1916) 'The transcendent function'. In *The Collected Works of C.G. Jung* (2nd ed., 1969/78) (vol. 8). Princeton: Princeton University Press.

Jung, C.G. (1927) 'The structure of the psyche'. In *The Collected Works of C.G. Jung* (2nd ed., 1969/78) (vol. 8). Princeton: Princeton University Press.

Jung, C.G. (1929) 'Commentary on "The secret of the golden flower."' In *The Collected Works of C.G. Jung* (1967) (vol. 13). Princeton: Princeton University Press.

Jung, C.G. (1935) 'The Tavistock lectures: On the theory and practice of analytical psychology'. In *The Collected Works of C.G. Jung* (1976) (vol. 18). Princeton: Princeton University Press.

Jung, C.G. (1938) *Dream Analysis* (1984). Princeton: Princeton University Press.

Jung, C.G. (1940) 'The psychology of the child archetype'. In *The Collected Works of C.G. Jung* (1972) (vol. 9). Princeton: Princeton University Press.

Jung, C.G. (1947) 'On the nature of the psyche'. In *The Collected Works of C.G. Jung* (2nd ed., 1969/78) (vol. 8). Princeton: Princeton University Press.

Jung, C.G. (1961) *Memories, Dreams, Reflections*. New York: Vintage Books, Random House.

Jung, C.G. (1963) 'Mysterium coniunctionis'. In *The collected works of C.G. Jung* (1974) (vol. 14). Princeton: Princeton University Press.

Kalff, D. (1980) *Sandplay*. Santa Monica, CA: Sigo Press.

Machtiger, H.G. (1984) 'Reflections on the transference/countertransference process with borderline patients'. In N. Schwartz-Salant and M. Stein (eds) *Transference/ Countertransference*. Wilmette, IL: Chiron.

Mindell, A. (1982) *Dreambody*. Los Angeles: Sigo Press.

Mindell, A. (1985) *Working with the Dreambody*. Boston: Routledge & Kegan Paul.

Neumann, E. (1973a) *The Child*. New York: G. P. Putnam's Sons.

Neumann, E. (1973b) 'The separation of the world parents: The principle of opposites'. In E. Neumann (ed) *The Origins and History of Consciousness*. Princeton: Princeton University Press. (Originally published in 1954.).

Piaget, J. (1952) *The Origins of Intelligence in Children*. New York: W. W. Norton.

Piaget, J. (1954) *The Construction of Reality in the Child*. New York: Basic Books.

Piaget, J. (1962) *Play, Dreams and Imitation in Childhood*. New York: W. W. Norton.

Perera, S. (1981) *Descent to the Goddess*. Toronto: Inner City Press.

Quintero, N. (1980) 'Coming of age'. *National Geographic 157*, 2, 62–71.

Sachs, C. (1937) *World History of the Dance.* New York: W. W. Norton.

Sandner, D. (1979) *Navaho Symbols of Healing.* New York: Harcourt, Brace & Jovanovich.

Schoop, T. with Mitchell, P. (1974) *Won't You Join the Dance?* Palo Alto, CA: National Press Books.

Schwartz-Salant, N. (1982) *Narcissism and Character Transformation.* Toronto: Inner City Books.

Stein, M. (1984) 'Power, shamanism and maieutics in the countertransference'. In N. Schwartz-Salant and M. Stein (eds) *Transference/Countertransference.* Wilmette: IL: Chiron.

Stewart, C.T. (1981) 'Developmental psychology of sandplay'. In G. Hill (ed) *Sandplay Studies: Origins, Theory and Practice.* San Francisco: C.G. Jung Institute.

Stewart, L.H. (1981) 'The play–dream continuum and the categories of the imagination'. Paper presented at the 7th Annual Conference of The Association for the Anthropological Study of Play (TAASP), Fort Worth.

Stewart, L.H. (1984) 'Play-eros'. In *Affects and Archetypes II.* Unpublished manuscript presented at the Active Imagination Seminar in Geneva, Switzerland.

Stewart, L.H. (1986) 'Work in progress: affect and archetype: A contribution to a comprehensive theory of the structure of the psyche'. In N. Schwartz-Salant and M. Stein (eds) *The Body in Analysis.* Wilmette, Ill: Chiron.

Stewart, C.T. and Stewart, L.H. (1981a) 'Play, games and affects: a contribution toward a comprehensive theory of play'. In A.T. Cheska (ed) *Play as Context.* Proceedings of The Association for the Anthropological Study of Play (TAASP). Westpoint, N.Y.: Leisure Press.

Stewart, C.T. and Stewart, L.H. (1981b) 'Play, games and stages of development: A contribution toward a comprehensive theory of play'. Paper presented at the 7th Annual Conference of The Association for the Anthropological Study of Play (TAASP), Fort Worth.

Tomkins, S. (1962–63) *Affect Imagery Consciousness.* Volumes I and II. New York: Springer.

Ulanov, A. (1982) 'Transference/Countertransference'. In M. Stein (ed) *Jungian Analysis.* La Salle, IL: Open Court.

Whitehouse, M. (1958) 'The Tao of the body'. In D.H. Johnson (ed) *Bone, Breath and Gesture: Practices of Embodiment.* (1995) Berkeley, CA: North Atlantic Books.

Whitehouse, M. (1963) 'Physical movement and personality'. *Contact Quarterly*, Winter 1987, 16–19.

Whitehouse, M. (1970) 'Reflections on a metamorphosis'. In R. Head, R.E. Rothenberg and D. Wesley (eds) *A Well of Living Waters: Festschrift for Hilde Kirsch.* Los Angeles: C.G. Jung Institute (1977).

Whitehouse, M. (1979) 'C.G. Jung and dance therapy'. In P. Lewis Bernstein (ed) *Eight Theoretical Approaches in Dance/Movement Therapy.* Dubuque, IA: Kendall/Hunt.

Whitmont, E. (1972) 'Body experience and psychological awareness'. *Quadrant 12*, 5–16.

Winnicott, D.W. (1954) 'Withdrawal and regression'. In D.W. Winnicott (ed) *Through Pediatrics to Psychoanalysis.* New York: Basic Books.

Woodman, M. (1980) *The Owl was a Baker's Daughter.* Toronto: Inner City Books.

Woodman, M. (1982) *Addiction to Perfection.* Toronto: Inner City Books.

Woodman, M. (1984) 'Psyche/soma awareness'. *Quadrant 17*, 2, 25–37.

CHAPTER 21

Active Imagination[1]

Joan Chodorow

My most fundamental views and ideas derive from these experiences. First I made the observations and only then did I hammer out my views. And so it is with the hand that guides the crayon or brush, the foot that executes the dance-step, with the eye and the ear, with the word and the thought: a dark impulse is the ultimate arbiter of the pattern, an unconscious 'a priori' precipitates itself into plastic form. (C.G. Jung 1947, p.204)

Jung developed his technique of active imagination in 1916. It became his primary method of psychotherapy. All of the creative art psychotherapies can trace their roots to Jung's early contribution. Active imagination is based on the natural, healing function of the imagination, which tends to take us directly to, and eventually through, the emotional core of our complexes. I shall begin this paper by taking a look at the nature of the emotionally toned complex, because it is our complexes that bring us to therapy in the first place. Then, I'll trace the development of active imagination, its origins in the symbolic play of childhood and its role in clinical practice. I shall close with a brief review of the contribution of Mary Whitehouse and some images of dance/movement as a form of active imagination.

---

1   Paper presented at the NCATA Conference in Washington, DC, November 1–5, 1990, as part of the symposium on Active Imagination. Adapted from *Dance Therapy and Depth Psychology: The Moving Imagination*. London: Routledge, 1991.

The emotionally toned complex

Jung's psychological theory was built on his early studies of the emotionally toned complex. Whereas Freud emphasized the drives as the source of human motivation, Jung held to the primacy of the emotions. In addition to understanding emotion as bridge between instinct and archetype, body and psyche, Jung also speaks of emotion as source of 'value' (Jung 1951), 'imagery' (Jung 1961), energy and new consciousness:

> Conflict engenders fire, the fire of affects and emotions, and like every other fire it has two aspects, that of combustion and that of creating light. On the one hand, emotion is the alchemical fire whose warmth brings everything into existence and whose heat burns all superfluities to ashes (*omnes superfluitates comburit*). But on the other hand, emotion is the moment when steel meets flint and a spark is struck forth, for emotion is the chief source of consciousness. There is no change from darkness to light or from inertia to movement without emotion. (Jung 1938, p.96)

For Jung, the emotionally toned complex is the key to understanding the unconscious processes that produce psychogenic symptoms. A complex is 'a collection of various ideas held together by an emotional tone common to all' (Jung 1911, p.599). The complex is usually formed when circumstances evoke an emotional response that cannot be borne. That unbearable emotion or emotional tone gets split off from consciousness and an autonomous complex begins to form. The affective core of the complex gathers around itself a collection of interrelated ideas, impressions, memory traces and behavior patterns. This network of affectively interwoven associations may include not only aspects of personal history but cultural and primordial themes as well.

The problematic aspect of the complex has to do with its autonomy. Although we may reject, deny and even structure our lives to avoid its emotional content, it remains active. The complex doesn't go away. Instead, it lives on in the unconscious, outside the control of the conscious mind. Emotionally toned complexes usually make themselves known through unconscious states of projection and possession, which often have a driven, compulsive, fanatic or even demonic quality. Complexes appear in dreams and visions as well as in mental disturbances. Complexes may convert and manifest as somatic symptoms. The phenomenon of ghosts and spirits, too, may be understood psychologically as projections of autonomous complexes.

When we are in a complex, its affective core engulfs us with its characteristic emotional tone or mood. It may compel us to think unwanted thoughts (that we may not even agree with) and act out in troublesome ways: 'Everyone knows nowadays that people "have complexes." What is not so well known, though far more important theoretically, is that complexes can *have us'* (Jung 1934, p.96).

The development of active imagination

After the break with Freud, Jung felt disoriented and sensed so much pressure inside himself that he suspected a psychic disturbance. Thinking there might be something in his past that was causing the pressure, he went over all the details of his entire life, twice, with particular attention to early memories. But he could find no logical explanation or solution.

Then he deliberately opened himself to the impulses and images of the unconscious and decided to do whatever occurred to him. The first thing that came up was a childhood memory. At the age of ten or eleven there was a period when he was fascinated with building games. This memory of spontaneous play was accompanied by a rush of emotion. Jung, now in his middle years, felt out of touch with his own creative life. He realized that he had to re-establish a relationship to that inner child. But how was he to bridge the distance between himself, a grown man, and the young boy? Since there seemed to be no rational way to do it, he submitted to his fantasies and began to enact them – that is, play exactly as he had when he was a boy:

> As a grown man it seemed impossible to me that I should be able to bridge the distance from the present back to my eleventh year. Yet if I wanted to re-establish contact with that period, I had no choice but to return to it and take up once more that child's life with his childish games. This moment was a turning point in my fate, but I gave in only after endless resistances and with a sense of resignation. For it was a painfully humiliating experience to realize that there was nothing to be done except play childish games. (Jung 1961, p.174)

We have to remember that the year was 1913. It was unheard of for a bourgeois Swiss husband, father, doctor, university professor, to gather stones and sit by the side of the lake, building a miniature village out of blocks, stones and mud! But, despite feelings of humiliation, Jung remained engrossed with the task and went on with the building game every day, weather permitting.

The small town he built included cottages, a castle, gates and arches. Then he realized the church was missing and made a square building with a dome. He knew the church needed an altar, too, but felt hesitant. It took him a long time to find the right stone:

> Suddenly I caught sight of a red stone, a four-sided pyramid about an inch and a half high. It was a fragment of stone which had been polished into this shape by the action of the water – a pure product of chance. I knew at once that this was the altar. I placed it in the middle under the dome, and as I did so, I recalled the underground phallus of my childhood dream. (Jung 1961, p.174)

As Jung placed the altar stone inside the church, a fearful dream from early childhood came back to him. It had haunted him for years but was then buried and forgotten. In the dream (Jung 1961) he descended into a large, sub-terranean temple where he found a terrifying God of the Underworld. It was an enormous ritual phallus set on a magnificent golden throne. Now, through the process of symbolic play, he was led directly to the core of one of his deepest complexes. He remembered this early dream again and sought to understand its meaning.

Jung wrote his memoirs many years later when he was in his eighties. By then he understood that his childhood dream about the fearful, underground God had a purpose:

> Who spoke to me then? Who talked of problems far beyond my knowledge? Who brought the Above and Below together, and laid the foundation for everything that was to fill the second half of my life with stormiest passion? Who but that alien guest who came both from above and from below? Through this childhood dream I was initiated into the secrets of the earth. What happened then was a kind of burial in the earth, and many years were to pass before I came out again. Today I know that it happened in order to bring the greatest possible amount of light into the darkness. It was an initiation into the realm of darkness. My intellectual life had its unconscious beginnings at that time. (Jung 1961, p.15)

As Jung continued the process of imaginative play, his thoughts clarified. The pressure he had been feeling was released as a flood of fantasies – that is, images and emotions – came to consciousness. He wrote them down as well as he could; he also drew and painted them. After giving the fantasies form, he made every effort to analyze and understand their meaning.

His building game turned out to be the beginning of a deep process of psychological development. In a beautifully written, thought provoking review of Jung's confrontation with the unconscious, Stewart (1982) points out that 'play did not necessarily lead down the slope of memory to childishness, but rather it led directly to the unfinished business of childhood' (p.210). Symbolic play inevitably involves some regression because the process takes us to the emotional core of our complexes. But play does more. Symbolic play activates the image producing function of the psyche (i.e., the imagination) which puts us in touch with ourselves. In Jung's case he not only retrieved long-forgotten memories from his past but a flood of fantasies was released that ultimately reshaped his future:

> The years when I was pursuing my inner images were the most important in my life – in them everything essential was decided. It all began then; the later details are only supplements and clarification of the material that burst forth from the unconscious, and at first swamped me. It was the *prima materia* for a lifetime's work. (Jung 1961, p.199)

Jung came to call this process 'active imagination.' As a psychotherapeutic method, it has two parts. The first half is 'letting the unconscious come up.' The second half consists in 'coming to terms with the unconscious' (Jung 1973, p.561). Another way of describing it is that you open to the unconscious and give free rein to fantasy. At the same time, you maintain an alert, attentive, active point of view.

The starting point of active imagination is an emotional state that may take the form of a dream image, a fragment of fantasy, an inner voice or simply a bad mood. Jung writes:

> To begin with, the task consists solely in observing objectively how a fragment of fantasy develops (1929, p.16).

> I...took up a dream-image or an association of the patient's, and, with this as a point of departure, set him the task of elaborating or developing his theme by giving free rein to his fantasy. This according to individual taste and talent could be done in any number of ways, dramatic, dialectic, visual, acoustic, or in the form of dancing, painting, drawing, or modelling. (1947, p.202)

> It is technically very simple to note down the 'other' voice in writing and to answer its statements from the standpoint of the ego. It is exactly as if a

dialogue were taking place between two human beings with equal rights. (1916, pp.88–89)

He must make the emotional state the basis or starting point of the procedure. He must make himself as conscious as possible of the mood he is in, sinking himself in it without reserve and noting down on paper all the fantasies and other associations that come up. Fantasy must be allowed the freest possible play, yet not in such a manner that it leaves the orbit of its object, namely the affect… The whole procedure is a kind of enrichment and clarification of the affect, whereby the affect and its contents are brought nearer to consciousness, becoming at the same time more impressive and more understandable. (1916, p.82)

Quite often, the patients themselves feel that certain material contains a tendency to visibility. They say, for instance: 'That dream was so impressive, if I only could paint I would try to express its atmosphere.' Or they feel that a certain idea should be expressed not rationally but in symbols. Or they are gripped by an emotion which, if given form, would be explainable, and so on. And so they begin to draw, to paint, or to shape their images plastically, and women sometimes do weaving. I have even had one or two women who danced their unconscious figures. Of course, they can also be expressed in writing. (1935, p.173)

My most fundamental views and ideas derive from these experiences. First I made the observations and only then did I hammer out my views. And so it is with the hand that guides the crayon or brush, the foot that executes the dance-step, with the eye and the ear, with the word and the thought: a dark impulse is the ultimate arbiter of the pattern, an unconscious *a priori* precipitates itself into plastic form. (1947, p.204)

As the unconscious material was given form, Jung always sought to understand its meaning. He also drew ethical conclusions from it, to be put to work in life:

I took great care to try to understand every single image, every item of my psychic inventory, and to classify them scientifically – so far as this was possible – and, above all, to realize them in actual life. That is what we usually neglect to do. We allow the images to rise up, and maybe we wonder about them, but that is all. We do not take the trouble to understand them, let alone draw ethical conclusions from them. This stopping-short conjures up the negative effects of the unconscious. It is equally a grave mistake to think that it is enough to gain some understanding of the images and that knowledge can here make a halt. Insight into them must be converted into an ethical obligation. Not to do so is to fall prey to the power principle. (1961, pp.192–193)

Some forms of active imagination are usually done by the patient alone, away from the analyst. Other forms, such as sandplay and dance/movement, usually include the presence of the analyst as witness. Early on in analysis, whether the endeavor is solitary or shared, the analytic relationship serves as container and process. But a long-term goal of active imagination is to liberate the patient through his or her own efforts rather than through dependence on the analyst. The analyst may serve as consultant and/or witness but the process is self-directed and usually needs no interpretation. When Jung worked with patients who needed some kind of interpretive response, he made it as tentative as possible and returned their material to them through open-ended questions:

I had to try to give provisional interpretations at least, so far as I was able, interspersing them with innumerable 'perhapses' and 'ifs' and 'buts' and never stepping beyond the bounds of the picture lying before me. I always took good care to let the interpretation of each image tail off into a question whose answer was left to the free fantasy activity of the patient. (p.203)

In his earlier works Jung speaks of active imagination and dream interpretation as two distinct psychotherapeutic methods. But if we follow the development of his thought, active imagination takes on an increasingly important role. In his later writings he says that his method of dream interpretation is based on active imagination and he describes active imagination as 'the analytical method of psychotherapy' (1975, p.222). In his final work he relates active imagination to the entire alchemical process, the development of self-knowledge (Know Thyself) and the process of individuation (1963).

Following Jung's late thought, we understand active imagination to be the fundamental method of analytic practice. The therapeutic relationship serves as container and process. Active imagination clearly includes the use of dance/movement, as well as sandplay and every type of artistic media. But it also includes imaginative exploration of dreams, fantasies, memories, present life experiences and issues in the analytic relationship. From this larger perspective, work with the transference and countertransference can be a form of active imagination (Davidson 1966; Schwartz-Salant 1982; Stewart

1987b). So can the scholarly-imaginative process that sends analysts and analysands to look up the roots of a particular word in the appendix of a dictionary (Lockhart 1983) or do library research on the natural, historical and mythic origins of a particular image. Shared images and enactments (Mindell 1982, 1985; Schwartz-Salant 1984; Dreifuss 1987) can also be understood as forms of active imagination.

Stewart points out that active imagination and creative imagination are the same process. Both are expressed through 'rhythm,' 'ritual,' 'reason' and 'relationship' (1987b, pp.138–142, 1987c). But creative imagination is turned to the creation of the cultural forms – art, religion, philosophy and society. Active imagination is turned to the creation of the personality. This leads to a new understanding of active imagination as rhythm (dance/ movement, sandplay, painting, poetry, sculpting, weaving, etc), ritual (imagination of the sacred, inner voices, dialogue with the gods), reason (imagination of number and origins, cosmos and meaning, scholarly amplification) and relationship (empathic imagination, especially work with the transference and countertransference). As active imagination, rhythm, ritual, reason and relationship serve the psychological attitude and foster the development of self-reflective consciousness.

Dance/Movement as active imagination

As a psychotherapeutic technique, dance/movement as active imagination was originated by Jung in 1916, but it remained largely undeveloped and its use in analytic practice was rare. In the 1950s and 1960s it was taken up by dance therapy pioneer Mary Whitehouse. Today, the work she developed is an approach to dance therapy as well as a form of active imagination in analysis.

Mary Whitehouse received her diploma from the Wigman School in Germany and also was a student of Martha Graham. Her personal analysis with Hilde Kirsch in Los Angeles and studies at the Jung Institute in Zürich resulted in the development of her approach, that she called 'movement-in-depth' and which others have termed 'authentic movement.' Her work has many aspects. She was the first to describe movement from different sources in the psyche:

> 'I move' is the clear knowledge that I, personally, am moving. The opposite of this is the sudden and astonishing moment when 'I am moved.' It is a moment when the ego gives up control, stops choosing, stops exerting demands, allowing the Self to take over moving the

physical body as it will. It is a moment of unpremeditated surrender that cannot be explained, repeated exactly, sought for, or tried out. (Whitehouse 1979, p.57)

The core of the movement experience is the sensation of moving and being moved. Ideally, both are present in the same instant. It is a moment of total awareness, the coming together of what I am doing and what is happening to me. (Whitehouse 1958, p.243)

As she developed her approach to movement, she taught her students to become aware of a specific inner impulse that has the quality of a bodily felt sensation:

Following the inner sensation, allowing the impulse to take the form of physical action, is active imagination in movement, just as following the visual image is active imagination in fantasy. It is here that the most dramatic psychophysical connections are made available to consciousness. (Whitehouse 1963, p.17)

She was also interested in the visual images that emerge in the midst of moving and emphasized the importance of staying with the image. In a conversation with Frantz (1972), she stated:

When the image is truly connected in certain people then the movement is authentic. There is no padding of movement just for the sake of moving. There is an ability to stand the inner tension until the next image moves them. They don't simply dance around. (p.41)

Dance/movement as active imagination involves a relationship between two people: a mover and a witness. It is within the relationship that the mover may begin to internalize the reflective function of the witness, to yield to the unconscious stream of bodily felt sensations and images, while at the same time bringing the experience into conscious awareness.

To begin, both mover and witness usually warm-up in silence, doing simple movements, each with their own inner focus. After the warm-up the mover closes his or her eyes, attends inwardly and waits for an impulse to move, while the witness finds a corner in the room where s/he can sit and watch. At the beginning, the witness carries a larger responsibility for consciousness – the mover is simply invited to immerse in his or her own fluctuating rhythms of movement and stillness. The movement itself may take no more than ten minutes or it can go on for a half an hour or more. Sometimes, it's helpful to decide in advance on a time period, something like ten or fifteen or twenty minutes, and have the analyst serve as timekeeper, letting the mover know when to (gradually) bring the movement process to an end.

In the early stages of the work the mover may remember very little. But, eventually, the mover learns to allow the movement to unfold and, at the same time, pays attention to what the body is doing. The mover also develops a more differentiated sense of where the movement comes from – that is, the inner world of bodily felt sensations and images. When the mover is aware of both the expressive action and its sensory-imaginal source, s/he is likely to be conscious of the emotion or emotional tone as well. But it doesn't always happen that way. For example, the emotion may be strongly felt on a visceral level but without awareness of the images that would give it meaning. On the other hand, there are movers who experience the unconscious as an inner landscape rich with mythic images yet their relationship to it may be curiously detached, as if it had nothing to do with them. In time, active imagination in movement tends to develop in us a more differentiated, balanced relationship to both the sensory and imaginal aspects of our emotional life.

Physical safety issues need to be discussed. The mover closes his or her eyes in order to listen for the inner sensations and images. But if he or she begins any large swinging, spinning, leaping movement – any kind of momentum that could lead to a collision with windows, furniture, or what have you – it is essential that the eyes be open. Even when the quality of movement is smaller and slower, movers have to learn to open their eyes from time to time to keep an orientation to the room. It is difficult to do this without losing the inner-directed focus. But if the work involves a true meeting of conscious and unconscious, maintaining a sense of where one is in a room becomes part of the conscious standpoint. This is easy to say but, often, extremely difficult to do. When one is moving in this way, the eyes usually 'want' to stay closed. To open the eyes (even a tiny slit) takes a major effort. At times, the mover's eyes feel as if they are glued shut. But this struggle is an essential part of active imagination – that is, to develop the capacity to bear the tension of the opposites, to open fully to the unconscious while, at the same time, maintaining a strong conscious orientation.

In the midst of moving, people often remember a particularly vivid aspect of a dream or an early childhood experience. For example, while moving low, close to the floor, an analysand suddenly remembered the full impact of what it was like when she fell and broke her leg at the age of six. In a seemingly random way, one of her legs had taken on a particular kind of twisted tension. The memory followed. This was the first time in recent years that she remembered the painful, helpless, humiliating feelings that came as she tried to get up but couldn't. These were exactly the feelings that had brought her into analysis. She felt unable to 'take a stand' or 'stand on her own two feet.' The process of active imagination in movement took her directly to the emotional core of the complex.

This brief description illustrates the vital link between memory and the moving body. It is as if certain memories are stored kinesthetically and can best be retrieved through the movements of the body. The great French novelist Marcel Proust (1932) wrote about this: 'Our arms and legs are full of sleeping memories of the past' (p.2). Sometimes, the movements seem to be random. Other times, we discover that a particular posture or gesture is always there, no matter what we do, we can't get away from it. But whether the movement that holds a particular memory appears randomly or consistently, it is our embodied link to the past.

It was very important for my analysand to retrieve such a long-forgotten memory. Continuing work was needed to understand and integrate it on a more conscious level. Verbal dialogue and exchange was an essential part of the process. Through her dreams, fantasies and exploration of feelings that arose in the transference relationship, we learned that the real problem was not the broken leg, rather it was a family atmosphere that could not tolerate feelings of helplessness, as if it were shameful to be in pain or to be in need of help.

When movement is part of Jungian analysis, people generally know when they want to move, but everyone seems to approach it differently. Some move every hour, others only when they feel drawn to explore a particular theme in movement. Some move in the middle of the hour, with time for verbal exchange before and after. Others begin the hour with dance/movement. It may consist only of a brief warm-up as a way to become more fully present and then the person sits down and talks about whatever is on his or her mind or the warm-up may lead into a deeply imaginative, emotional process that opens material for us to explore for the rest of the hour.

Eliade (1975) wrote: 'Life cannot be *repaired*, it can only be *recreated*' (p.30). Active imagination is the essence of that re-creative process.

Bibliography

Adler, J. (1972) 'Integrity of body and psyche: Some notes on work in process'. In B.F. Govine and J. Chodorow (eds) *What is Dance Therapy Really? Proceedings of the Seventh Annual Dance Therapy Conference,* pp.42–53. Columbia, MD: American Dance Therapy Association.

Bernstein, P.L. (ed) (1984) *Theoretical Approaches in Dance/Movement Therapy.* Vol.2. pp.321–342. Dubuque, IA: Kendall/Hunt.

Chodorow, J. (1986) 'The body as symbol: Dance/movement in analysis'. In N.Schwartz-Salant and M. Stein (eds) *The Body in Analysis.* Wilmette, IL: Chiron Publications.

Chodorow, J. (1991) *Dance Therapy and Depth Psychology: The Moving Imagination.* London and New York: Routledge.

Dallett, J. (1982) 'Active imagination in practice'. In M. Stein (ed) *Jungian Analysis.* La Salle: Open Court.

Darwin, C. (1872) *The Expression of the Emotions in Man and Animals.* Chicago: The University of Chicago Press, 1965.

Davidson, D. (1966) 'Transference as a form of active imagination'. *Journal of Analytical Psychology 11,* 2, 135–146.

Dreifuss, G. (1987) 'Voice dialogue and holocaust'. In M.A. Mattoon (ed) *The Archetype of Shadow in a Split World.* Einsiedeln, Switzerland: Daimon Verlag.

Ekman, P. (1982) *Emotion in the Human Face,* 2nd ed. Cambridge: Cambridge University Press.

Eliade, M. (1975) *Myth and Reality.* New York: Harper & Row.

Frantz, G. (1972) 'An approach to the center: An interview with Mary Whitehouse'. *Psychological Perspectives 3,* 1, 37–46.

Hannah, B. (1953) 'Some remarks on active imagination'. *Spring,* 38–58.

Hannah, B. (1981) *Active Imagination.* Santa Monica: Sigo Press.

Hawkins, A. (1972) Dance therapy today: Points of view and ways of working. In B.F. Govine and J. Chodorow (eds) What is dance therapy really? *Proceedings of the Seventh Annual Dance Therapy Conference,* pp.61–68. Columbia, MD: American Dance Therapy Association.

Henderson, J.L. (1984) *Cultural Attitudes in Psychological Perspective.* Toronto: Inner City Books.

Hillman, J. (1961) *Emotion: A Comprehensive Phenomenology of Theories and Their Meanings for Therapy.* Evanston, IL: Northwestern University Press.

Hillman, J. (1983) 'Active imagination: The healing art'. In J. Hillman, *Healing Fiction.* Barrytown, NY: Station Hill Press.

Humbert, E. (1971) 'Active imagination: Theory and practice'. *Spring,* 101–114.

Izard, C.E. (1977) *Human Emotions.* New York: Plenum Press.

Johnson, R.A. (1986) *Inner Work.* San Francisco: Harper and Row.

Jung, C.G. (1911) 'On the doctrine of complexes'. In *The Collected Works of C.G. Jung* (1973) (vol. 2). Princeton: Princeton University Press.

Jung, C.G. (1912) 'The concept of libido'. In *The Collected Works of C.G. Jung* (1967) (vol. 5). Princeton: Princeton University Press.

Jung, C.G. (1912) 'The transformation of libido'. In *The Collected Works of C.G. Jung* (1956/67) (vol. 5). Princeton: Princeton University Press.

Jung, C.G. (1912) 'Two kinds of thinking'. In *The Collected Works of C.G. Jung* (1967) (vol. 5). Princeton: Princeton University Press.

Jung, C.G. (1916) 'The transcendent function'. In *The Collected Works of C.G. Jung* (2nd ed., 1969/78) (vol. 8). Princeton: Princeton University Press.

Jung, C.G. (1928) 'The technique of differentiation between the ego and the figures of the unconscious'. In *The Collected Works of C.G. Jung* (1966) (vol.7). Princeton: Princeton University Press.

Jung, C.G. (1929) 'Commentary on "The secret of the golden flower."' In *The Collected Works of C.G. Jung* (1967) (vol. 13). Princeton: Princeton University Press.

Jung, C.G. (1931) 'The aims of psychotherapy'. In *The Collected Works of C.G. Jung* (1975) (vol.16). Princeton: Princeton University Press.

Jung, C.G. (1934) 'A review of the complex theory'. In *The Collected Works of C.G. Jung* (1975) (vol.8). Princeton: Princeton University Press.

Jung, C.G. (1935) 'The Tavistock lectures: On the theory and practice of analytical psychology'. In *The Collected Works of C.G. Jung* (1976) (vol. 18). Princeton: Princeton University Press.

Jung, C.G. (1938) 'Psychological aspects of the mother archetype'. In *The Collected Works of C.G. Jung.* (1968) *(vol. 9, part I).* Princeton: Princeton University Press.

Jung, C.G. (1947) 'On the nature of the psyche'. In *The Collected Works of C.G. Jung* (2nd ed., 1969/78) (vol. 8). Princeton: Princeton University Press.

Jung, C.G. (1951) 'Aion: Researches into the phenomenology of the Self'. In *The Collected Works of C.G. Jung.* (1968) *(vol. 9, part II).* Princeton: Princeton University Press.

Jung, C.G. (1961) *Memories, Dreams. Reflections.* New York: Vintage Books, Random House.

Jung, C.G. (1963) 'Mysterium coniunctionis'. In *The collected works of C.G. Jung* (1974) (vol. 14). Princeton: Princeton University Press.

Jung, C.G. (1973) *Letters. Vol. 1.* Princeton: Princeton University Press.

Jung, C.G. (1975) *Letters. Vol. 2.* Princeton: Princeton University Press.

Lockhart, R. (1983) *Words as Eggs.* Dallas, TX: Spring Publications.

Lynd, H. (1958) *On Shame and the Search for Identity.* New York: Harcourt and Brace.

Mindell, A. (1982) *Dreambody.* Los Angeles: Sigo Press.

Mindell, A. (1985) *Working with the Dreambody.* Boston: Routledge & Kegan.

Nathanson, D.L. (ed) (1987) *The Many Faces of Shame.* New York: The Guilford Press.

Otto, R. (1923) *The Idea of the Holy.* Oxford: Oxford University Press, 1981.

Proust, M. (1932) *The Past Recaptured.* New York: Random House.

Schwartz-Salant, N. (1982) *Narcissism and Character Transformation.* Toronto: Inner City Books.

Schwartz-Salant, N. (1984) 'Review of Jungian analysis'. *The San Francisco Institute Library Journal 5*, 2, 14–27.

Sherman, F. (1978) 'Conversation with Mary Whitehouse'. *American Journal of Dance Therapy 2*, 2, 3–4.

Stewart, C.T. (1981) 'Developmental psychology of sandplay'. In G. Hill (ed) *Sandplay Studies: Origins, Theory and Practice.* San Francisco: C.G. Jung Institute.

Stewart, C.T. and Stewart, L.H. (1981) 'Play, games and affects: a contribution toward a comprehensive theory of play'. In A.T. Cheska (ed) *Play as Context.* Proceedings of The

Association for the Anthropological Study of Play (TAASP). Westpoint, N.Y.: Leisure Press.

Stewart, L.H. (1981) 'Play and sandplay'. In G. Hill (ed) *Sand Play Studies: Origins, Theory and Practice* (pp.21–37). San Francisco: C.G. Jung Institute.

Stewart, L.H. (1982) 'Sandplay and analysis'. In M. Stein (ed) *Jungian Analysis*. La Salle: Open Court.

Stewart, L.H. (1985) 'Affect and archetype: A contribution to a comprehensive therapy of the structure of the psyche'. *Proceedings of the 1985 California Spring Conference*, pp.89–120. San Francisco: C.G. Jung Institute.

Stewart, L.H. (1986) 'Work in progress: affect and archetype: A contribution to a comprehensive theory of the structure of the psyche'. In N. Schwartz-Salant and M. Stein (eds) *The Body in Analysis*. Wilmette, IL: Chiron.

Stewart, L.H. (1987a) 'A brief report: Affect and archetype'. *Journal of Analytical Psychology, 32,* 1, 35–46.

Stewart, L.H. (1987b) 'Affect and archetype in analysis'. In N. Schwartz-Salant and M. Stein (eds) *Archetypal Processes in Psychotherapy*. Wilmette, IL: Chiron.

Stewart, L.H. (1987c) 'Kinship libido: Shadow in marriage and family'. In M.A. Mattoon (ed) *The Archetype of Shadow in a Split World*. Einsiedeln, Switzerland: Daimon Verlag.

Stewart, L.H. (1992) *Changemakers: A Jungian Perspective on Sibling Position and the Family Atmosphere*. London: Routledge.

Stewart, L.H. (in press) 'Jealousy and envy: Complex family emotions'. In L.H. Stewart and J. Chodorow (eds) *The Family: Personal, Cultural and Archetypal Dimensions*. Boston: Sigo Press.

Tomkins, S. (1962–1963) *Affect Imagery Consciousness*. Volume I and II. New York: Springer.

Watkins, M. (1977) *Waking Dreams*. New York: Harper and Row.

Whitehouse, M. (1958) 'The Tao of the body'. In D.H. Johnson (ed) *Bone, Breath and Gesture: Practices of Embodiment*. Berkeley, CA: North Atlantic Books. (1995)

Whitehouse, M. (1963) 'Physical movement and personality'. *Contact Quarterly*, Winter 1987, 16–19.

Whitehouse, M. (1970) 'Reflections on a metamorphosis'. In R. Head, R.E. Rothenberg and D. Wesley (eds) *A Well of Living Waters: Festschrift for Hilde Kirsch*. Los Angeles: C.G. Jung Institute. (1977)

Whitehouse, M.S. (1977) 'The transference and dance therapy'. *American Journal of Dance Therapy 1,* 1, 3–7.

Whitehouse, M.S. (1979) 'C.G. Jung and dance therapy'. In P. Lewis Bernstein (ed) *Eight Theoretical Approaches in Dance/Movement Therapy,* pp.51–70. Dubuque, IA: Kendall/Hunt.

Subject Index

Author Index

320